WE ARE ALL FAST-FOOD WORKERS NOW"

THE GLOBAL UPRISING AGAINST POVERTY WAGES

ANNELISE ORLECK
Photographs by Liz Cooke

BEACON PRESS
BOSTON

BEACON PRESS
Boston, Massachusetts
www.beacon.org

Beacon Press books
are published under the auspices of
the Unitarian Universalist Association of Congregations.

21 20 19 18   8 7 6 5 4 3 2 1

This book is printed on acid-free paper that meets the uncoated paper
ANSI/NISO specifications for permanence as revised in 1992.

Text design and composition by Kim Arney

Photographs by Liz Cooke

Use of Messenger Band song lyrics by permission of the
Messenger Band.

Library of Congress Cataloging-in-Publication Data

Names: Orleck, Annelise, author.
Title: "We are all fast-food workers now" : the global uprising against
    poverty wages / Annelise Orleck.
Description: Boston : Beacon Press, 2018. | Includes bibliographical
    references and index.
Identifiers: LCCN 2017037792 (print) | LCCN 2017056512 (ebook) |
    ISBN 9780807081785 (e-book) | ISBN 9780807081778 (paperback)
Subjects: LCSH: Working poor—Interviews. | Living wage movement. |
    BISAC: SOCIAL SCIENCE / Social Classes. | HISTORY / Modern /
    21st Century. | POLITICAL SCIENCE / Labor & Industrial Relations.
Classification: LCC HD4901 (ebook) | LCC HD4901 .O75 2018 (print) |
    DDC 331.5/4—dc23
LC record available at https://lccn.loc.gov/2017037792

"We are all fast-food workers now."

—KEEGAN SHEPARD,
graduate student and Fight for $15 activist, 2015

"WE ARE ALL FAST-FOOD WORKERS NOW"

CONTENTS

AUTHOR'S NOTE · xi

PART I POVERTY WAGES, WE'RE NOT LOVIN' IT: ROOTS AND BRANCHES OF A GLOBAL UPRISING

PROLOGUE   Brands of Wage Slavery, Marks of Labor Solidarity · 2

CHAPTER 1   Inequality Rising · 4

CHAPTER 2   All We're Asking for Is a Little Respect · 9

CHAPTER 3   "We Are Workers, Not Slaves" · 13

CHAPTER 4   "I Consider the Union My Second Mother" · 17

CHAPTER 5   Hotel Housekeepers Go Norma Rae · 21

CHAPTER 6   United for Respect: OUR Walmart and the Uprising of Retail Workers · 29

CHAPTER 7   Supersize My Wages: Fast-Food Workers and the March of History · 33

CHAPTER 8   1911–2011: History and the Global Labor Struggle · 37

CHAPTER 9   People Power Movements in the Twenty-First Century · 42

CHAPTER 10   "You Can't Dismantle Capitalism Without Dismantling Patriarchy" · 48

CHAPTER 11   This Is What Solidarity Feels Like · 56

PART II THE RISING OF THE GLOBAL PRECARIAT

CHAPTER 12   Respect, Let It Go, 'Cause Baby, You're a Firework · 62

CHAPTER 13   Realizing Precarity: "We Are All Fast-Food Workers Now" · 65

CHAPTER 14   Days of Disruption, 2016 · 69

CHAPTER 15   The New Civil Rights Movement · 75

CHAPTER 16 Counting Victories, Girding for an Uphill Struggle · 78

CHAPTER 17 *Huelga de Hambre:* Hunger and Hunger Strikes Rising · 83

CHAPTER 18 Social Movement Unionism and the Souls of Workers · 93

CHAPTER 19 "Contractualization" · 99

CHAPTER 20 "Stand Up, Live Better": Organizing for Respect at Walmart · 102

PART III GARMENT WORKERS' ORGANIZING IN THE AGE OF FAST FASHION

CHAPTER 21 "If People Would Think About Us, We Wouldn't Die": Beautiful Clothes, Ugly Reality · 118

CHAPTER 22 How the Rag Trade Went Global · 125

CHAPTER 23 "The Girl Effect" · 130

CHAPTER 24 "Made with Love in Bangladesh" · 134

CHAPTER 25 "We Are Not a Pocket Revolution": Bangladeshi Garment Workers Since Rana Plaza · 141

CHAPTER 26 "A Khmer Would Rather Work for Free Than Work Without Dignity" · 149

CHAPTER 27 "After Pol Pot, We Need a Good Life" · 153

CHAPTER 28 Consciousness-Raising, Cambodia Style · 160

CHAPTER 29 Filipina Garment Workers: Organizing in the Zone · 166

PART IV NO RICE WITHOUT FREEDOM, NO FREEDOM WITHOUT RICE: THE GLOBAL UPRISING OF PEASANTS AND FARMWORKERS

CHAPTER 30 "No Land No Life": Uprisings of the "Landless," 2017 · 180

CHAPTER 31 "Agrarian Reform in Reverse": Food Crises, Land Grabs, and Migrant Labor · 187

CHAPTER 32 Milk with Dignity · 192

CHAPTER 33 "Like the Time of Cesar Chavez": Strawberry Fields, Exploitation Forever · 200

CHAPTER 34 Bitter Grapes · 207

CHAPTER 35 "What Are We Rising For?" · 212

CHAPTER 36 "These Borders Are Not Our Borders" · 218

CHAPTER 37 After the Colonizers, RICE · 227

PART V "THEY SAID IT WAS IMPOSSIBLE": LOCAL VICTORIES AND TRANSFORMATIVE VISIONS

CHAPTER 38 "We Can Turn Around the Labor Movement. We Can
Rebuild Power and We Can Win!" · 240

CHAPTER 39 Flashes of Hope · 242

CHAPTER 40 Big Ideas, New Models, Small Courtesies Build
a New World · 253

ACKNOWLEDGMENTS · 260
NOTES · 262
INDEX · 281

AUTHOR'S NOTE

THIS BOOK IS A DEPARTURE FOR ME. It is the work of an Americanist thinking globally, a historian reflecting on the present and recent past. It is not a conventional work of scholarship, though it is based on abundant research: 140 interviews; government documents; foundation reports; news coverage; organizational websites and records; insights from scholars of labor, globalization, transnational capitalism, and agribusiness. I make no pretense of objectivity. This is an uneasy hybrid: data, storytelling and analysis, politics, polemics and poetry. And it *is* a history of sorts, I have come to realize—an urgent history of now.

I began this work because I felt called on in a time of globalization, as an ever-spreading flood of capital transforms our world, to better understand how low-wage workers are starting to resist, to think and act globally as well as locally. Since that time, I have spoken to many workers about what moved them to rise against poverty wages. These conversations transformed what I see, think, and feel every time I buy a shirt or a flat of berries, shop at a big-box store, check out of a hotel, or drink clean water from my kitchen faucet.

Researching this book was revelatory. I traveled across the United States and to parts of the world I had never before visited. I drove, flew, walked, rode in open-air tuk-tuks and on the backs of motorcycles. With photographer Elizabeth Cooke, I conducted interviews in windowless worker dormitories, union offices, and on the streets, at protest marches, in city council hearing rooms, in brightly lit restaurants and shaded back rooms, in elegantly shabby colonial hotels, at factory gates, by phone and via Skype.

I interviewed in English, my native tongue, and with interpreters, in Spanish, Khmer, Tagalog, Visayan languages, Bangla, Mixtec, and Zapotec. Oxnard translator Yessica Ramirez navigated the distinct dialects spoken by indigenous Oaxacans. In Manila, Joanna Bernice Coronacion deftly switched back and forth between Tagalog and English, and Jamaia

Montenegro translated from the Visayan languages spoken in the southern Philippines.

And then there was Vathanak Serry Sim, who works for Solidarity Center in Phnom Penh. Vathanak translated from the Khmer language but also revealed Phnom Penh as an incredible text—beautiful, ugly, inspiring, devastating, punctuated by traffic circles and imposing government buildings, colorful Buddhist temple complexes and labyrinthine alleyways. He seemed to know every trade unionist in the country, along with the nuances of their politics, battles, and backstories. As a child survivor of the Khmer Rouge death camps, Vathanak also bridged the profound chasm that divides Cambodians who lived through the genocide from the young millions who were born afterward. Again and again, Vathanak tried to explain, as best he could, much that is impossible to understand.

I learned also from those who did a different kind of translation, opening to me worker cultures of resistance and struggle: Tampa organizers Kelly Benjamin and Bleu Rainer introduced me to Fight for $15 activists; Tg Albert and Heather Nichols to Southern California Walmart activists and Providence hotel workers; Donna Foster and Arcenio Lopez to the Mixteco farmworkers of Oxnard; and Rutgers graduate student Nafisa Tanjeem to the garment worker–activists of Bangladesh. It was an enduring gift to spend time with Kalpona Akter—as she passionately, patiently, humorously, and angrily reflected on the long and ongoing struggle of the women and men who make clothing for the world.

There were moments in the process of researching and writing this book when I felt a gnawing sense of worry as I wondered how I would tie together and make sense of all that I was seeing and hearing. I paused for a deep breath. But for the most part, I didn't panic. Because deep inside me, I felt certain that the people I was meeting, the kaleidoscopic fragments of stories and experiences they shared, were part of one larger story.

What I saw in New York City and Los Angeles, Manila and Phnom Penh, were ravages of neoliberalism—the brand of global capitalism that has swept our world since the late twentieth century. And the forms of resistance I encountered were, similarly, part of a larger struggle. Though rooted in and motivated by local politics and history, the activists I spoke with were all engaged in fighting the same things: poverty wages, the disappearance of public services (education, healthcare, water), the transformation of workers into independent contractors (and with that a loss of seniority, benefits, pensions), disrespect, sexual harassment and violence, mass evictions and disregard of people's land rights. What follows are some stories of their resistance—their struggles, their losses, their victories, their visions for the future.

When I began this book Donald Trump had not yet been elected president of the United States. As the book goes to press, the US and many parts of the world are just coming out of a period of shock and mourning that followed the election. Listening to the activists whose words animate this book has been healing for me, inspiring.

US activists, especially African American and Latinx workers, reminded me that their battles had begun long before Trump, and that they planned to keep on struggling as they had for centuries. Outside the US, activists facing crackdowns by the murderous Duterte regime in the Philippines, as well as the brutal regimes of Sheikh Hasina in Bangladesh and Hun Sen in Cambodia, put our inward-looking American grief in perspective. The world is both bigger and smaller than I ever knew before I began work on this book. And though the forces arrayed against low-wage workers are powerful, and often violent, the spirit, creativity, courage, and stamina of this global uprising are seemingly endless. With all that I have learned as I researched this book, I am left with feelings of hope and possibility. I hope you will be too.

This book is arranged in four parts. The first is a broad view, a sweep, an attempt to frame how our world has changed and to sketch the roots and spreading branches of global rebellion. The second traces the rising of the global precariat. The third examines garment organizing in the age of fast fashion. And in the fourth section, I trace local and global activism by farmers and farmworkers. I try to cast some sparks of light by sketching small successes that can be seen as models. Finally, I reflect on some quite ambitious visions for a more humane future in which a system based on poverty wages gives way to a living wage and dignified work for everyone.

PART I

POVERTY WAGES, WE'RE NOT LOVIN' IT

Roots and Branches of a Global Uprising

BRANDS OF WAGE SLAVERY, MARKS OF LABOR SOLIDARITY

IN SOUTHERN CALIFORNIA, a fifty-eight-year-old Oaxacan immigrant shows her knees—scarred and swollen from years of picking strawberries. In Vermont, a twenty-four-year-old dairy worker from Chiapas rolls his pants up, revealing knees bruised and painful from long nights of milking and mucking out stalls. Thai berry workers in Scandinavia and women grape pickers in South Africa rub the ache from their limbs every night. In Boston and London, Manila and the Maldives, hotel housekeepers struggle to stand after scrubbing twenty bathrooms on their knees. Their scarred limbs are a bane and a bond.

In Bangladesh, Cambodia, Myanmar, India, Vietnam, and Ethiopia, garment workers have taken to the streets. They are sick from breathing toxic fumes and tired of factory owners who flee to other countries owing workers months of back pay. Hundreds of thousands have joined these protests.

Many of the Cambodian protesters bear a diagonal white scar on their foreheads. Some were beaten by angry foremen who thought they were working too slowly; others had their skulls smashed by rocks—punishment for organizing. Undeterred, these workers—mostly women—rally before imposing government buildings, face off against steely guards, un-flinchingly demand their rights. The jagged indentations on their fore-heads are combat ribbons, marks of struggle, badges of quiet courage.[1]

On a hot August day at a conference in Brazil, three young men in their twenties roll their sleeves up. Their arms are scored by burns that have blistered, then healed, leaving darkened scars, symmetrical stripes. They are fast-food workers—from Tampa, Tokyo, and Manila. And each has been branded by the labor they do for McDonald's. Expected to turn around orders in ninety seconds, they do a dance all day over boiling oil and searing grills. The men have come to Brazil to speak with politicians and with workers from other countries, to share stories, strategize, compare scars. As they speak, each feels a sense of purpose and shared struggle. A new global labor movement is awakening.

CHAPTER I

INEQUALITY RISING

SOMETIME AROUND 2011, people began talking again about poverty and inequality. A sense of urgency seeped into our collective consciousness with smoke from the campfires of Occupy Wall Street. As Occupy encampments arose in financial districts from New York to Hong Kong, people who had been made homeless by medical bills, student debt, or predatory mortgages began to tell their stories.

They spoke with a ragged eloquence that sometimes even broke through the cynicism of jaded reporters. Or maybe their tales resonated because most of us already understood. Almost everyone, everywhere, was being screwed—one way or another—by the twenty-first-century economy and by the widespread belief that increasing shareholder value is more important than any other collective human endeavor.

Scholarly tomes on the subject became surprisingly popular. Economists probed the sources of unequal wealth distribution. Historians and geographers argued that galloping capitalism had become the "new imperialism," that Exxon, Walmart, and McDonald's were the global empires of our age. Then Occupy changed the conversation forever, burning a simple indelible image into our collective psyches. There were always haves and have-nots. But the idea of a 1 percent and a 99 percent endured long after the ragtag Occupy camps were broken up by militarized police. The notion that 1 percent of the world's people dominated and exploited the rest of us was a call for broad coalition-building to which people have responded around the world.[1]

There have been true believers in the power and glory of capitalism for hundreds of years. But by the mid-twentieth century, most people agreed that some regulation was necessary, that governments must protect people as well as property. Even in that heyday of liberalism there were those who argued that any regulation of trade and commerce, any government programs to diminish economic inequality, constrained and weakened individual freedoms. Ronald Reagan popularized that view in his critical 1964 speech "A Time for Choosing," a clarion call to cut "big government." But that argument did not become dominant until the 1980s, with the elections of Reagan in the United States, Margaret Thatcher in the United Kingdom, and the rise of Deng Xiaoping in China. The new era they heralded did more than limit progressive taxation and shred the social safety net. The creation of the World Trade Organization (WTO) in 1995 institutionalized the "neoliberal" vision that profit-taking was a virtue in and of itself. Over the next two decades almost all the world's countries joined the WTO. But it always was—and still is—run by and for the wealthiest and most powerful nations.[2]

The global economy that neoliberals celebrated did not emerge overnight. But by the twenty-first century, the idea that unrestrained global capitalism is the best way to reduce poverty and expand freedom had become dogma for political and economic elites worldwide. Still, they only espoused certain kinds of freedom: from trade barriers and labor regulations; from robust taxes to redistribute wealth and fund education, infrastructure, and healthcare; from environmental regulations that might limit profits as they slowed climate change and reduced poisons in our air and water. This new regime sparked fierce global protest, beginning with the Battle of Seattle in 1999 in which trade unionists, students, and environmental groups took to the streets to highlight the dangers posed by World Trade Organization tribunals and secret negotiations. This resistance moved world leaders to place some environmental and human rights limitations on the new global economy. But they were often weak and ineffectual, by design.

In a twenty-first-century update of Andrew Carnegie's nineteenth-century "Gospel of Wealth," corporate titans espoused a gospel of global profit-taking. Politicians—many with ties to global corporations—signed on, passing tax cuts for the wealthy, slashing labor and environmental protections, Social Security, education and healthcare programs. Like Carnegie, they have argued that philanthropy obviates the need for rights. But from Donald Trump to the Walton family, the 1 percent has given selectively and stingily.[3]

In many ways, Trump's election as president of the United States in 2016 was a culminating moment in the rise of the twenty-first-century Gospel of Wealth. The oil-magnate Koch brothers had long worked to dismantle welfare-state provisions and worker protections. They continue to. Walmart had long used government food and cash aid programs to supplement poverty wages, while arguing that corporate employers should not have to pay into workers' compensation programs for those injured on the job. Trump railed against global trade agreements on the campaign trail, promising to help American workers harmed by neoliberalism. But after his inauguration, he and a GOP-run Congress quickly moved to slash federal programs for the poor and the sick and to restructure US political and economic institutions to serve the wealthiest few (even more than they already did).

In the twenty-first century, the World Trade Organization, the International Monetary Fund, the World Bank, and select transnational corporations have become more powerful than many, if not most, nation-states. Buying the debt of poor nations, they have pressured governments worldwide to cut or privatize essential services: water, transportation, education, healthcare, housing, social welfare, and energy. Indigenous lands have been mined and logged, rivers dammed. Wholesale land grabs by agribusiness and mining, energy, and timber companies have driven hundreds of millions from farms to urban slums, export-processing zones, and migrant worker camps.

It all happened so fast, and in so many parts of the world at once, that it took time for people to grasp what was happening. Far-flung supply chains linking myriad subcontractors obscured the role that global brands played in gutting worker wages, safety protections, smallholders' land rights, and environmental regulations. Many workers no longer knew who their employers were. Consumers did not know where and how their clothes were made, where their food was grown and harvested, and under what conditions. They enjoyed the low prices and chose not ask uncomfortable questions.

Why question low prices when almost everyone was feeling stretched? And that's because they were. In 2016, British-based charity Oxfam reported that the poorer half of the world's people had lost 38 percent of their wealth since 2010, while food, housing, and healthcare costs skyrocketed. In the same period, an ever-increasing share of wealth had flowed to the top 1 percent. By 2016, the 62 richest people on earth controlled more wealth than 3.8 billion people. Occupy Wall Street's rallying cry no longer seemed hyperbolic. It had become cold, hard fact.[4]

This was not simply a problem in developing nations. Wealth and income were more concentrated at the top in the US than in any other affluent nation. As deindustrialization, automation, and financial deregulation transformed the labor market, massive tax cuts for the wealthy deepened government deficits and provided a rationale for program cuts. The top marginal tax rate in the US during the prosperous 1950s and 1960s approached 90 percent. By the mid-1980s, it had fallen below 30 percent. Federal aid to cities and states dried up; public services were gutted. Private unions withered and public unions, already struggling, faced relentless legislative assaults.

The Great Recession of 2008 made these inequalities worse, erasing savings for tens of millions. Spiraling healthcare and housing costs and predatory lending drove millions of Americans into bankruptcy. Many literally ended up in the streets.

The recovery since that time has done little for the poor or middle class. Unemployment rates dropped below 5 percent in 2016, but two-thirds of the jobs created in the US since 2008 do not pay a living wage or provide benefits, job security, or potential for growth. By 2014, 71 percent of American workers earned less than $50,000 a year. More than half earned less than $30,000; 38 percent earned less than $20,000. The American middle class has evaporated.

Unemployment is still an issue, but poverty wages are a greater problem—in the US and around the world. Growing numbers of impoverished workers (worldwide) mark a dramatic shift from the mid-twentieth-century high-water mark of liberalism with its generous government subsidies. Then incomes grew all along the wealth scale, unions and public services were strong, and public colleges were affordable for millions. The twenty-first century is starkly different, a new Gilded Age, in many ways more like the 1870s than the 1970s.[5]

Since 2008, the wealthiest 1 percent of Americans have seen incomes increase by 31.4 percent while everyone else's grew by less than half a percent. Six members of the Walton family control as much wealth as 40 percent of Americans. Half of fast-food workers, retail sales and non-union manufacturing workers require food stamps or other aid programs to survive. And education is no longer a sure path out of poverty. In 2015, three-quarters of US college professors worked on term-to-term contracts. Between one-quarter and one-third needed some form of public aid—cash assistance, food, or medical services—to support themselves, especially if they had children.

In expensive cities—New York, Los Angeles, Boston—three and four generations live together. They pool resources so that they can afford rent. Employed workers sleep on relatives' couches. Some commute to work from homeless shelters.[6]

Secure jobs are disappearing. Employees are reduced to "independent" contractors, as corporate managers relentlessly cut costs. College graduates stagger under crushing levels of debt, unable to purchase homes or even cars. Stagnant wages erode workers' living standards. Wage theft runs rampant. Marx's proletariat has grown scarce, replaced by an expanding global "precariat"—contingent, commodified labor to whom no one owes anything.

Not surprisingly, many people are angered by the cruelties of the twenty-first-century economy. And their fury has fueled worldwide protest. Simultaneously, and almost everywhere, low-wage workers and small farmers began to revolt: in New York City restaurants, laundries, and warehouses, in Western Cape wineries and the garment shops of Phnom Penh, in Southern California Walmarts, and the big hotels of Providence, Oslo, Karachi, and Abuja. As capital has globalized, so has the labor movement. Marches, strikes, protests, and sit-ins from Tampa to Mali have changed the global conversation about workers' rights.

This book offers sketches of these uprisings. Whenever possible, I try to tell the story through workers' eyes, using their words. If, by the end, you come to believe that we are all fast-food workers now, then you will realize that this is not a story about other people. It is our story, a history of our times.

CHAPTER 2

ALL WE'RE ASKING
FOR IS A LITTLE RESPECT

IN JULY 2015, Bleu Rainer, a twenty-six-year-old Tampa, Florida, Mc-Donald's worker, opened his mail and found an invitation to testify before the Brazilian Senate. "I was kind of shocked," he laughs. McDonald's workers in Brazil had filed charges of wage theft, unsafe working conditions, and violations of Brazil's labor laws. This moved the Senate Human Rights Commission to convene an unprecedented hearing. Their goal was to determine if McDonald's, with operations in more than a hundred countries, was driving down wages and eroding safety conditions worldwide. So they invited fast-food workers from the US, Europe, Latin America, and Asia to testify about Brazil's and the world's second-largest private employer.[1]

Legislators from many nations were also invited to offer their views on whether McDonald's adversely affected wages and labor conditions in their countries. McDonald's was then being investigated by the European Parliament. European unions had accused the company of tax evasion, overcharging franchise owners, and illegally suppressing worker wages.[2]

On August 16, 2015, Rainer and colleagues from the Philippines, Korea, Japan, New Zealand, and many other countries came to tell their stories. They were greeted by cheering crowds at the Brasília airport. "People from different unions and politicians from all over Brazil and all over the globe were coming to talk about how McDonald's tries to keep us at the bottom," Rainer recalls. "It was amazing. Because McDonald's has employees everywhere, everything they do has a global impact that affects all workers."

Rainer's life had been marked by starvation wages, uncertain scheduling, and boiling oil. "In eight years, I made no more than eight dollars and five cents an hour. I witnessed the torture of not having enough to afford rent, which led to me sleeping from house to house. I even had to sleep at bus stops because I was homeless. There have been nights that I had to go without food so I could buy a bus pass, so that I could get to work the next day. I have had to rely on food stamps to get a good meal and when those food stamps run out, it's back to square one—which is nothing at all. Sometimes I think: I'm working so hard every day. Why am I not making a living wage? Why can't I feed myself? Why am I still hungry?"

Though Rainer had already joined the fight for a living wage, he experienced moments in Brazil that opened his eyes. "I met this really cool guy from Japan, another McDonald's worker. He showed me his arm full of burns." Rainer raised his arm and held it alongside. The men were burned in the same places. Stripes. Rainer knew how his colleague had been scarred. "They make you get orders out in ninety seconds," he explains. "You're constantly behind. So, you're not thinking about safety. You're worried that your manager is going to push you."

A chill passed through him when he saw the matching burns. The men had more in common than their injuries. "Me and him have the exact same story," Rainer learned as they talked. "I didn't know it would be that way." Both men had enrolled in college but had to drop out. "He wasn't earning enough to pay tuition and neither was I. It was my whole story except he was in Japan." Rainer felt the pieces fall into place.

When Benedict Murillo, from Manila, heard the men's stories, he rolled up his sleeves and held out his arms. He had the same burns. He also had left college because he couldn't pay tuition. Their skin colors, languages, backgrounds were different, Murillo says. Still the three were, in Murillo's view, "McBrothers"—members of the new global working class. Later, when Murillo told the story in a union hall in Quezon City, fast-food workers placed their arms on the table—fist-to-fist like spokes in a wheel. Identical lines of burns scored each arm.[3]

At the hearing in Brasília, Rainer learned that some fast-food workers have it worse than he does. He heard testimony from a Seoul worker who delivered "Happy Meals" on a bicycle. "This dude had to cover his face when he testified because he was afraid of retaliation." In South Korea, the government had been cracking down hard, Rainer learned: police clubs, water cannons, summary imprisonment, and torture. And brutal work conditions.

"This dude told a story about one of his friends who got killed delivering meals. That guy had to deliver three or four meals every thirty minutes. That's fast riding. And there's a lot of hills there and lots of traffic." Brazil's Arcos Dorados (Golden Arches) bike deliverymen also testified. "They were going through the same thing," says Rainer.

Deliverymen from several countries exchanged stories. Some spoke through interpreters, others in rudimentary English. What angered Bleu was that "nobody takes responsibility for what fast-food workers go through. But someone *is* responsible: McDonald's. Someone needs to take responsibility. We *are* starting to do that."

Rainer, Murillo, and other activists who came to Brasília in the summer of 2015 are part of a new global labor movement whose members connect using a mix of old-fashioned and new tactics: face-to-face organizing, cell phones, and social media. They adapt pop-culture references and embed them in local cultures and languages. Disney theme songs, Justin Timberlake jingles, even an electronic dance tune called "Barbra Streisand" are recast and repurposed.

Their protests are not your grandmother's revolution. Repeated one-day flash strikes have largely replaced months-long sieges that often hurt workers more than management. Activists still march, chant, go door-to-door. But they also use social media, perform street theater, and engage in pop-culture civil disobedience actions. They hold mock trials of Ronald McDonalds. Singing, dancing flash mobs invade fast-food restaurants and shopping malls, posting online about everything they do.

Many twenty-first-century labor activists are under thirty-five and savvy about communications, social media, and popular culture. They take pleasure in subverting expensive advertising slogans, cracking the glossy shell of consumerism. McDonald's paid pop star Justin Timberlake $6 million to sing "I'm Lovin' It." It was the burger giant's first global television ad. Fast-food workers tweaked the slogan to: "Poverty Wages: Not Lovin' It." Anti-sweatshop activists turned Nike's "Just Do It" into a boycott chant: "Just Don't Do It." Walmart's "Save Money, Live Better" slogan became: "Stand Up, Live Better." And when Walmart workers staged the first retail sit-in since the 1930s, their signs said: "Sit Down, Live Better."

Even more than a living wage, these movements are fighting for respect. In Manila, fast-food workers sing the 1967 Otis Redding/Aretha Franklin anthem as they block rush-hour traffic: "R-E-S-P-E-C-T. Find out what it means to me." I have heard that word from hotel workers in Providence, strawberry pickers in Oxnard, garment workers in Phnom

Penh, airport workers in New York City. "You need to respect the job and the role we play," says airport security guard Canute Drayton. "Bosses need to know that we are not garbage."

Around the world, low-wage workers are outlining a coherent vision of what a human-centered, post-neoliberal world might look like. What RESPECT means to them is this: a living wage; freedom of assembly, the right to unionize; job security, benefits; safe working conditions; an end to dispossessions, an end to deportations, and restraints on plunder of the earth for profit.

Low-wage workers also speak in terms of freedom. But their idea of freedom is distinct from that of neoliberals, says Filipina fast-food organizer Joanna Bernice Coronacion. Freedom means a decent life for all workers, clean, free water, free time to spend with families, freedom from sexual harassment and violence, wage equity for women and men, an end to labor slavery.

Denise Barlage, a longtime activist in Organization United for Respect at Walmart (OUR Walmart) says: "We're not asking to be rich. We are asking for respect, dignity, decent benefits, to be treated like human beings." In so many ways, that sums up the spirit and ethos of the new global uprising against poverty wages.[4]

Researching this book, I have met and spoken with remarkable activists from New York City to Tampa, from Los Angeles to Dhaka, Manila, and Phnom Penh, from Geneva to Brasília. Some are union officials with political clout, big budgets, and armies of members behind them. Others are on-the-ground organizers who work seven-day weeks and eighteen-hour days, for little pay, dedicated to the cause, lit by the promise of change. Most moving and profound have been my conversations with the people who make our clothing, serve our food, care for our elderly and sick, clean our hotel rooms, kitchens, and bedrooms, plant and pick our food.

These workers are the human beings behind the big abstract concepts associated with the twenty-first-century economy: globalization; free trade treaties; World Bank loans; austerity regimes; multinational capital and contingent labor. Meeting them, listening to their stories, has revealed those economic and political forces in fresh ways, from the bones out. It is my hope that they will do the same for those who read this book.

CHAPTER 3

"WE ARE WORKERS, NOT SLAVES"

IN MARCH 2015, tens of thousands of indigenous berry pickers walked out of the vast agribusiness fields of the San Quintín Valley in northern Mexico, launching the largest agricultural strike Mexico had seen in decades. Strikers carried signs that explain much about the world in which twenty-first-century workers operate. "*Somos Trabajadores, No Esclavos. We Are Workers, Not Slaves.*" When police cracked down violently, the Mexican newspaper *La Jornada* ran a cartoon of police beating strikers. "Haven't thirty years of neoliberalism taught you anything?" the caption asked. The answer, in short, is: Yes. A lot.

As neoliberalism has spread, so have mass evictions, involuntary migrations, and many forms of unfree labor. Among those who grow grapes for the global wine market, pick berries, apples, and tomatoes for global grocery chains, are many who would rather have stayed on their own lands, growing their own food. In China alone, tens of millions of farmers were displaced by agribusiness, factories, and real estate development in the 2010s. Many became factory workers, in vast export zones, making products for export. In 2015, China unveiled a plan to move 250 million more farmers to cities by 2025. Meanwhile, food multinationals Cargill, Monsanto, and John Deere sell maize and soybeans grown in Brazil to Chinese consumers.

On Luzon, the largest island of the Philippines, farmers flooded the cities in the early twenty-first century as two-thousand-year-old rice terraces fell into disrepair, says rice activist Vicky Carlos Garcia. Indigenous farmers on the southern island of Mindanao, forced off their lands at gunpoint to make way for banana and palm oil plantations, also have resettled in the vast shantytowns at the center of Manila—the infamous slums of Tondo. "Ask them why they are there," says Garcia. "No one ever asks them. They just call them problems."[1]

13

In South Africa, more than two million farmers and farmworkers were evicted between 1994 and 2013. Cambodia, Taiwan, India, Japan, and Indonesia passed new laws in the 2010s opening their countries to foreign ownership and leasing, leaving tens of millions of farmers landless. After the 1994 North American Free Trade Agreement, an estimated two million Mexican farmers left their lands as corn prices plummeted and common lands were privatized.

Displaced farmers have become cheap labor for global industry and for agribusiness farms. Some become "guest workers"; many endure slave labor conditions. Undocumented migrants, laboring in the shadows, unprotected by labor laws, live in fear of deportation.

These migrants fill the mega-slums of Asia, Latin America, and Africa, living in cardboard shacks and tin huts along polluted rivers. They survive on food scavenged from fast-food Dumpsters, recooked and resold. They pick and resell garbage—waste from the global economy. Profiteers sell them water and access to illegal electric lines at exorbitant rates.

Increasingly fed up, farmers and farmworkers have been organizing globally. In 1993, they created La Via Campesina—"The Peasant's Way." By 2014, the group represented 164 farmers' organizations in 72 countries and held conventions from Indonesia to Turkey. Its headquarters move every few years—from Brussels to Honduras to Zimbabwe. In 2015, Zimbabwean organic farmer Elizabeth Mpofu became "coordinator of the international peasant movement." She is leading the fight against transnational corporations grabbing land and water, making people landless, poisoning the earth, destroying traditional farming practices. Via Campesina has helped to tie farmers, farmworkers, and landless and indigenous activists together around the world. "We are organized," she said in 2016, "and we know what we want."

In China, protests that the government calls "mass incidents" have skyrocketed, from a few thousand annually in the early 1990s to more than 180,000 per year in the 2010s. Most have been sparked by evictions and land expropriations. It's the same story around the world. In 2012, Via Campesina began to push the United Nations to adopt an International Declaration of the Rights of Peasants to enshrine rights to land, clean water, and freedom from violence.[2]

"In most regions where Via Campesina is present, the leaders are women," Mpofu says. Women are "the backbone of agriculture" and have been at the forefront of farm protests. In South Africa in 2012, women grape pickers sparked the largest farmworker strike the country had seen in decades. In the Western Cape Winelands, thousands laid down their hoes and scythes to demand gender and race equity in pay, clean water, decent housing, and an end to sexual harassment and violence. By strike's end, they had nearly doubled their wage to $10 daily. Most importantly, they overcame their fear and learned they could win gains if they fought.[3]

When Oaxacan migrant berry pickers in the US and Mexico began organizing en masse in the twenty-first century, women played a crucial role as well. One Mixteca woman, who had picked berries in the San Quintín Valley of northern Mexico since she was seven, explained that she was tired of being yelled at and made fun of for being indigenous, tired of being sexually harassed and abused. "That's how it was for many years." But the stirrings of militancy among other indigenous workers changed her. "We were asleep but now people have stood up and we will continue in this struggle for what is right so that our grandchildren will have a better future."[4]

In the mountain towns of Oaxaca, after NAFTA flooded Mexico with cheap industrial American corn, Triqui, Mixteco, and Zapoteco farmers could longer survive on their meager earnings from native corn and beans. Mexico stopped subsidizing domestically grown corn in 2008. Hunger raged as millions transitioned from subsistence farming to purchasing staple foods.[5]

Tens of thousands of Mixtecos headed north. Arcenio Lopez walked through desert mountains under cover of night, paying *"coyotes"* (human smugglers) to guide him from Tijuana to California. He dodged snakes and bandits to join his father who had found work picking berries in Oxnard and lettuce in Watsonville. Now director of the Mixteco/Indígena Community Organizing Project (MICOP), Arcenio trains indigenous farmworkers to stand up for their rights.[6]

The migrants MICOP serves often have spent years following crops from Mexico through California, Oregon, and Washington. They pick berries, apples, and grapes, pack kale, lettuce, and cilantro. At the end of the season they start again.

But the border has been increasingly militarized and it is more difficult to cross back and forth these days. Families have been separated. Some remain in California, Texas, or Arizona. Others work on the Mexican side—planting and picking tomatoes in Sinaloa, berries in San Quintín. They are the people behind the fresh-food revolution that has transformed the diets of affluent consumers worldwide.[7]

Theirs, too, is a struggle for respect and against violence. In 2012, Mixteco and Triqui farmworkers in Oxnard brought a case to the California Agricultural Labor Relations Board against employers who had used Tasers to stop field-workers from unionizing. When he was fired for organizing, Mixteco migrant Bernardino Martinez sued in court, and a judge ordered his reinstatement. "Most workers are too scared to go to court," Martinez says. "They are afraid they'll be deported. I was scared too, but even more, I was mad. And I was tired. I had been doing this for seven years, and it never got better."

For it to get better, indigenous field-workers in the US and Mexico knew they would have to build coalitions that wielded economic power. When workers struck Washington State's largest blueberry grower in 2013, they reached out to consumers and college students and organized a boycott of Sakuma berries. It quickly broadened into a boycott of Driscoll's berries. To make that work, they knew, meant organizing globally. Driscoll's employs migrants from Canada to Mexico, Egypt to Portugal, and exports berries to Europe, China, and Australia.

Transnational networking produced impressive results. In the spring of 2015, fifty thousand berry pickers in Baja California walked out of the fields, threatening the immensely lucrative harvest. Like their South African counterparts, many of these workers were migrants, forced to flee their ancestral farmlands by falling produce prices and international trade agreements. Bernardino Martinez believes that it is time for migrant farmworkers to be offered a path to citizenship, in the US and around the world. Giving migrant workers citizenship rights, he says, "is the least you can do. Remember, we feed you all."[8]

CHAPTER 4

"I CONSIDER THE UNION MY SECOND MOTHER"

THE WORD "UNION" evokes images of brawny brotherhoods, working-class fraternities. And it is true that, even today, most union leaders are male. But in a low-wage workers' movement that is majority female, activists have started to see unions in softer ways: as family, offering love, support, and financial help. Cambodian beer promoter Tep Saroeung describes her union as "my second mother. She stands by her children and shows them how to survive."[1]

Tep comes from about an hour outside Phnom Penh. She bore children young and had no way to support them beyond the meager living her family earned growing rice. So when recruiters came to her village looking for pretty young women to promote Cambrew beer—the top-selling beer in Cambodia, owned by the transnational Danish brewer Carlsberg—her parents urged her to go.

Tep lives in a lightless warren of rooms on the edge of a leafy Phnom Penh neighborhood. Most of Tep's colleagues are in their teens and early twenties. At thirty-two, Tep is one of the oldest beer promotion "girls." Noticeably, there are few children. Those who do have children leave them in the villages, cared for by grandparents.

Tep rents a $35-a-month room for herself so that she has privacy if her husband and children visit. Hers is one of the few rooms with a flush toilet and shower. Carefully washed uniforms hang on a line above her bed. A white plush bear sits on her pillow.

The beer promoters' "worker dormitory" is a series of ten-by-ten-by-five-foot rooms connected by narrow alleyways. Three young women live in each, sharing one full-size bed. They also share an outdoor toilet and shower with scores of neighbors. In November, the rooms are damp. The cement walls sweat; the women are alternately hot and chilled.

Many beer promoters have been driven to the city by land grabs in their villages. Since 2003, family farmlands across the country have been seized and leased to foreign sugar and rubber planters. "Entertainment work" offers a lifeline. Some start as garment workers, but are forced to find other work when factory owners "run away." Most "beer girls" have little education, and so have few other options. Besides beer promotion there is sex work.

The line between the two fields is often faint. Beer promoters are chosen for their youth, good looks, and, frankly, their desperation. They wear skimpy, colorful, glossy uniforms, showing the logo of whatever beer they are pushing. At midday when I visit, some are resting in bed, gossiping, checking their phones. They work nights in bars, restaurants, and beer gardens, flirt with male customers, pour their beers and encourage the men to buy another round.

The more men drink, the more the women earn. Though they are employed by beer companies, bar and restaurant owners press promoters to clean and cook for free. Owners also push women to drink with customers, flirt, maybe agree to sex on the side. The possibility of sex sells more beer. And it helps the women pay bills. They are far from home, and their families need not know.

Alcoholism, drug addiction, and STDs are rampant. With promoters drinking up to seven beers a night, the work takes a toll on their health and spirits. Wage theft is common. It's one reason the women like to work for tips: cash on the spot, pocketed quickly.

For Tep, who has been doing the work for eleven years, the job is an unpleasant necessity. "I don't like it," she says, "but I have very little education so I don't have a choice." The worst part for her is when customers take liberties with women servers. "When the worker pours the beer into the customer's glass, the man uses his hands to touch the lady as she pours. If the woman objects, the customer says—'Oh.' As if it's an accident that he touched her." Worse things happen too, she says, when women leave work late at night and men are waiting.

Cambodian beer promoters, karaoke singers, and massage workers have been organizing and striking frequently since 2010. Tep has helped organize strikes and protests by the Cambodian Food and Service Workers' Federation. Founded in 2007 by charismatic young activist Sar Mora, CFSWF has built a militant movement of service workers in Cambodia.

Tep helps women file charges of sexual harassment and assault, but even with the union's help, justice is elusive, she says. "We had one customer who grabbed a woman in such a way that she became very angry and wanted him arrested. The union helped us, but he disappeared. The woman even knew what his motorbike looked like, but we never found him." Male customers come and go, she says. Servers rarely know their names. And when they do, says Tep, men threaten to hurt women if they complain.

So the women prefer campaigns for systemic change. Transnational Danish brewer Carlsberg was not happy to have its labor abuses in Asia exposed back in Europe, and especially not in union-friendly Denmark, where the Cambodian strikers made TV news. Danish union officials announced a campaign to change "Carlsberg's behavior in Cambodia." When global labor federations with 175 million members called for a boycott, Carlsberg announced it would work with Danish unions to improve conditions for its Asian beer promoters. Tep watched it all closely, she says. "Lessons in global capitalism." She smiles. "My education."[2]

The union educates the women well, she says. "The rep comes to see the women at least twenty times a year and invites us to classes. We learn about labor rights and gender-based violence at work. They teach us how to organize, how to negotiate a collective bargaining agreement."

But there is a deeper connection, an emotional bond. "I consider the union my second mother," she says. "When I have problems, union members care about me, about my working conditions. And when we are challenged the union helps us."

Before she became a union member, Tep was earning $30–$40 a month. By 2015, after several strikes, she was earning $160, enough to keep her parents in their home and her children in school. Her children motivated her to become a leader, she says, as did younger workers, who she helped win eighteen paid days off a year and three months' paid maternity leave. I tell her that this is more than most American workers have. Tep smiles. "I'm going to tell my friends on Facebook."

In 2016, when Carlsberg failed to honor its promises, Tep helped organize a strike. Sympathetic coverage in the Danish press sparked consumer protest. Some stores stopped carrying Carlsberg. Meanwhile, Tep and her colleagues picketed at the beer maker's corporate headquarters in Phnom Penh.

Wearing bright red shirts and loudly condemning violence against women, they also protested at the Cambodian Department of Labor and Ministry of Women. After months of struggle, workers won a 300 percent pay increase and a change in schedule. Workdays would now end at 9:30 p.m. instead of 11. And their new contracts offered clear procedures for grieving sexual harassment. Tep sits up straighter. "We won a lot."

But Tep believes that Cambrew retaliated by assigning union members to less lucrative bars and to restaurants in isolated areas, where they had to wait late at night at dark crossroads for private vans to take them home. As women and as known activists, they feared for their safety. Tep and her coworkers again turned to consumers and unionists abroad, inviting Danish union food servers, hotel workers, and bartenders to visit Phnom Penh and observe working conditions up close. Sar Mora traveled through Europe, seeking allies. Carlsberg profits from a strong reputation for social responsibility, he said. "We have to hold them to that."[3]

Tep says she will keep fighting. "Before the union, we had nothing to live on after we gave birth. Now we get full maternity pay for three months and fifty dollars extra each month to buy food. We can spend more time with our children and our families. I love my union mother."

CHAPTER 5

HOTEL HOUSEKEEPERS GO NORMA RAE

"FEW PEOPLE KNOW ABOUT HOTEL HOUSEKEEPERS," reflected Milan hotel organizer Massimo Frattini as he sat in his tiny Geneva office planning a global housekeepers' week of action for "decent, safe jobs." Frattini, who works for the IUF (a century-old international federation of food, farm, and hotel workers), has, since 2014, been the nerve center for worldwide low-wage workers' protests. He reaches out to local affiliates of the IUF, which claims twelve million members in 120 countries. "It was easier than I ever imagined," he says. "I was surprised. But the feeling was strong among our affiliates. They all wanted to do something big for worker power."

For hotel housekeepers, the challenge has always been how to make the invisible visible. "When customers leave a hotel room," Frattini quips, "many of them must think there is a fairy who comes and cleans. Or they do not think about it at all. In either case, they have no idea how punishing the work is, how hard it is on workers' bodies. Making people see that it's a human being who cleans your room—that is the first step to change."[1]

The labor that service workers do is, by design, invisible. Domestic workers come and go. Often employers are out and, as if by magic, their houses become sparkling clean. Waitresses and waiters, bartenders and baggage handlers appear to customers as little more than outstretched arms and serving hands. "Back of the house" labor in hotels is even more hidden. That's intentional. It shines the magic that hotels sell.

Behind the fantasy that hotel consumers buy are housekeepers: a mostly immigrant and almost exclusively female labor force. They strip and remake rumpled, sweaty beds, scrub dirty linens, food waste, cigarette ash, and unmentionable bodily fluids from ten to twenty-five rooms daily, making them appear fresh and new. It is brutal on their bodies. The International Labour Organization (ILO) says that ten rooms a day is the most anyone can clean safely. Still, some housekeepers must clean fifteen, twenty, even twenty-four rooms daily. And not just in Karachi but also in Providence, Reno, and Seattle.[2]

It used to be that way in Phnom Penh, says Chhim Sitthar, a slight, fierce twenty-seven-year-old who leads a union of more than three thousand workers at the glittering NagaWorld casino, which sits at the confluence of the Mekong and Tonlé Sap Rivers. "But we protested on International Women's Day, and we joined the Global Week of Action for Housekeepers. Now sexual-harassment cases are down. The number of rooms we clean are down. We have three thousand members in our union. And women are the leaders. That's unusual for Cambodia."[3]

Until 2005, Diamond Island was home to fishing families. Some were bought out, others forcibly evicted. The island was a green oasis, says Vathanak Serry Sim, labor activist and child survivor of the 1970s Khmer Rouge death camps. "I used to come with my parents for picnics."[4]

If the river island of Sim's memories recalled the sleepy post-colonial feel of Phnom Penh before globalization, the metal and glass NagaWorld casino embodies the bustle of the new Cambodia. It brims with foreign capital, businesspeople, and NGO staff from the US, France, China, Japan, Australia, Malaysia, and South Korea. Outside, construction workers line up beams and girders for new hotels and condo towers. Young men who were farmers not so long ago now build glossy spaces where Phnom Penh's multinational elite live and work.

It is a dangerous job, says Sok Kin, leader of Phnom Penh's largest construction workers' union. "Men sleep piled together in garages and inadequate shelters. Construction workers die every year in building collapses or bad falls." Sok Kin's union is one of the fastest growing in Cambodia, because construction is booming.[5]

The buildings on which they labor are sleek and modern, rapidly changing the face of a city once known for its mix of French colonial and Buddhist architecture. NagaWorld's vast lobby, with crystal chandeliers and plaster reproductions of ancient Khmer statues rising over chiming slot machines, would fit well on the Las Vegas Strip. So would the hotel's large and militant union.

Like Las Vegas workers, Chhim Sitthar and her comrades have had to fight some scary characters. Cambodia's gambling industry is run by shady investors, international fugitives, and online gambling billionaires. And then there is the repressive Hun Sen regime, which will do pretty much anything to keep foreign capital flowing into Cambodia.

By 2013, says Chhim, NagaWorld housekeepers were tired of abusive managers, sexual harassment, and a monthly wage of $80, half of what they needed to live in the expensive capital. They sent a delegation to demand a raise. The company refused to negotiate. Chhim, and the older union men who had taught her to organize, persuaded 90 percent of the hotel's staff to go on strike. "The company had no intention of seeking a solution," Chhim recalls. The walkout changed that. Still, Chhim was worried. She feared the protests would cost her fellow workers their jobs. Unintimidated, they voted to strike anyway. "When I'm feeling disappointed I keep fighting," she says. "The same is true for my members."

Chhim and union vice president Pao Chhumony are proud that most members and leaders in their union are women. At their airy headquarters, a tight-knit group of women in their twenties plan intently for their next action. "These are the union counselors," Chhim explains. "They talk directly to workers, help with their problems, speak to management for them."

These slight young women have led tense strikes involving hundreds of workers. They've faced physical violence from police and company guards. And they have prevailed. When NagaWorld fired four hundred workers, Chhim negotiated hard and won them their jobs back. Journalists compared the women's militancy to that of textile workers in the 1970s American South. "NagaWorld Staff Go Norma Rae," one headline blared. Norma Rae was the fictional name given to North Carolina textile union organizer Crystal Lee Sutton, played by Sally Field in the 1979 Oscar-winning film.

In Cambodia, where two-thirds of workers are under thirty, Norma Rae and the J. P. Stevens textile strike immortalized in the film are relics of a distant time and place. Still, the young Cambodian rebel girls enjoyed the comparison. Like so many in this new global uprising, Chhim is serious about teaching her members labor history. Once compared to Norma Rae, she watched the film and learned the history. Now she wears the name proudly as she continues to fight for her members. They want maternity leave, higher pay, a reasonable workload, and an end to sexual harassment.[6]

With funding from the Service Employees International Union (SEIU) and the IUF, Chhim and Pao travel to international meetings. They strategize with housekeepers from Myanmar, Pakistan, India, Nepal, Malaysia, and the Philippines. Together, they are developing labor standards across Asia, Chhim says. The slim, dark young woman hopes one day to become an attorney. Meanwhile, she says, she is working on "global actions and to have our friends in other countries help us." Are you a twenty-first-century Norma Rae? I ask. She nods. "Maybe yes."[7]

As the world sweltered through the summer of 2017, hotel workers were fighting hard to keep from sliding backward. In Manila, hotels that had once been union were turning thousands of full-time jobs into "temporary contracts." Union activists were being fired en masse. The Philippine Labor Department ordered hotels to reinstate union workers. Some hotels outright refused, insisting that the workers were not covered by labor laws because they were not permanent. This is the new reality. In Spain, hotel chains outsourced 120,000 jobs to third-party labor suppliers after 2012, so they would not be covered by federal labor protections. Massimo Frattini says the IUF is learning to reckon with this new reality.[8]

Organizers for NUWHRAIN, the Philippine hotel workers' union, wear a special T-shirt to reach workers. As international hotels are increasingly run by third-party management companies, surveillance has intensified. Organizers can't easily approach even workers who have the legal right to join a union. Activists wear the shirts, says organizer Edwin Bustos, so workers will come to them. *Dignified Housekeeper*, the shirts say, in bold red on a black background. On the back are their demands. "Regular Employment, 8-Hour Workday, No Room Quota, Just Wages, Safe Workplace."

When housekeepers talk of health and safety, Bustos says, they are focused on three problems. More than half, globally, are sexually harassed or assaulted. Housekeepers are fighting for hotels to adopt zero tolerance policies, to fire or arrest perpetrators. Toxic cleaning products destroy housekeepers' health. They want the right to refuse to work with poisons. And housekeepers no longer accept managers' insistence that they scrub bathrooms on their hands and knees. It is unnecessary. It's degrading, and it hurts. Housekeepers suffer daily pain and long-term injury more frequently than any other profession.[9]

The other big issue is that hotels are constantly changing owners. They have become a hot investment for private equity firms who move their money in and out quickly. Investors have little to do with daily operations. Most large hotels are now run by professional managers who ramp up workloads, slash wages, and try to break unions. Brand names no longer mean much, says veteran hotel organizer Maria Elena Durazo: "One Hilton is not like the other." International investors own a piece of a Starwood here, there a Marriott, in another city, a Hilton.

To organize, workers must first figure out who owns their hotel. That involves a fair amount of digging, and it can change in an instant. This is a common problem for twenty-first-century unions. Whether it's garment factories or hotels, workers often don't know who profits from their labor. Usually it's not the same people who set their wages, but it is precisely these faceless investors whom workers must pressure if things are to improve.

Santa Brito learned this the hard way. When Brito first arrived in Providence from the Dominican Republic, she was hired in a nonunion housekeeping job at the Renaissance hotel. "The boss was decent. He was a human being and he treated us with care." Then the hotel changed hands. The new owners brought in the Procaccianti Group to manage.

Procaccianti runs hotels for Marriott, Intercontinental, Wyndham, and other brands, providing "management through an owner's lens." What this means, says Brito, is that "they don't think of us as human beings. All they want is to torture our bodies, to wring everything out of us, as if we are rags." Brutal disregard, she says, drove her into the arms of UNITE HERE, the hotel and restaurant workers' union.

"After the Procacciantis took over, they laid a lot of people off," says Brito. "Then they cut wages for everyone else. The new supervisors were abusive. And they made us work so hard." The threat of firing was unspoken but omnipresent. So even after her daily quota was upped to eighteen rooms, Brito didn't complain. "They even stopped giving extra credit for checkouts, which take much longer than cleaning for guests who are staying." Brito says she knew other Providence housekeepers had it worse. "In some hotels, housekeepers have to clean twenty-four rooms a day. You can't work like that for long without getting hurt."

When she became pregnant, Brito worried that the heavy workload might harm her baby or send her into labor early. Like most low-wage workers who do not belong to unions, Brito had no paid time off for illness or maternity leave. "I had to work. I needed to pay for my house and the baby." She was afraid to ask even for unpaid time off. "I thought they'd fire me."

Brito was changing bed linens when her contractions began. She asked to leave. Her shift supervisor said, "No." Her water broke and Brito decided, "I don't care." And she left. "I went to the hospital to have my baby still wearing my uniform." She says she barely had time to wash the cleaning solvents from her hands. Two weeks later, she was fired. As she hung up the phone, she realized that if she didn't want to feel helpless, the only answer was to organize. Since that time, she has not stopped.[10]

Maria Elena Durazo says that a reasonable workload tops the list of demands for hotel housekeepers "because their bodies hurt like hell." Hotel housekeepers have the highest rates of pain and permanent musculoskeletal injury of any labor sector. And Latinas have the highest injury rates of all housekeepers. In Las Vegas, one study found that 66 percent of hotel housekeepers had experienced pain in the past month, 75 percent in the previous year. These injuries were avoidable, say activists. Of the five-largest hotel management companies, three had injury rates that were twice those of the other two. This was something that unions could organize around.[11]

Durazo remembers being at a meeting in Los Angeles in 2011 at which a group of housekeepers were asked to mark an X on a diagram of the human body to show where they hurt. "These were housekeepers from different hotels. They didn't know each other. But when they sat down we all saw they had marked the same places. They all hurt in exactly the same places."

The veteran organizer pauses as she tells this story. Traffic noises echo in a loud Los Angeles café. "There was almost no dry eye in the room. We were crying. They were crying." Durazo thought she knew what the women were thinking: "'I was always told it's me. It's my fault that I get hurt.' It was an amazing moment for them to realize that they were being told lies by management. The next step was, 'What are we going to do about it?'"[12]

What they did was organize globally. In 2009, Hyatt hotels laid off one hundred housekeepers in Boston and replaced them with new immigrants earning half their salary. Though they were not union members, the laid-off workers appealed to UNITE HERE. The union's decision to support them marked an important change in labor-organizing strategy. Facing the extinction of the American labor movement, a new generation of union leaders had decided to devote organizers, resources, and political capital to help low-wage workers who were not, and might never become, union members.

Laphonza Butler, just thirty-five when she became president of the California United Long Term Care Workers Union, the largest union local in the country, believes that strategy is working. She explains: "At a time when public opinion of unions was at an all-time low in the US, we had to make people understand that unions were there to defend all workers, not just their own."

Rusty Hicks, the young head of the Los Angeles Federation of Labor, believes that unions must prioritize "raising the wages and the working conditions of all workers, whether they are in unions or not." It is the job of unions "to ensure that all workers are empowered, that they come together and that their voices will be heard."[13]

Hotel housekeepers helped to drive that strategy. In a 2006 campaign called "Profits, Pain, and Pillows," UNITE HERE activists fought to establish national hotel wage and safety standards. There were protests and civil disobedience, lobbying and economic suasion. Hotel workers marched, picketed, and went on hunger strikes across the US. Hundreds were arrested.[14]

Three years after the Boston layoffs, UNITE HERE, the IUF, and affiliates in other countries launched a global "Hyatt Hurts" boycott. It worked, says Massimo Frattini. "A group of little housekeeping ladies" from the US, Europe, Asia, and Africa brought mighty Hyatt to the bargaining table. They were helped when President Barack Obama nominated Hyatt heiress Penny Pritzker to be secretary of commerce in 2013. Worried about union protests at her confirmation hearings, the Pritzkers granted raises and union recognition to workers in all hotels still owned by the family. (It didn't improve things for workers at franchised Hyatts, but it was still a huge victory.)[15]

That same year, a local hotel battle in San Diego raised another big issue—the way the hotel industry exploits undocumented immigrants. When a San Diego Hilton changed hands and workers complained about layoffs, heavier workloads, and reduced wages, they were fired. And information on the undocumented among them was sent to Immigration and Customs Enforcement (ICE). The workers faced arrest and deportation. Nine fired workers went on hunger strike, fasting in a tent in front of the hotel. The mayor and state legislators visited. United Farm Workers cofounder Dolores Huerta fasted with them, drawing attention to the deep ties between the UFW and UNITE HERE.

Maria Elena Durazo, child of farmworkers turned UNITE HERE organizer, was trained as an organizer by the UFW. Both unions understand that there can be no labor justice without a path to citizenship for all workers, she says. And that will only come when unions register members to vote and fight for immigration reform. "That was true in the early twentieth century," Durazo says, "and it's just as true now."[16]

Massimo Frattini believes that workers' transnational networking is equally important in a global economy. He has organized worldwide weeks of action by hotel housekeepers each year since 2014. Workers from Massachusetts to California, from Manila to Buenos Aires, in the Maldives, Addis Ababa, Reykjavík, Oslo, and hundreds of other locales have participated. Some hotels have retaliated, firing workers. But the attention generated by global campaigns and boycott threats has given them power to fight back—which, says Chhim Sitthar, gives "meaning and excitement" to lives too often consumed by backbreaking drudgery.

"International attention provides a bit of clout for the most marginal workers in the world," says Frattini. Ultimately, he hopes the housekeepers' movement will be able to establish global hotel labor standards. Meanwhile, small victories can make the difference between a living wage and poverty, between feeling safe on the job and working in fear, between good health and a body racked with pain.

As for Frattini, who once hauled bags in a Milan hotel, he loves being the nexus for global labor actions. He works phones and computers like a dervish and travels incessantly, not only coordinating global actions by hotel workers but also by retail, farm, and fast-food workers. Strong coffee is essential, he says with a laugh. "This is just the beginning."[17]

CHAPTER 6

UNITED FOR RESPECT

OUR Walmart and the Uprising of Retail Workers

IN OCTOBER 2012, associates from nine stores in the Los Angeles area decided to wage the first strike ever against a Walmart on US soil. Thirty-four-year-old deli manager Venanzi Luna was the spark plug at the hot center of the strike: Pico Rivera, a dusty, Latino working-class town near Los Angeles. Workers there knew the stakes were high. After a strike in Quebec a few years earlier, Walmart had simply shut down the store. "It was scary. Really scary," Luna says.[1]

A child of Mexican immigrants, Luna says her father—a union trucker—taught her not to accept abuse. She didn't. Nor did the older activist workers Luna called "mamas": Evelin Cruz, daughter of Salvadoran civil war refugees, and Denise Barlage, who says she is "spawn of French immigrants on one side and hardworking Tennesseans on the other." Riled up, pissed off, and ready to rise, they knew they needed help and training. They got both from the Organization United for Respect at Walmart, funded by the United Food and Commercial Workers (UFCW).

No one in the US had challenged the retail giant in this way before. Luna says they didn't know if there would be anybody behind them. But "I looked at Denise, and Evelin looked at me. And I said, 'Mamas, we're going out.'" When they got to the parking lot, more than a hundred workers and hundreds of supporters picketed. The *New York Times*, CNN, and other mainstream outlets noted the strike's importance. *Democracy Now!* called it historic. The *Nation* lauded "the great Wal-Mart walkout."[2]

They knew they were making history, but mostly associates were sick of the ways that store managers punished them for "every little thing," subjecting them to a ritual reprimand called "coaching." It felt both racist and sexist, Cruz recalled. "In a store that was 90 percent Latina, it was almost always a white man calling a scared Latina into his office and closing the door."

Barlage says Cruz taught women: "'Tell the manager, you can't close the door.' That's not OK. And the second thing she taught us was that we could demand that one of us from OUR Walmart be allowed to go in with the person being coached."

The managers were usually big men, says Barlage, and some seemed to enjoy "leaning over these small women." It was intimidating. Implied threats and verbal abuse motivated a lot of workers to join the movement, Barlage believes. It did her. A self-described "Southern girl with LA attitude," Barlage says she wasn't easily intimidated. "Still, it can get to you."[3]

Evelin Cruz worried about what Walmart might do to workers who organized. "Anytime a worker stood up for herself there was extreme retaliation. People were being fired for crazy reasons. The point was to intimidate." Managers knew the workers who could least afford to be fired, Cruz says. "The financial burden was tremendous. Many associates are single mothers who can't even afford notebooks or pencils for their kids to take to school."

Cruz joined OUR Walmart because she couldn't stand watching "how people were being disrespected." It hurt the "bleeding heart," she inherited from her mother. As for her knowledge of workers' rights, Cruz says she was taught by the UFCW.

Managers tried to pit her against her colleagues, Cruz recalled. They let her take vacations, gave her full-time work "when almost no one at Walmart had that." But the cruelty got to her. "Managers would yell at employees on the sales floor in front of customers. It was outrageous. Calling them stupid, ignorant when they were trying their best to serve people."[4]

"We found out we didn't have to just take it," says Luna. She was then supporting two elderly parents and worried what it would mean if she lost her job. But the UFCW taught her that she could file Unfair Labor Practices complaints to the state and federal governments when Walmart violated workers' rights. She was afraid the first time she did. Soon she really enjoyed it. "I told my managers they have to put up a poster on the wall so workers can see their legal rights. They didn't like me for that." She strikes a pose, flashes a bad-ass sneer.

When the Pico workers walked out in October 2012, Luna learned something else that surprised her. Walmart associates in other countries were unionized. She remembers watching in amazement as a bus rolled up to the Pico store and workers from Italy, Spain, Uruguay, South Africa, and other countries poured out. "They walked us into the store and the manager came over. He said: 'Everyone who is not a Walmart employee has to leave.' They all started pulling out their Walmart IDs. Then they sang union songs." That was the moment Luna understood: it had to be about global solidarity. Before the international delegation left, they met with US associates to establish the Walmart Global Union Alliance. They were backed by the UFCW and UNI Global Union, an international federation of twenty million workers.[5]

Going global was not a choice if Walmart workers had any hope of changing the culture of the world's largest private employer. Only the US and Chinese militaries employed more people than Walmart. The company controlled 25 percent of the US grocery market, was the second-largest grocer in the United Kingdom, the largest retailer in Mexico, the largest food and department store chain in China, and the third-largest retailer in Brazil. It was majority owner of the largest supermarket chain in Central America. And with the help of the US Agency for International Development (AID), Walmart was then breaking into India and fourteen African nations.

By 2015, Walmart claimed 11,500 stores on five continents—with 2.2 million direct employees. Add to that, those who worked for its 100,000 suppliers. Walmart was the largest importer of Chinese low-cost goods in the US. By some estimates, those imports cost 400,000 American workers their jobs. If ever there was a David versus Goliath battle, this was it.[6]

The Walmart workers' protests spread quickly. Truckers and warehouse workers, retail salespeople and managers held labor actions across the US. On "Black Friday," the day after Thanksgiving and the busiest day of the American shopping year, OUR Walmart protested in front of hundreds of stores. They blocked entrances and sat down on busy streets and highways, singing half-century-old civil rights songs and seventy-five-year-old labor anthems. Cruz, Barlage, and Luna happily held their wrists behind them as police applied plastic zip-tie handcuffs. "This is what I want to do for the rest of my life," Barlage said.

. . .

Since 2012, Walmart workers have struck on every Black Friday—in the US and around the world. In 2014, Chilean workers shut every Walmart in that country. Walmart workers across India marched for higher wages and safer conditions. And in June 2013, less than two months after the Rana Plaza factory collapse in Bangladesh, the worst industrial disaster in the history of the garment trades, Walmart associates chipped in to help bring garment union leader Kalpona Akter to the annual Walmart shareholders meeting in Arkansas.

There Akter joined with a hundred OUR Walmart activists who had crossed the country on a "Ride for Respect" to speak out for a living wage and safe, dignified jobs. Actor Tom Cruise spoke first, praising Walmart for "using its size and scale to improve women's lives around the world." Akter followed, describing what it felt like to find Walmart labels in the charred ruins of the Tazreen factory, where 112 workers had died in a fire the year before. She faced Walmart family members on the dais. Then she called on them to personally ensure that the workers producing the clothing sold by Walmart would never again have to die for their jobs. It was a powerful moment, shared widely on social media, covered sympathetically by the press.[7]

Walmart did what it often does when unrest surfaces. In the spring of 2015, the Pico store was suddenly closed for "plumbing problems." When the store reopened a few months later, none of the OUR Walmart leaders were rehired. Walmart corporate set up an anti-union hotline, encouraging managers to report even casual conversations about organizing. Luna says her social media accounts were hacked, as were those of other activists. Sometimes, they would post or text false information about labor actions, "just to watch the company spies scurry."

In 2015, *Fortune* magazine found that Walmart had hired defense contractor Lockheed Martin to keep tabs on OUR Walmart activists. They knew they were not supposed to interfere with workers' right to organize, so they kept their surveillance hidden from state labor inspectors, Barlage says. But she later found proof that Walmart corporate had warned store managers not to rehire activist workers. Barlage says OUR Walmart activists should be proud: "We must be making a difference," she says feistily, "if Walmart is going to all that trouble."[8]

CHAPTER 7

SUPERSIZE MY WAGES

Fast-Food Workers and the March of History

TWENTY-ONE-YEAR-OLD CARL'S JR. and CVS worker Vance "Stretch" Sanders attended the first national Fight for $15 convention in Richmond, Virginia, in August 2016. Visiting the capital of the Confederacy, he could not help thinking about the lingering effects of slavery. Ten thousand activists, most of them African American, marched up Monument Avenue, lined by statues of Confederate generals. "I heard Reverend William Barber speak about the morality of our movement," he says. Barber is the founder and leader of Moral Mondays, a mass civil-disobedience campaign that began in North Carolina and spread to Georgia, South Carolina, Illinois, and New Mexico. Protesting legislation restricting voting rights, minimum wage increases, and union rights, clergy, professors, students, and low-wage workers would get themselves arrested on repeated Mondays. Sanders, who also preaches the gospel, felt inspired.

"It took us four hundred years to get from zero to $7.25," Barber told the crowd. "We can't wait another four hundred years. Labor without a living wage is nothing but a pseudo form of slavery." The crowd roared in agreement. Sanders says: "It was really something."[1]

For three days, Sanders listened as fast-food, retail, and home-healthcare workers insisted it was no accident that half of African American workers in the US earned under $15 an hour. "We always did the grunt work for low wages," said Virginia home-healthcare worker Lauralyn Clark. "White babies drank from our breasts, but we couldn't drink from their fountains. White families relied on us to care for their elderly parents, but we couldn't ride the bus with them. We cleaned their schools, but our children couldn't attend. We cooked their food, but we couldn't sit at their table. Well, enough is enough."[2]

It all began four years earlier. Weeks after the Walmart walkout, a few fast-food workers in New York City decided to strike. One of the organizers was twenty-two-year-old Brooklyn Kentucky Fried Chicken worker Naquasia LeGrand. In 2016, she looked back amazed. Her little group had kicked off something bigger than they ever expected: a global uprising against poverty wages. "We triggered something epic that had never been done," she marveled. In 2014, LeGrand was invited to the White House to witness President Obama sign an increase in the minimum wage for workers on federal contracts. "We never thought it would even get this far," she said that day. "We're just sick and tired of being sick and tired."[3]

From its beginnings, the low-wage workers' struggle in the US was rooted in the long history of African American protest: against exploitation of black labor, violation of black bodies, and attempts to break the spirit of black workers. Fast-food activists have repeatedly quoted the famous words uttered by former sharecropper and voting rights activist Fannie Lou Hamer when asked why black people could wait no longer for freedom. "You always hear this sob story," she said in 1964. "You know it takes time. For three hundred years, we've given them time. And I've been tired so long now, I am sick and tired of being sick and tired."[4]

I've heard it from fast-food workers everywhere. Bleu Rainer told me he was "sick and tired of being sick and tired." Marching down Monument Avenue, Stretch Sanders saw black workers holding signs that said: "Sick and Tired of Being Sick and Tired." Sanders told that story with the same fervor and weariness Hamer had displayed a half century earlier. "We're young," he says, "but we understand that black folk have been at this for a very long time. We're picking up an old struggle."

Under twenty-first-century conditions. At a Fight for $15 march, Bleu Rainer held up a paycheck for $109. "That's for two weeks' work," he said incredulously. His schedule at McDonald's was decided by algorithm, he explained, and the computer called him in only when managers felt like it. Schedules are changed at the drop of a hat. Parents can't plan child care, or know for sure if they will be able to pay their bills.

The movement's focus on scheduling has started to make a difference. In May 2017, the New York City Council passed bills mandating that employers give fast-food workers fourteen days' notice about schedule changes. It also banned back-to-back shifts. The movement started with

New York fast-food workers, activists say. They believe these bills will send out ripples.[5]

Before they started organizing, normal life was impossible, workers say. LeGrand was working three jobs to make rent on a two-bedroom apartment she shared with five other people. Most people she knew worked two or three jobs. Bleu Rainer was sleeping in bus stations because he didn't earn enough to pay Tampa rent. The decision to protest was not that hard, says Rainer. "We really had nothing to lose."[6]

Between 2012 and 2015, fast-food workers staged hundreds of one-day flash strikes, every few months in an ever-growing number of cities. And they took advantage of social media to maximize the impact of their actions. Images of shamefaced or weeping Ronald McDonalds went viral. So did the word "McJobs," denoting dead-end work without benefits. They called on McDonald's to "Supersize My Wages" and asked customers if they wanted "poverty fries."

These actions spread around the globe. In 2013, the National Guest-worker Alliance asked Massimo Frattini and the IUF to support foreign student workers protesting horrific labor conditions at US fast-food restaurants. In Pennsylvania, "exchange students" were being forced to work eighty-hour weeks at McDonald's and sleep in jammed basement dorms. When Frattini reached out to affiliate unions in Europe, Asia, and Africa, he was stunned by their response.

"We had no idea how ready they were," he says. During the summer of 2013, fast-food workers staged "days of action" in more than thirty countries. Eleven months later, fast-food workers in 230 cities, in thirty-four countries on six continents, walked off the job to demand a living wage, full-time work, and union recognition. It was the most global strike in history.

A series of international conversations enhanced fast-food workers' sense that they were part of a rising global movement. Workers from New York, Chicago, and 150 US cities met with counterparts from Denmark, Argentina, Thailand, South Korea, the Philippines, and other countries. Los Angeles McDonald's workers flew to speak with counterparts in Tokyo. Workers from Chicago and New York traveled to the Philippines. They planned global campaigns and talked of negotiating global labor agreements with the world's largest corporations.

And they shared experiences. LeGrand remembers meeting a McDonald's worker from Thailand who made her realize that there were fast-food workers who had it worse than she did. But American workers also learned that some in other countries had it better. In unionized Denmark, Bleu Rainer found out, fast-food workers earned the equivalent of $21 an hour, with paid vacations, health benefits, and subsidies to attend college. He was impressed. It could be done. He learned a lot more when he joined workers from twenty-two countries at the Brazilian Senate hearings in the summer of 2015.

On April 14, 2016, low-wage workers struck in three hundred cities and forty-plus countries. Momentum continues to grow. Nineteen-year-old Los Angeles activist Samuel Homer Williams believes that this movement, like the black freedom struggle fifty years earlier, will be remembered as a turning point: "For me it's about being a part of history," he says, "part of something bigger than myself. I kind of feel like a hero, knowing that I'm helping people stay in their homes, pay their bills, and be able to eat. That's something that a lot of people haven't been able to do lately. We're trying to change that. And I think we will."[7]

CHAPTER 8

1911–2011

History and the Global Labor Struggle

FOR GARMENT WORKERS, March 25, 2011, was a critical moment. Hundreds poured into the Great Hall at Cooper Union in New York City to commemorate the one hundredth anniversary of the Triangle Shirtwaist Factory fire. Many famous political figures had spoken in the column-lined auditorium during the nineteenth and twentieth centuries: suffragist Elizabeth Cady Stanton, President Abraham Lincoln, antislavery activists Frederick Douglass and William Lloyd Garrison, Lakota chief Red Cloud and Arapahoe chief Little Raven. Now, the room buzzed as a thirty-five-year-old Bangladeshi garment union leader named Kalpona Akter slowly climbed the stairs to the stage. "In Bangladesh," she said quietly, fiercely, "it is not 2011; it's 1911."

Students, teachers, garment workers, union retirees, and low-wage workers had come together to remember a terrible fire that, one hundred years earlier, had changed the course of American history. Crowding the Great Hall that night there were also coal miners, catfish processors, construction workers, hotel workers, and taxi drivers, representing millions of others who perform the twenty-first century's most dangerous jobs. They were not there to commemorate the 1911 fire as a moment burned into the lives of long-dead workers, a catastrophe that changed everything for the better. They were there to remind us all that danger is still a daily reality for workers in this country and, even more so, around the world.

One hundred and two years earlier, in November 1909, a twenty-three-year-old Jewish immigrant dressmaker named Clara Lemlich gave a brief, impassioned speech from the same stage to an audience of garment workers in their teens and twenties. After a parade of male union leaders and middle-class women advised the young women not to go on strike, Lemlich had jumped onto the stage. "I have something to say," she shouted, interrupting the official program.

It was a bold assertion for a lowly "girl worker," one of millions of poor immigrants then living and working in New York. Speaking in Yiddish, Lemlich described the dangerous conditions for workers in the new ready-to-wear industry. She was angry, as were the women who listened that evening. "I am one of those who suffer from the conditions being described here," she said. "And I move that we call a general strike."

It was as if a tide had broken. The cautious elders could not hold them back. Hundreds of women threw their hats into the air, pledging to uphold the strike. Over the next few months, between twenty thousand and forty thousand young garment workers, immigrant Jews from Eastern Europe, Catholics from Ireland and southern Italy, and a few native-born white and black Protestants marched and picketed along the streets of Lower Manhattan. It was the largest women's strike the country had ever seen.[1]

In the years that followed, women garment workers across the US organized, struck, and unionized. But they found that unionism could only take them so far. They also needed enforceable labor law. That need was indelibly burned into the national consciousness on March 25, 1911, when a fire at the Triangle Shirtwaist Factory, in the heart of Greenwich Village, took 146 young workers' lives. In a terrible half hour, thousands watched as young people jumped to their deaths from eighth-story windows, some burning even as they fell.

Between 1911 and 1938, outrage over the fire galvanized support for the passage of minimum wage, maximum hours, and safety laws. Triangle seared the conscience of a nation, forging a new consensus that workers should not have to put their lives on the line to earn their daily bread. The political fallout from Triangle transformed American law, putting state and federal governments in the business of guaranteeing the safety of workers. There was a backlash. Labor laws were struck down by conservative courts. But they were rewritten and passed again. A new era had begun for American labor. Few could imagine going backward.

For nearly a hundred years, garment unions convened annual commemorations of the fire—solemn events marked by cautionary tales about how bad labor conditions were before unions grew strong, protective legislation was passed, and governments began to enforce workplace safety standards. These commemorations were reminders that unions and government inspectors needed to stay vigilant. But overall, they radiated a sense that much had changed—and for the good. Then, as the fire's centennial approached, Kalpona Akter and other twenty-first-century labor activists insisted that there was another story to tell. The past was present again.

Akter began to travel the world in 2010, not just to publicize the killing conditions under which clothing was now being made but to let European, Asian, and American consumers know that Bangladeshi garment workers had reached their limit and were rising. They wanted safe working conditions and wages sufficient to support their families. Their protests were huge. Hundreds of thousands of workers were in the streets, blocking roads, staging sit-ins.

A handful of newspapers in the UK covered the turmoil, but the US press paid little attention. Our cities were awash in a flood tide of "fast fashion"—cheap, colorful, plentiful clothing. It was intoxicating and fun. No one wanted to think about where it came from.

Akter began to tour the world to ensure that the cries of Bangladeshi garment workers could be heard beyond the crowded streets and export-processing zones of Dhaka and Chittagong. She was sponsored by UNITE HERE, Canadian public employee unions, the European consumer group Clean Clothes Campaign, and the US-based International Labor Rights Forum, Worker Rights Consortium, and United Students Against Sweatshops. Akter's tours helped forge a new global alliance to stand with Bangladeshi workers who make the clothing sold on Fifth Avenue, Oxford Street, and the Champs-Élysées, in Tokyo's Ginza district and Seoul's Myeongdong district. As the centennial of the 1911 Triangle fire approached, they used the occasion to help consumers see and understand the human costs of the fast-fashion revolution.

Since the 1990s, thousands of workers had been killed and injured in garment factory fires and building collapses in Bangladesh. As a teen, Akter had lived through a garment factory fire. She described it to audiences to make the fear real.

In a crowd of panicked workers she had rushed for the exits. "Then we realized they had locked us in, because they believed maybe we will steal merchandise." She is still angry, decades later. Staircases were blocked by piles of clothing bound for the US and Europe. When eight hundred workers tried to pour down smoke-filled steps, some were trampled.

Others passed out from smoke inhalation. "Finally, we screamed and cried so loud that they opened the door." On that day, Akter says, she learned the importance of making noise.

Bangladeshi garment workers have been speaking out since then, especially since 2005—protesting, striking, and putting pressure on famous retail brands. As this book goes to press, they are still in the streets. Like berry pickers and fast-food workers, they hope to embarrass major brands into behaving more humanely. After factory fires, Akter sorts through smoking rubble to find labels she knows are there: for Disney, Walmart, Gap, the Children's Place, Primark, Top Shop, and H&M. Globalized youth culture. Globalized capital. Burned skin and crushed bones. Far from London, New York, and Tokyo where the clothes are sold, Akter holds charred labels up to the cameras so the world can see and understand.[2]

A few months before the Triangle centennial, a garment factory fire in Dhaka killed scores. The doors were locked. Workers had no other way to flee the burning building than by jumping from the eleventh floor. Horrified crowds watched from the sidewalks below. The falling bodies, burning as they dropped through the sky, looked the same as they had in Greenwich Village one hundred years earlier. Grief-stricken Dhaka families searched bodies lined up on the sidewalk, hoping not to find a loved one. Photographs of their grisly search echoed grim images of makeshift street morgues in 1911 New York, where Triangle's victims were arrayed.[3]

As she looked out from the Great Hall stage on March 25, 2011, Kalpona Akter says she thought about Clara Lemlich, whose ninety-five-year-old daughter, Rita Margules, was in the audience. "I came to know that this was the hall where Clara Lemlich spoke," Akter says. "I was proud to speak from that same stage. UNITE HERE made a poster with Clara Lemlich and me both saying 'I Have Something to Say.' That is really a very moving sentence. It speaks volumes."[4]

Akter left the stage at the end of her speech, knelt before Rita Margules, and took the old woman's hand. Lemlich had inspired a generation of Bangladeshi garment workers, she told her. The tiny woman smiled. Then the New York City Labor Chorus, white-haired veterans of earlier union struggles, sang "Solidarity Forever."

In Dhaka, Akter had made sure that garment workers knew that the Triangle centennial was coming. They marched with banners expressing the solidarity of Bangladeshis with the struggles of American workers, past and present. When Akter came to New York, she brought with her purple T-shirts emblazoned with images of Bangladeshi garment workers and the women of Triangle. They said in English and Bengali: "1911 to 2011: Not One More Fire."

Akter recalls her first visit to the Triangle site. She was deeply moved to be "walking on that street where so many people worked, where there was so much loss of life. Touching the wall of the building, walking on the sidewalk where so many women jumped to their deaths, hurt so much." But, says Akter, as she stood with her fingers pressed against the wrought-iron early-twentieth-century building, she felt more than sorrow. She believed that the shirtwaist makers of Triangle were speaking to the women who, in 2011, still worked fourteen-hour days sewing dresses, shorts, and shirts; who still, a century after Triangle, put their lives on the line every day.

What US labor activists won in the aftermath of Triangle, Akter says, "was everything we have worked for, everything we are fighting for." She believes those gains came in part because American trade unionists kept "the women who died there alive—through prayer, through protest, through anger." So Akter began to teach Bangladeshi garment workers that history. "We in Bangladesh began to keep them alive too."

When Akter speaks to audiences in New York and Stockholm, Montreal and Seoul, she echoes arguments that Clara Lemlich made in a 1912 *Good Housekeeping* article. Lemlich exhorted consumers to be conscious, to demand safer conditions for workers who risked death to make the beautiful clothes they loved. A century later, Akter says, she asks of American and European consumers the same.

But when she speaks of Triangle to Bangladeshi workers, Akter says, her focus is on labor's victories. "Talking about the fire's victims," she believes, "is a way of telling women who are working today, it doesn't matter what part of the world you work in. If you stand up and fight for change, you can win."[5]

CHAPTER 9

PEOPLE POWER MOVEMENTS IN THE TWENTY-FIRST CENTURY

AKTER'S ASSERTION THAT "in Bangladesh it is not 2011; it's 1911" explains a lot. For, it is true not just of Bangladesh but of low-wage workers everywhere. Four decades into the neoliberal revolution, the repeal and erosion of labor protections, shrinking labor unions, precarious employment, stagnant wages, declining buying power, and a global race to the bottom in safety standards have turned the clock back for workers. And it has not been a small step back, but a giant leap. From Arkansas chicken processing plants to Philippine flip-flop factories, low-wage workers are having to again fight for rights already fought for and won one hundred years earlier.

Regression is a difficult concept to absorb, especially for those who live in the world's most affluent countries. We have been schooled in the ideology of progress, and we like to believe that life for workers has steadily improved. Instead, millions of workers have lost ground. They have less security than workers did forty years ago. Their wages buy less. Their factories are more dangerous.

Low-wage workers understand this all too well. It is the root of their global uprising. From New York City to southern China, Brasília to Cape Town, thousands of twenty-first-century labor stoppages, strikes, civil-disobedience actions, and street protests have called into question the boundless expansion of capital. And that has prompted a violent backlash. There have been targeted murders of movement leaders—in the Philippines, Bangladesh, and Cambodia, in Honduras, Mexico, and Colombia. Indigenous activists, who have led the resistance to dam building, land expropriations, and pipelines from Honduras to Standing Rock, have been particularly hard-hit.[1]

Honduran environmental leader Berta Cáceres, who fought to prevent eviction of Lenca villagers for a dam project, was assassinated in her home in 2016. At least 111 Honduran land rights activists from different communities have been killed since 2000. In Brazil, more than 400 indigenous activists have died defending their lands. In Mexico and Colombia, indigenous land rights activists continue to be murdered. Around the world, uprisings for workers' and women's rights and against dams and mines have touched a nerve. "The answer is to keep on fighting," Kalpona Akter insists. "If you are always worrying about dying, you can't live."

Activists know that their struggles have also brought change: wage increases, hours reductions, enhanced maternity leave, and investigations of labor conditions in complicated global supply chains. The geographic scope and scale of the protests, the vast numbers of people involved, the militancy and the courage of the protesters have been stunning. Many of those rising are the poorest of the poor, willing to risk what little they have for the next generation.

We are witnessing the first truly global uprisings since the 1980s "People Power" movements that toppled Duvalier in Haiti, Marcos in the Philippines, Ershad in Bangladesh, and Communist dictatorships across Central and Eastern Europe. That same wave of mass movements unsuccessfully challenged dictators in Nepal, Thailand, Burma, and Tibet. China's Tiananmen Square student uprising in 1989 was the last of the People Power movements, a tragically suppressed move to weld political freedoms onto the market forces that Deng Xiaoping had unleashed. Like the global 1968 student uprisings before them, the People Power movements of the 1980s spread across national borders, sweeping many parts of the globe. Resistance is contagious; rebellion feels good.

The uprisings against poverty wages that are the subject of this book have spread with similar speed. Like other poor people's movements, they have had to depend on support from allies—labor unions, consumer groups, insurgent politicians, progressive businesspeople. But the sparks and fuel have come from mass discontent at the grass roots.

They have pulled off remarkable organizing feats—work stoppages in hundreds of cities, in scores of countries, on every continent. And they have had real successes. Between 2012 and 2015, their organizing yielded wage increases in South Africa, Bangladesh, Cambodia, and Myanmar, among other places. Some workers doubled their wages and more. In New Zealand, workers won regular schedules, and in Britain, more than one hundred thousand won guaranteed hours and then proceeded to strike McDonald's for the right to unionize. The struggle continues. But workers have seen that if they keep the pressure on, wages will rise, and conditions will improve.[2]

In the US, the Fight for $15 movement begun by fast-food and Walmart workers has grown to include adjunct professors, retail and airport workers, and gas station and home-healthcare attendants. Since most American workers no longer earn a living wage, activists see unlimited possibilities for growth. Many cities have passed the $15 minimum wage. New York and California enacted $15 state minimums. And new living-wage bills are considered every term by cities and towns across the US.[3]

Will these victories survive the presidency of Donald Trump, and the rise of authoritarian regimes in the Philippines, Brazil, and other parts of Africa, Latin America, and Asia? Activists believe they will, because rising inequality and falling real wages are so widespread, and are sparking anger across political divides.

Some movement gains will likely not survive. In 2016, the US National Labor Relations Board limited "on-demand scheduling," under which workers must always be on call but have no guaranteed hours. In another case, the NLRB ruled McDonald's a "joint employer," responsible for the treatment of workers in restaurants owned by franchisees. Also in 2016, the NLRB ruled that graduate students are workers and entitled to unionize. Because NLRB members are political appointees, these rulings are endangered under President Trump. Still, activists insist "We Will Not Go Back"—even if the forces arrayed against them are overwhelming. To continue the struggle they use all the tools at their disposal.

Social media, accessible via inexpensive smartphones, have enabled activists to publicize their struggles and to let the world know when their leaders are endangered or assaulted. It also helps them to make connections and build coalitions globally. They need no longer depend on corporate media for coverage. In countries like Bangladesh, where garment factory owners control newspapers and television stations, this has been essential. But the sword is double-edged: social media is easily monitored.[4]

Filipina activist Em Atienza—a diminutive twenty-four-year-old student who has organized street protests for labor rights and against gender-based violence, says that activists "can't afford to be afraid. We are young, so we must and will keep fighting." Cambodian hotel organizer Chhim Sitthar says she knows that she might die before she achieves her goals. "That's OK with me," she says. "It really is. If I can help the next generation, I don't mind."[5]

The courage of youth is powerful, says veteran Maria Elena Durazo. But these movements have not risen without careful planning by labor veterans. Bangladeshi activist Moshrefa Mishu, who led a 2014 hunger strike of 1,600 garment workers, and Josua Mata, who has helped drive a labor resurgence in the Philippines, argue that the mass protests of the twenty-first century have come from decades of organizing, debate, splintering, and rebuilding.[6]

Bangladeshi students and workers have organized ceaselessly for at least forty years, Mishu says—for women's and workers' rights, against Islamists, against a repressive state. "Organizing and protest are what we do. We're good at it. We fight. We win a little. We lose. They beat us and we fight again."[7]

In the Philippines, say activists Walden Bello and Josua Mata, the struggle has also been very long. Union workers helped power the peaceful 1986 revolution that brought down Ferdinand Marcos. It is ironic, Bello has noted, that post-Marcos "democracy" has not helped Filipino workers and small landholders much. Perhaps the opposite.

Offering a different vision, Bello ran for the Philippine Senate in 2016, demanding justice for low-wage workers and small landholders. American observers, noting the impassioned rhetoric and the devotion of his young supporters, compared him to Vermont's democratic socialist senator Bernie Sanders, then running for president of the United States. Though both were ultimately unsuccessful, supporters believe that their campaigns sowed seeds that continue to sprout.[8]

In Mexico, rebellion against the damages of globalization and neoliberalism has been ongoing since the 1990s. Historian Iain Boal compared the breakup of Mexico's *ejido* common lands and the displacement of millions of Mexican peasants in the 1980s and 1990s to the industrialization of England four centuries earlier, when enclosures of "the commons" sparked decades of rebellions, land occupations, and the rise of early labor unions.[9]

The Zapatistas weren't quite the machine-smashing Luddites, but they offered indigenous community and traditional knowledge as resistance and solution. Boal wrote of their rebellion: "The longing for a better world will need to arise at the imagined meeting place of many movements of resistance, as many as there are sites of closure and exclusion. The resistance will be as transnational as capital. Because enclosure takes myriad forms, so shall resistance to it."

Indigenous resistance has continued unbroken worldwide. The Zapatistas did not disappear. They built autonomous communities in Chiapas that remain vibrant in the twenty-first century. And chants of "Berta Cáceres Vive!" (Berta Cáceres Lives!) animate indigenous land rights protests from Chiapas to Chile.

A decade after the Zapatista uprising, seventy thousand Oaxacan teachers from indigenous Mixteco, Zapoteco, and Triqui communities struck for a living wage and for basic supplies for their students: books, pencils, toilets, and potable water. The state government deployed police helicopters, bullets, and tear gas. Teachers and journalists alike were shot. After the brutal police assault, the strike mushroomed into a movement that ultimately involved over a million people.

Protesters occupied the city's zócalo (central square). Police cut down the ancient trees so they would have no shade. Oaxacans quietly reclaimed their commons, offering food and water to striking teachers. Together they erected barricades to keep police and military vehicles from entering the city. One night, my family and I drove into Oaxaca past groups of teachers sitting on folding chairs behind burned-out buses. They waved us around the charred metal and onto a dry riverbed. River rocks pinged and echoed as we drove through the smoke of campfires in Oaxaca's streets.

In the months that followed, grassroots groups governed themselves via teacher and peasant assemblies. Two thousand indigenous women banging "pots and pans" marched into a government-run television station they said had spread false stories about the protests. For three weeks, the women ran their own "Channel of the Oaxacan People." When police stormed the station, the women fled but soon occupied eleven other TV and radio stations, creating grassroots media of their own: the "voice" of the rebellion.

Death squads and hundreds of arrests finally stilled the protest. Thousands of armed police stormed the city center, posting signs purported to be from city residents thanking the government for "reclaiming our park." But graffiti sprayed on city walls told of transformations that could not be undone. "We will never be the same again." And: "This seed will grow."[10]

Sprouting seeds, spreading vines, global rebellion grew. Five years later, Occupy Wall Street laid claim to city centers from New York to Hong Kong, building alternative communal institutions, challenging city authorities, battling with police, questioning global capitalism. They launched a discussion that has not yet ended.

In 2016, Mexican teachers were still protesting school privatization, funding cuts, and mandatory teaching of English in place of indigenous languages. As the 2016–17 school year began, Mexican teachers were on strike in four states. Many were still angry about the disappearance and murder of forty-three student teacher activists in 2014. The repression in 2016 was almost as bloody. Twelve teacher-activists and supporters were killed.

In the aftermath, parents, teachers, and students came together to reflect. Teacher-turned-journalist Luis Hernandez Navarro, like so many activists in the new labor movement, argued that workers must study history to understand what is happening to them. Quoting a teacher active in the Paris Commune uprising of 1871, Navarro wrote of the 2016 strike: "The task of teachers . . . is to give the people the intellectual means to rebel." It is that gift that veterans like Mishu, Durazo, and Mata are passing on to a new generation of activists.[11]

CHAPTER 10

"YOU CAN'T DISMANTLE CAPITALISM WITHOUT DISMANTLING PATRIARCHY"

MOST OF THE WORLD'S service and retail workers, small farmers and contract workers are women. Desire for gender justice fuels their militancy. From the tomato fields of Florida to the export zones of the Dominican Republic and Rangoon, women workers are organizing. And it is not just for a living wage but for freedom from sexual violence and pregnancy discrimination.

Twenty-seven-year-old Manila fast-food organizer Joanna Bernice Coronacion is one of that new generation of feminist labor activists. Coronacion, who goes by the nickname "Sister Nice," is a serious young woman with an easy grin. As a child, she lived in a squatters' *barangay* (neighborhood) in Metro Manila, in a vast network of slums that are home to millions of displaced farmers and fishing families. Her father went abroad to work in Japan, one of more than ten million Filipinos forced to emigrate by lack of opportunity at home. Her mother did the best she could.[1]

Coronacion's experiences left her with a visceral sense that the fight for workers' rights is inseparable from struggles for women's rights. "You can't dismantle capitalism without dismantling patriarchy," she says. "We have a lot of work to do."

Sister Nice Coronacion credits her mother with politicizing her. "She was a community leader who fought for land tenure for squatters. Growing up, I called where I lived a home because, if there is love it is a home, but . . ." She pauses. "Still, I know we were lucky. We never lived in the danger zone, near the rivers where it floods." We visit the Manila danger zone. Small children squat in the dirt, diligently sweeping makeshift drains so that no water seeps into the rooms, lean-tos, and shacks where millions of families live, eat, and sleep.

Coronacion says her life changed when the Alliance of Progressive Labor awarded her a scholarship to college. She became a fervent convert to class struggle and feminism. "My mother made me sign up for a labor youth orientation." She was not enthusiastic at first.

"Now I'm a full-blown activist." She laughs. "But in high school I wanted to be a Miss Universe. I wanted to be a millionaire. I wanted to be a doctor. I thought of activists as violent people who make a rah-rah sis-boom-bah in the streets, people who make traffic, people who make trouble. Everything changed for me because the labor movement gave me an education. It allowed me to learn about the world and myself."

Coronacion has helped spread fast-food workers' organizing across Asia. A well-known international firebrand, she was denied entry to South Korea at the tender age of twenty-two, for fear she would infect Seoul fast-food workers with her militancy. She is unabashed and unapologetic. "I have loved what I do from the get-go," she says. "The movement captured my vision. The workers captured my interest. The movement made me a better person."

Like many low-wage worker-activists, Coronacion is a radical Christian. Faith gives her confidence to face armed police and paramilitary amid the violence of Metro Manila. The fusion of faith with activism drives many young Filipinas, says Em Atienza. "You can give me a thousand reasons to leave the movement and I will give you a million why I never will. The movement is my breath, my rhythm, my music, my life."

Coronacion, Atienza, and other young Filipina labor activists march against domestic violence and sexual assault. Each year, on International Women's Day, March 8, they lead flash mobs of young women in singing, dancing protests. "We believe in socialism *and* feminism," Coronacion announces. "We seek a just, peaceful society where working people are empowered through democratic processes, gender equity is recognized, and there is an equitable distribution of wealth."[2]

Young Filipinas like Coronacion and Atienza were drawn into the global women's movement through the Philippine chapter of the World March of Women, founded in Quebec in 1995, in response to the creation of the World Trade Organization. World March founders argued that globalization and neoliberalism fueled violence against women and intensified the feminization of poverty. "In an increasingly globalized world," the group vowed to organize against "dominance of the most vulnerable" by "patriarchy" and "neoliberal capitalism," which "sustain and reinforce one another."[3]

World March has fostered conversations among women trade unionists, antipoverty activists, and peace workers worldwide, by staging transnational women's marches every five years. In 2000, women from 161 countries marched and staged rallies from Mozambique to Morocco. They gathered five million signatures demanding an end to violence against women and remediation of the damages to women and children wrought by neoliberalism and war.

On October 16–17, ten thousand women from many countries marched to the United Nations in New York City to deliver the signatures. They met with the leaders of the World Bank, the International Monetary Fund, and the United Nations. They summed those meetings up tersely: "unprecedented, vigorous denunciations by the women and . . . bureaucratic or smug speeches by the other side."[4]

Since 2000, World March has held annual gatherings in Montreal, New Delhi, Kigali, Lima, Galicia, Quezon City, and São Paulo. In Mozambique and Burkina Faso, its organizers have fought women's disproportionate poverty and violence against women. Youth activists in other African chapters have fought for improved sexual health and reproductive education. In Venezuela, organizers fought successfully to criminalize spousal violence. In Morocco, they won a self-described "peaceful revolution," earning women the right to divorce, raising the minimum age for marriage to eighteen, and restricting polygamy.[5]

In 2010, World March events involved eighty thousand participants in seventy-six countries. Miriam Nobre of the Democratic Republic of Congo was lead organizer. The march concluded with a rally of twenty thousand women in Bukavu, the site of "horrific acts of sexual violence" during Congo's civil war. Delegates from forty-eight countries heard moving testimony from Congolese witnesses, documenting violence against women by armies on both sides.

Witnesses linked global capitalism to lethal conflict, condemning corporations who funded the war in Congo by purchasing "conflict minerals"—tantalum, tungsten, tin, and gold. They called on Apple, Google, Amazon, GE, and Victoria's Secret to stop using these to make smartphones, lightbulbs, and underwire bras. (Congress did include a provision in the 2010 Dodd-Frank bill banning conflict minerals in products sold in the United States.)[6]

They also composed a "Women's Manifesto for Peace," in which they argued that "the language of violence, at the root of capitalism and patriarchy, and supported by transnational companies, mercenaries and paramilitary forces, brings about war." Women and girls are turned into weapons and commodities, trafficked and sold to profit competing armies, they said, and they blamed politicians who make "false speeches about safety . . . and the war on terrorism, while meanwhile, the arms industry, the installation of military bases and the privatization and destruction of natural resources keeps growing."[7]

Women must continue organizing globally, they concluded, because "in different regions of the world, our experiences and testimonies are similar. Women and girls are sexually harassed at military control posts, raped by groups of armed men, to be then rejected by their own communities. Women flee their homes, under a sky of bullets, carrying their belongings and their children on their shoulders, moving towards shelter or an unknown destination, far from their culture and their history, with the hopes of a new dawn."[8]

Five years later, during the 2015 World Marches, women activists aided refugees fleeing a new generation of wars. They helped build women's libraries in Kurdish regions of Turkey and brought books to refugee camps for women fleeing the Syrian civil war. They brought seeds and helped mothers plant nourishing grains and vegetables for their families. Over seven months, thirty thousand women staged 89 street protests, 147 performances, and 163 public meetings in Greece, the Balkans, Italy, Germany, France, Spain, and Portugal.[9]

The young women of the Manila-based RESPECT Fast Food Workers Alliance enjoyed and adapted some of these performative forms of protest. On International Women's Day, they staged flash mobs in shopping malls across the Philippines. Posing as shoppers, young activists filled mall atria. There they sang "Bread and Roses," adapting lyrics written about women mill workers in 1912 Massachusetts to conditions faced by twenty-first-century Filipinas.

Dancing as they sang, they shocked shoppers by stripping off white button-down shirts, only to reveal pink undershirts that said: "Stop Corporate Land Grabs and Enforce the Reproductive Health Law." RESPECT had fought hard for a new reproductive justice law that was being blocked by the Catholic Church. "No to Corporate Occupation of Our Lands," they chanted. "No to Occupation of Our Bodies." Said one protester: "It's all colonialism."

Then they read their manifesto: "We celebrate the joys and triumphs of women all over the world advancing struggles for land, food, water, reproductive rights, and for a life free from violence, marginalization, and discrimination. . . . Urban poor communities are demolished with no regard for the dignity of women and children; as government pursues relentlessly corporate-led privatization, public hospitals are privatized, public lands are now to be developed. . . . Farmers and indigenous peoples defending their lands are harassed, even killed. . . . Give us peace, equity, equality, and opportunities. Give us bread. Give us roses!"[10]

Jamaia Montenegro uses the idea of bread and roses in organizing Manila domestic workers. The soft-spoken, dark-eyed woman emigrated from the southern Philippines to Manila because she needed income. But she also wanted roses: a college education. She was determined.

Many domestic workers in Manila are Visayan speakers forced from their lands by foreign mining, lumber, and palm oil companies, she says. Like her, they end up as servants for Tagalog-speaking Manilans who see them as "less than," she says: "less smart, less capable of learning." Montenegro defied that stereotype, attending university classes while organizing and working. Still, employers mocked her Tagalog accent, she says. She learned to speak English because "it rolls off my tongue with less pain. Tagalog is a language of colonizers."

Montenegro's experience with wage theft turned her into an organizer. "The woman I worked for still hasn't paid me. I was humiliated by her. The husband was always leering and touching me. I stayed because I loved the children and because I needed a place to live. I was a very long way from my home.[11]

Montenegro reached out to the Alliance of Progressive Labor. Through them, she found the International Domestic Workers Federation, the first global union founded and led entirely by women. On the ground in Manila, she organized four hundred domestic workers into a new union.

Though it is difficult to organize domestic workers, Montenegro had a plan. She designed and handed out leaflets at bus stops in *barangays* where she knew women from the southern islands lived. "I would figure out who was a domestic worker. She was taking a bus to a rich neighborhood. I knew what they were going through. I lived it. That's why they trusted me."

Montenegro attended international domestic workers' conferences where she learned from other activists. Yim Sothy, who organized eight hundred domestic workers in Phnom Penh, negotiated an agreement with Maid in Cambodia, an agency that matches domestic workers with employers. Now anyone who hires a worker from that agency must sign a contract promising decent wages, hours, and safety standards. The contracts also expressly forbid sexual overtures.

Montenegro says she learned immeasurably from these meetings. "I was amazed by how much our experiences are the same. The pain in our knees and backs, the harassment, the wage theft—everything."

Thirty-one-year-old Vun Em says that she too was educated and politicized by her exposure to global feminism. Vun was a teenage garment worker in Phnom Penh when she encountered an Australian Oxfam-funded NGO called Womyn's Agenda for Change (WAC). Soon she was organizing for a labor coalition they founded, United Sisterhood Alliance, and performing in an all-woman music group called the Messenger Band, singing about the lives of women garment workers.

Vun moved to Phnom Penh at sixteen from Kampong Cham province. Like so much of Cambodia's rural population, Vun's family was struggling to eke out a living growing rice. Then Cambodia leased one million acres of land to foreign companies for rice, sugar, and rubber plantations. Vun's family was no longer able to earn a living. Products grown for export were replacing subsistence farming. Farm families were violently evicted and tropical forests were cleared. Vun would later sing about those experiences.[12]

Like so many other young Cambodian women of her generation, she moved to Phnom Penh to find work in the garment industry to help support her family. At night, she returned to a labyrinth of windowless rooms enclosed by a six-foot-tall cyclone fence. When she learned that English classes were being offered by Womyn's Agenda for Change, Vun began burrowing under the fence for 5 a.m. classes. "Other women couldn't understand why I wanted to go to school so early," she says, "but I needed to learn. And I did."

WAC funds programs to empower garment and sex workers and Vun became deeply engaged. "You could say I grew up in United Sisterhood," she reflects. She and her colleagues are militant about advocating for sex workers and challenge anyone who stigmatizes either profession. Young women stranded in the city may have few other options, she says. Sell their bodies or end up on the streets. Garment and sex workers both suffer from misogynistic violence. Both have families in the countryside desperate for the cash they send. United Sisterhood fights for both, says Vun. And it also works to create other opportunities. They help seamstresses and cooks start their own businesses. They promote Cambodian women's crafts abroad, as another income option for rural families.[13]

Vun also records garment worker stories and turns them into songs and music videos that she plays for workers, farm families, and schoolchildren. Setting off in crowded vans, the women of the Messenger Band bounce down pothole-pitted roads through the countryside. They help rural parents understand the lives their daughters lead in the city and encourage those facing displacement to write and stage plays about their lives.

In a country where violence against activists is systemic, says Shalmali Guttal, director of Focus on the Global South, these young activists show remarkable courage. Dissidents have been beaten and murdered with impunity in Cambodia. "I tell police and soldiers I am just a musician," Vun says coolly. "This is just a concert." The willowy young woman, who is training to become a yoga teacher, flashes a brave grin. "It's worked so far."[14]

On November 25, 2016, Vun Em, Nice Coronacion, Kalpona Akter, and millions of other women labor activists took part in a Global Day of Action to Stop Gender-Based Violence in the Workplace. It was organized by the International Trade Union Confederation (ITUC), created in 2006 to promote transnational worker organizing. Headed by Sharan Burrow, an Australian woman unionist, the ITUC links the IUF, which represents fast-food and hotel workers, IndustriALL, which represents manufacturing employees, and UNI Global Union, which represents Walmart and other retail workers. The ITUC claims 181 million members in 162 countries. Burrow leverages that global heft to give workers a "voice" at World Bank and International Monetary Fund negotiations, demanding stronger protections for workers and an end to demands that poor countries privatize public utilities.

Under Burrow, the ITUC has foregrounded issues of sexual violence, human rights, and labor slavery. The ITUC is campaigning for an ILO convention banning gender-based violence in the workplace. "No workplace is immune from harassment and violence—whether it's the anchorwoman at Fox News, or the leaf picker on a tea plantation."[15]

As part of the global campaign, women janitors in Los Angeles have demanded protection from sexual assault on the job—a constant threat for those who work alone, late at night, in large office buildings. In Johannesburg, Accra, Providence, Karachi, and London, hotel housekeepers demanded lighter duties for pregnant workers, and panic buttons that housekeepers can push to bring help if a man corners them inside a room. In Chicago, workers staged "Hands Off, Pants On" protests. Before the protests, UNITE HERE released a study showing that half of hotel housekeepers and three-quarters of casino workers experience unwanted sexual advances. The need is clear.[16]

Philippine garment union organizer Asuncion Binos held a press conference condemning politicians for placing corporate profits over the safety of women workers. "It is lamentable that our lawmakers have always struggled to pass laws and craft policies for . . . global competitiveness," she said, "but leave behind women's protection."

Failure to grant generous maternity leave harms women and children, she said. "Studies show that mothers need 120 days to fully recover from giving birth, to breast-feed and establish the routine for her newborn, and to make arrangements necessary for a smooth transition back to work." Binos is part of a global network of women trade unionists working to pass labor laws in their own countries to help women workers. "If we can get countries to pass good policy," she says, "then we can use those to push for global standards."[17]

Kalpona Akter says the campaign against workplace violence is an urgent priority. "Women workers get raped, get touched inappropriately by men. If you talk you are the bad one," she says. "We organize against it all—the beatings and the mental pressure—every way we know." It will be a long slog to pass an ILO convention, she says. Even if they get it through, women trade unionists will have an uphill battle pushing their own governments to ratify it. But the ILO gives workers international presence, she says, and a legal basis for struggle. In countries where wages are low, protections few, and governments repressive, that is worth fighting for.[18]

CHAPTER 11

THIS IS WHAT SOLIDARITY FEELS LIKE

WHEN CAMBODIAN GARMENT WORKERS won a wage increase in the fall of 2015, Kalpona Akter saw Bangladeshi garment workers smiling as they watched cell phone videos of celebrations in Phnom Penh. Massimo Frattini has seen European workers watch Fight for $15 videos on their phones. Cell phones help workers feel part of something global—the electricity of rebellion. But transnational movements predate cell service.[1]

Sociologist George Katsiaficas, who has studied the global protests in 1968 and "People Power" movements in the 1980s, argues that uprisings are infectious. The pleasures of revolt spark currents of change that spread across national borders. Katsiaficas calls this "the eros effect."

A buzz sweeps marginalized communities, an elation at the possibility that they might be able to enact change. Las Vegas antipoverty activist Ruby Duncan remembers how she felt as a welfare rights activist in the 1970s. After a lifetime of taking orders, she says poor mothers finally became "the ones doing the demanding." She felt it like a surge of power.[2]

"As people are transformed through insurgencies," Katsiaficas writes, "they refuse to tolerate previously accepted forms of domination. Popular wisdom grows in each iteration of the movement's emergence; ever-new aspirations animate action."[3]

Adrenaline spreads grassroots protest from one city to the next, one country to another. Hope is an important, and understudied, political force. Amid genocidal wars, refugee crises, and violent repression, a disappearing middle class and a planet grown hotter, currents of hope began running through the world in the 2010s, animating worker movements and connecting them. On days of global action, one can feel electricity crackling.

On April 15, 2015, low-wage workers in two hundred US cities and in forty countries on six continents struck and rallied for a living wage. They marched in New York, Boston, Los Angeles, Chicago, and hundreds of other American cities. They marched in London, Brussels, Paris, Stockholm, Manila, Seoul, Tokyo, Rio, Tegucigalpa, Buenos Aires, Brasília, Cape Town, Freetown, and Accra.

It wasn't only economic gains that moved them. The marchers sought to reoccupy cities where all but the wealthiest have been marginalized by rising costs, to make visible the people whose labor makes cities run. While workers are relegated to far-flung fringe neighborhoods or marooned in bleak, poor "ethno-burbs," cities that were once economically diverse, home to manufacturing as well as banking and luxury real estate, became sanitized and gentrified amusement parks for the rich.

In perhaps the most famous theme park for the wealthy, a place called Manhattan, tens of thousands marched that day. They revealed in all its astounding diversity the working class of a truly global city where nearly two-thirds of children lived with a foreign-born parent. Korean, Vietnamese, Cambodian, Afro-Caribbean, Polish and Bulgarian, Russian and Irish, Dominican, Mexican, indigenous Central American immigrants, and their American kids marched. American-born union workers marched too: Puerto Ricans, African Americans, Chinese, Irish, Italian.

Among the low-wage workers who came out that day, many were legal residents but many others were undocumented. Hotel workers, home-healthcare providers, restaurant and bakery workers, car service and school bus drivers, crossing guards, airport baggage handlers, "car washeros," fast-food servers. They made a conscious choice to come out of the shadows, riding subways and commuter trains from apartments in East New York, Flatlands, Brownsville, and the Bronx where two and three generations shared lodging.

It took a leap of faith for them to come out into the light, says Dominican organizer Virgilio Aran, to lift their heads, to walk freely down the streets of the city center where they worked but could not afford to live. Undocumented workers well understand that employers pay them too little and work them too hard because they are sure that workers without green cards are too frightened to report abuses. Aran has fought for a long time to change that.

On April 15, 2015, he walked with his wife and fellow activist Rosanna Rodriguez, greeting marchers in emotion-filled Spanish, shaking hands and giving hugs. A few years earlier the couple had founded the Laundry Workers Center (LWC) to organize undocumented Spanish-speaking workers across New York. Working with Restaurant Opportunities Centers (ROC), they sparked a wave of labor uprisings in restaurants, bakeries, warehouses, and laundries across the city and around the region. As this book goes to press, their movement is ongoing.

The LWC and ROC organize immigrants who work not for large companies but for small businesses and family-run chains. Often they are exploited by bosses from their home countries who try to intimidate workers by threatening to harm family members living abroad. In spite of this, restaurant workers in the Bronx and Queens, warehouse workers in Brooklyn, and retail workers in Manhattan have repeatedly struck since 2012, signed union cards, filed court complaints, and brought cases before the NLRB. And they have won. A 2012 campaign led by Mexican immigrant Mahoma Lopez to organize the Hot & Crusty bakeries, and a 2016–17 union drive at the B&H photo warehouse, resulted in new unions, no small feat.[4]

Still, Aran and Rodriguez say that the most radical work they do is psychological. To transform scared workers into labor activists, organizers must help them overcome legitimate fears and anxieties. Undocumented migrants must transcend lifetimes of being told that they are good only for cheap labor, says Aran. To foster that, the LWC runs consciousness-raising and peer education groups. Workers teach one another about labor history, racism, and women's oppression. "Since so many of the workers are women, everyone must understand the history of sexism," says Aran. Dominicans teach about white-skin privilege in the Dominican Republic and in the US. "Racism affects workers negatively," he says. "We try to help them fight that feeling."

When a worker feels strong enough to step into the light, Aran says, that's a breakthrough. "If you're an undocumented immigrant, you get up every single day and you get on the train to go to work and someone might say, 'Give me your papers.' If you don't have documents, then you're facing deportation." To do that every day takes incredible courage, he says. "You've made such hard choices: to come to another country, to cross borders, to learn a new language, to adapt and find work and face deportation every day. When you realize that"—he pauses—"you understand that you are a superhero! It's my job to help workers find that feeling."

Most undocumented immigrants are warned not to reveal their real names, says Aran. In the age of Donald Trump, those fears have deepened.

But the only path to freedom is to reject terror. "When you no longer fear," Aran insists, "when you tell your own story, when you know your own history and that of the workers who have struggled before you, when you say your own name, when you show your face, then you have power. Then you know that employers can't report you or they too will face government sanctions. Then intimidation in the workplace doesn't affect you so much." He takes a slow breath. "Then you can fight back."

Aran, Rodriguez, and Mahoma Lopez, president of the LWC, believe that transformation can come only when disrespected workers become teachers. So every Sunday, in the Bronx, Washington Heights, and Lower Manhattan, restaurant, bakery, and warehouse workers meet to hear one of their own lecture. Then the group talks together—about labor history, sexism, racism, wage theft, and labor law. These are twenty-first-century freedom schools. As Rodriguez describes how they work, I think of Ella Baker and Septima Clark, civil rights pioneers who insisted in the 1950s and 1960s that poor, uneducated African Americans had wisdom to teach—and then created schools where they did so. At a Sunday class, as a Dominican waitress teaches immigrant restaurant workers about the black freedom struggle in the US South, I imagine Baker and Clark nodding with satisfaction.

On April 15, 2015, Laundry Workers Center activists joined a march in which more than half of the participants earned too little to properly feed their families. But for that day they controlled the streets of Midtown Manhattan. They flooded Columbus Circle, dancing beneath the gates to Central Park, poured onto Broadway, marched to Times Square. Singing and cheering, they said their names aloud.[5]

Bleu Rainer and hundreds of fast-food workers marched wearing "Black Lives Matter: I Can't Breathe" sweatshirts, tying the movement for higher wages to the struggle against police violence—highlighting the last words uttered by Staten Island street vendor Eric Garner as he was choked to death by police a year earlier. "It's the same struggle," says Rainer. "We are the same people. We all want the same thing. We deserve dignity and a decent life."

Some marchers carried Ronald McDonald puppets. They waved the corporate clown high. In some versions, he wept in shame. "McJobs Cost Us All," said a popular shirt. The McDonald's logo appeared on banners, covered by the words "Poverty Wages: Not Lovin' It." High school students mugged for the cameras. Wheelchair-bound veterans in neon-green OUR Walmart shirts wheeled with the marchers. Kids ran and laughed under signs that said: "Everybody Deserves Respect."

As we reached Times Square, daylight fading, city lights flickering on, hundreds of home-healthcare providers, clad in white lab coats, began to sing and dance to the tune of "When the Saints Go Marching In." With a Caribbean lilt, they sang: "We're overworked, and underpaid . . . All we ask is fifteen dollars. We're overworked and underpaid."

They repeated it again and again, dancing and singing, block after block. Humming, clapping, twirling. Tourists smiled and sang along. Twilight descended over Times Square, electronic billboards flashed. And for a few minutes on a warm spring evening, middle-aged, immigrant, black, Asian, and Latina home-healthcare workers owned Broadway.

The recognition came in a rush. It was the kind of feeling that enables people to keep mounting protests. Marching en masse, they were more than low-wage workers. Fear was replaced by strength. Hunger was sated by solidarity.

Against the twilit sky, an untold number of hands raised their cell phones to record and upload videos to social media. People shared and commented on cell phone videos of sister marches in London and Tokyo, Manila, Nairobi, and Seoul. One woman started showing around a photograph of a march in Dhaka. There, a young woman held a sign that said: "Bangladeshi Workers Support the $15 Minimum Wage." She had photographed herself and posted a selfie—as so many teenage girls do every day.

PART II

THE RISING OF
THE GLOBAL PRECARIAT

CHAPTER 12

RESPECT, LET IT GO, 'CAUSE BABY, YOU'RE A FIREWORK

IT'S A STEAMY DAWN in downtown Manila—already hot though it's only six thirty. A group of slim young men and women in their teens and twenties file out into the middle of a busy avenue, wearing white shirts, black pants, and purple headbands. The strains of Katy Perry's "Firework" rise from a boom box, heavy on the bass. At other times, they dance to Aretha Franklin's "Respect" or the Disney theme "Let It Go." But this is a morning for fireworks.

The kids start to dance, with verve, as perfectly synchronized as a Broadway chorus line. They sing as they move, improvising as they go, riffing on Katy Perry's lyrics in a mix of Tagalog and English—igniting the light inside them, letting it shine, showing the world what they are worth. They shout, strike poses, pump fists. "'Cause baby, we are fireworks." Cars roar in from all directions. Drivers honk, or tap their fingers through open windows. Motorcycles grind to a halt. Some yell at the dancers to move; others sing along. Then comes the chant: "What do we want? Decent jobs!" Again and again to the beat of the song. "Decent jobs for all."

It takes forever to get anywhere in Metro Manila. One of the world's most densely populated cities, it is also vast. In 2016, Manila had thirteen million people, twenty-three million if you count suburbs and ring-towns. The city center is choked by sprawling, smoky slums that are home to many young activists in the RESPECT Fast Food Workers Alliance. The poorest among them come from what Joanna Bernice Coronacion calls "danger zones"—where tin and cardboard shacks sit below sea level, flooding every time the inevitable rains and typhoons hit. It's a world of mud and sewage, but also of song and dance.

Many of the best performers come from Bagong Silangan, a *barangay* known for high unemployment and excellent dancers, says Lei Catamin, a twenty-three-year-old choreographer, theater student, and labor organizer. When Coronacion and Catamin realized that poor kids were entering dance contests to make money for their families, they helped them create a Dancers' Union of Bagong Silangan—DUBS. The name is an allusion to a globally popular genre of electronic dance music that grew out of reggae, hip-hop, and techno.[1]

Much of the Philippine workforce is under thirty and jobs are increasingly precarious; using young dancers to lead labor protests drew attention to these issues, Catamin says. "I was totally nervous, my first time to dance in the street," says DUBS member Irene Remontal. "But seeing all the people stopped on the overpass and the vehicles watching us, at that moment, I felt joy." Dancing for a cause feels great, says a nineteen-year-old male DUBS member. "Before I only danced to brag. Now with DUBS I dance for a purpose. Decent and secure jobs. Upholding women's rights. These issues have impact on my and my family's lives."[2]

Lei Catamin used to represent his university in dance competitions. Then he realized that he could put his musical theater training to work for "something larger, more important. It's good when you can use your talent and skills to show that young people need respect, that we need rights." Now a youth organizer for the Alliance of Progressive Labor, Catamin has turned down higher-paying work "for the cause."

Song and dance, Catamin believes, has attracted a new generation to a graying Philippine labor movement. "We started doing flash mobs to appeal to young people," he says. "Instead of carrying protest signs, same old, same old, we perform. When people start to listen, clap their hands, maybe sing along, we know we are succeeding. The young dancers all understand that we are not performing for the sake of performance but for a larger purpose."

And organizers work hard to ensure that performers understand the issues, says Catamin. "Before we take youth to a mobilization, we do education about wage theft, about sexual harassment, about labor rights. What is the impact on your life? On your community? On your family? They get it. They say: 'Wow. I have been cheated, my mother, my brother have been cheated, for so many years.' Then they know not just where they are going to dance, but *why*."

Though music has been an important part of many social movements, young Filipino workers have turned musical theater into protest art. So much so that Manilans are used to encountering street scenes that appear to have been ripped from the sets of television musicals. On May 14, 2014, a day of global action, teenage fast-food workers line-danced their way through Manila, singing to the music from Disney's animated hit *Frozen*.

Singing loudly, they urged fellow workers: "Let it go. Don't hold back anymore. Let it go. Turn away. Slam the door." They made up lyrics as they danced. Holding hands, they pulled workers from behind counters and into the streets, into the strike. They sang about rising as a new dawn broke. And they celebrated the end of fear. "Here I stand in the light of day," they sang. If that brought a raging storm, that was fine. "McDonald's never bothered me anyway."

Flash mobs have become a signature of the Philippine labor movement. On International Women's Day 2015, five thousand trade unionists danced in front of Manila's Malacanang presidential palace, singing Helen Reddy's 1972 hit "I Am Woman." One year later, men danced wearing women's shoes because "Walk a Day in My Shoes" is a slogan of the low-wage workers' struggle everywhere. And during the 2016 global week of action by hotel housekeepers, DUBS dancers made the march a chorus line as hotel workers sang: "Women's voices can shake the world."

RESPECT's best-known musical protest dance is the Aretha Franklin 1967 megahit for which the group is named. It's Lei Catamin's favorite. He breaks into dance, demonstrating his flashiest moves. Breathing hard, he chants, "R-E-S-P-E-C-T. I'll tell you what it means to me." Dancing and running. Then he freezes with his fist raised. He looks up and shouts: "Respect!" It's not as easily quantified as a living wage. But it's crucial.

CHAPTER 13

REALIZING PRECARITY

"We Are All Fast-Food Workers Now"

LA TERESITA IS A BELOVED OLD TAMPA, Florida, café. It is crowded, boisterous, inexpensive, and redolent of smoky Cuban food. The place is jammed at 7 p.m. on a weeknight. Diners in construction clothes, nurses' whites, and UPS uniforms line a long, winding counter. The din of conversation echoes off the tile. Most customers are speaking Spanish. A few speak Caribbean-, Florida-, or New York-accented English. Steam rises from plates of grilled fish, *chuleta* (pork), plantains, rice, and black beans. A damp sweetness wafts off baskets of Cuban bread.

A group of Fight for $15 activists sit jammed around one small table. They are a young and surprisingly diverse group for any American dinner table: white, black, and Latinx, men and women, deeply engaged in conversation, sometimes all speaking at once. Several are gay, lesbian, or transgender, I am told later. None are over thirty-five. They are college professors, community organizers, graduate students, and fast-food workers.

Home-healthcare workers are also part of the South Florida living wage movement but could not attend the meeting because they work up to 120 hours a week. African American, Afro-Caribbean, and Puerto Rican women, they are older than the group gathered at La Teresita. Their union local of four hundred care workers was organized almost entirely on Facebook because members don't have time to meet in person. Their "fight for 15" isn't just a fight for $15 an hour, says home-care worker-organizer Ann Buckner. "It is also a fight for fifteen-minute breaks. Our clients are so frail, we work twenty-four-hour shifts. Sometimes I need to step outside and feel the sun."[1]

They are the new working class and their solidarity crosses many lines. Activists have varying levels of education. Their politics are diverse.

Some belong to labor unions. Others were involved in Occupy, in campaigns for Florida's migrant tomato pickers, in environmental justice struggles. Some are military vets. Some have PhDs. Others never finished high school. To an old labor historian like myself, it seems unlikely that these very different people would be bound together in one movement. And yet, there is a strong feeling of solidarity, grounded in a shared belief that the American Dream is no longer attainable for most people.

"That's what it is," says Bleu Rainer, a Tampa McDonald's employee who worked for Arby's in North Carolina as a teen. "People used to say to us: 'If you want to be paid more, go back to school and get a better job.' But my professors in college aren't paid much more than I am. We're all fighting for the American Dream but it's broken."

Cole Bellamy's dream of being an English professor turned on him. Stitching together various temporary contracts, Bellamy taught twelve courses in 2015, three times the teaching load of tenure-track professors at research universities. He works at three different campuses, bucking the endless Tampa Bay traffic to earn $30,000 per year. With two children to support, his income put him just a few thousand dollars above the federal poverty level for a family of four. His employers did not provide health benefits but the family qualified for Medicaid. Like most low-wage workers, his benefits are paid not by employers but by taxpayers.

In 2015, three-quarters of American college professors were contract workers, paid by the course. One in four qualified for some form of public assistance: the Earned Income Tax Credit, Supplemental Nutrition Assistance Program (SNAP), Medicaid. "We are low-wage workers," the professors at La Teresita insist. "It doesn't matter how many degrees we have."

The professors say they love organizing together with fast-food servers, home-care providers, and airport workers. Adjunct history professor Eric Webb-Fiske says that fast-food and home-care workers have taught the professors a lot about resilience and tenacity. "This economy is not sustainable," says Bellamy. "Unless we do something, the university as we know it will disappear in the next ten years." Bleu Rainer chimes in: "Hell, jobs a worker can live on may disappear. They're almost gone now. So many workers I know don't earn enough to put a roof over their heads, or their kids' heads. You can work for years for the same company and have nothing."

"Regardless of what educational background you come from," Webb-Fiske says, "a contract employee is a contract employee. The issues a worker faces at McDonald's are similar to those I face as an adjunct professor at a community college. It's the same for home-care workers. The working conditions are brutal. The hours are too long. There's no security. The pay is nowhere near what it should be." Webb-Fiske figures that he makes about $8 an hour when he factors in time spent writing lectures, advising students, and grading papers. Many adjuncts say they earn less. And that's after six years in graduate school and lots of loans.

Graduate student Keegan Shepard points out that up to half of academic and research work at universities is performed "for free by graduate students." The university dresses it up as part of their education, insisting that graduate student workers are therefore not entitled to labor protections. Though public universities are strapped in an age of state and federal budget cuts, wealthy private universities take the same tack. Yale and NYU, to name two, challenged a 2016 National Labor Relations Board ruling that graduate students have the right to organize. American higher education would come crashing to a halt without unpaid labor by graduate students, says Shepard. It's wage theft, he says. Plain and simple.

"They try to fool us, to make us believe we're special because we have advanced degrees. But that is just a lie to keep us quiet, because the truth is: We are all fast-food workers now." Bleu Rainer laughs. "Or maybe, we are all professor adjuncts," he says. Either way, almost everyone is working longer hours for less pay.[2]

If the first half of the twentieth century was marked by uprisings of the industrial proletariat, the twenty-first century has been characterized by civil unrest among the postindustrial working class—the precariat. Whoever coined the term, and many have claimed credit, the precariat represents an ever-growing share of all workers. They have no security, seniority, or benefits. They earn too little to comfortably live on. And the corporations, hospitals, universities, and government agencies for which they work evade legal responsibility for meeting minimum wage, maximum hours, and safety standards by classifying them as "temporary" or as "contract" employees provided by third-party labor suppliers.

In many countries, full-time employees are protected by federal and state labor laws, fought for by labor unions and passed between the 1910s and the 1950s. But few people are classified as full-time employees these days. Suddenly almost everyone is an "independent contractor." Welcome to the so-called "gig economy."

Twenty dollars an hour, most studies show, is the minimum required to comfortably support a family with two children in the US. Nearly two-thirds of American workers earn less. And though the 2016 election sparked discussion of falling real wages among high school-educated white men, only a quarter of low-wage workers in the US are men. Two-thirds of the country's lowest-paid workers are women. Sixty percent of Latinx workers in the US earned less than $15 an hour in 2016. Half of African American workers did.[3]

With so many working people living at, or just above, the poverty line, the speed with which the living-wage movement caught fire in the 2010s should not have surprised anyone. Nor should the growing appeal of populist politicians from Bernie Sanders, Walden Bello, and Jeremy Corbyn on the left to Donald Trump, Nigel Farage, and Marine Le Pen on the right. Bleu Rainer and Keegan Shepard insist that broad coalition-building represents the only real solution. For we are all fast-food workers now.

CHAPTER 14

DAYS OF DISRUPTION, 2016

NOVEMBER 29, 2016: Picketers appeared with the first light. During the breakfast rush they delayed harried commuters hoping for an Egg Mc-Muffin before work. They rallied in Central Square in Cambridge, on Fulton Street in Brooklyn, on Broadway in Los Angeles. In St. Louis, adjunct professors sat down in the middle of a busy avenue; in Detroit, McDonald's workers stepped off the curb into traffic, arms crossed. In Phoenix, they shut down a McDonald's drive-through, then marched to City Hall and sat in for a $15 wage.

In Manhattan, fast-food workers, Uber drivers, and bike messengers sat down calmly in the middle of Broadway. "We shall not be moved," they sang, and for a time, police seemed content to let them be. Baggage handlers and wheelchair attendants struck at Logan, O'Hare, and nineteen other big-city airports. Crossing guards sat in the way of parents driving their children to school. In Boston, low-wage workers streamed into the legislature to demand a state minimum wage of $15. They had succeeded in raising the state minimum from $8 to $11 in the past two years. But it was not nearly enough. "Fifteen dollars! No less!" they shouted.

Three weeks after the stunning election of the most far-right president in US history, low-wage workers protested in 340 US cities for a living wage, paid sick leave, and union rights. Hundreds were arrested in civil disobedience actions across the country. Undocumented workers joined in despite the risk. They called it Day of Disruption.

The disrupters were mostly African American and Latina but they were also white, Native, and Asian. A majority were women, but thousands of men joined in. Fast-food worker Samuel Homer Williams and OUR Walmart activist Denise Barlage marched in Los Angeles. Bleu Rainer, Cole Bellamy, and Ann Buckner came out in the dark Tampa morning to stage sit-ins as the sun rose. In New York, Laundry Workers Center members were there.

Protesters offered an analysis of the twenty-first-century economy from the bottom up. Nearly two-thirds of jobs created in the United States between 2008 and 2012 do not pay a living wage. And the US Bureau of Labor Statistics predicts that 60 percent of new jobs created through 2023 will pay too little for workers to live on. "These are the jobs now," said Richard Eiker as he sat down in front of a Kansas City McDonald's. So workers are fighting "to make these jobs good jobs."[1]

North Carolina home-healthcare aide Hilde Edmundson, who was arrested blocking traffic in Durham on the Day of Disruption, had explained her reasoning a year earlier: "I love caring for people. It's my calling in life. But because I only make $9 an hour . . . I can't afford my own place. I catch the bus to work because I can't afford a car. I depend on food stamps and I can't afford health care insurance. . . . I've been homeless because of my wages. All I'm asking for is justice. People depend on home care workers but as a home care worker I can't afford to take care of my own health."[2]

Conditions for low-wage workers had been deteriorating for years, but the 2016 election dramatically worsened their situation. Fiercely anti-union Republicans had expanded their control of state legislatures, governors' mansions, and the US Congress. Speaker of the House Paul Ryan vowed to dismantle the social safety net put in place by Franklin D. Roosevelt during the 1930s and expanded by Lyndon Johnson in the 1960s. And Donald Trump's Cabinet promised to roll back hard-fought victories won by low-wage workers since 2012. Immigrants' and women's rights were also on the chopping block. Fight for $15 activists swore "unrelenting opposition." "We won't back down. We won't go back," disrupters chanted.

Vance "Stretch" Sanders, a twenty-one-year-old homeless rights activist, Christian minister, and CVS cashier, woke up at 4 a.m. on November 29 to get to the Fight for $15 office before the sun came up. He enjoyed the quiet morning. Clear desert light illuminated the purple-red mountains that ring the city, as retail workers, fast-food servers, home-healthcare aides, preschool teachers, and adjunct professors marched slowly down the Strip.[3]

McDonald's employees wore bright yellow vests emblazoned with a "Menu of Scandals: McShame, McSlavery, and McHumiliation." They riffed on McDonald's jingles. "I hate this very much," they sang. And

"McJobs hurt us all." Near the Mirage hotel, where a man-made volcano explodes every fifteen minutes then turns into a flickering-orange waterfall, the protesters called for magic of a different kind: $15 and a union.

Why target McDonald's? With a worldwide workforce of 1.9 million, it is the second-largest private employer in the world. Only Walmart employs more. In 2016, there were 36,899 McDonald's restaurants in 119 countries, serving 69 million people a day. One McDonald's CFO boasted that, like the British empire of old, the sun never sets on the Golden Arches. *New York Times* columnist Thomas Friedman argued, only somewhat tongue in cheek, that the transnationalism of McDonald's might bring world peace.[4]

Instead, the Golden Arches have come to symbolize all that is wrong with the twenty-first-century global economy. McDonald's has driven down wages in every country where it operates, activists say, shredding job security, robbing workers of overtime pay, and fighting compensation for those injured on the job. The corporation claimed that it was not responsible for labor violations by franchise owners. Prompted by workers and unions, courts and government agencies have begun to lift the veil on McDonald's.

In 2015, the National Labor Relations Board ruled McDonald's a "joint employer," making the corporation liable for how all its workers are treated. A Brazilian court handed McDonald's a whopping $30 million fine for labor law violations. And the European Parliament began investigating McDonald's for tax evasion and exorbitant charges to franchise owners who were being charged rents way above market value.

McDonald's makes much of its profit on real estate. When land values dropped worldwide in 2008, McDonald's went on a buying spree, becoming one of the largest real estate companies on earth. Charging franchisees rents of between 8 and 15 percent of their revenues, it earns up to $14,000 a month per store. Some say McDonald's is a real estate empire financed by burgers and fries. One former chief financial officer said that store sales just about cover franchisees' rent. There is little profit. So franchise owners cut costs by squeezing workers.[5]

That's how we got "McJobs," says Bleu Rainer. A "McJob" is defined by *Webster's* and *The Oxford English Dictionary* as low-paid work that offers little satisfaction and few prospects for advancement. Living-wage activists say we don't need dictionary definitions. People around the world have worked in McJobs. Many remain stuck in McJobs for their entire working lives. An estimated one in eight Americans has worked for Mc-Donald's itself, and with little to show for it. "I was even promoted to manager," says Rainer, "but I never made more than $9.15 an hour or had a schedule I could depend on. That's a McJob." Stretch Sanders also knows about McJobs. He is trying to put himself through college on his CVS cashier's salary.[6]

Sanders used to work for Carl's Jr., owned by Andrew Puzder, Donald Trump's first nominee to head the federal labor department. Charged with stealing $20 million from his workers in California, Puzder was the target of thirty-three investigations for workers' rights abuses. While earning a salary three hundred times that of his lowest-paid employees, Puzder told reporters he'd rather replace his workers with robots than raise their wages. Robots "are always polite," he said. "They never take a vacation, they never show up late, there's never a slip-and-fall, or an age, sex, or race discrimination case."[7]

Views like that invite protest. In September 2016, Sanders led an occupation of Nevada governor Brian Sandoval's office. Protesters demanded a $15 state wage and an end to mistreatment of undocumented workers. Las Vegas preschool teacher Luc Perez joined the sit-in. After eight years of teaching, she did not earn enough to pay her bills. Even that doesn't hurt as much, she said, as seeing three- and four-year-old students whose parents have just been arrested for immigration violations. They say: "My mom is not with me. Someone took her away."[8]

Sanders was upset by the 2016 election results, he says, but not as frightened as many people he knew. "My brothers and sisters were already being shot down in the streets by police. My coworkers were already having their doors broken down at dawn by ICE. Parents were being dragged away and taken someplace their children couldn't find them. That's why we started fighting. That's why we won't stop. I honestly don't know how much worse it can get."

For Sanders, Rainer, and many others, the living-wage campaign is inextricably tied to the struggle against police violence and for immigration reform. Fight for $15 activists at a McDonald's in Ferguson, Missouri, provided safe space during the unrest after police killed teenager Michael Brown in the summer of 2014. Living-wage marchers in New York wore shirts emblazoned with the last words of Eric Garner, father of six, killed by the NYPD that summer. "We're the same people," says Rainer. "We have to hold down three jobs, and when we are done and tired, walking home from work, then we are abused by police, raided by immigration cops."

Sanders says, "I was a Black Lives Matter activist before I was born." He is the nephew of Chicago Black Panthers who were close to Fred Hampton, the young Panther leader murdered by the FBI and Chicago police in 1969. Sanders's uncle was in the apartment with Hampton the night he was killed. He grew up on those stories.

Police violence, government crackdowns, and charges of corruption also fueled worker protest around the world at the end of 2016. On November 30, hundreds of thousands of South Korean workers struck as students nationwide boycotted classes. Unrest had been building for months as President Park Geun-hye's crackdowns on labor and farmer protest grew increasingly brutal. Trade unions, farmers, and student groups were enraged by her administration's assaults on labor rights and coziness with transnational corporations. Retail and fast-food workers' unions protested deteriorating conditions for workers. Vast street demonstrations, involving over a million people, ultimately led to her trial and removal.[9]

But her impeachment did not end the protests. Seoul McDonald's workers had been marching for months, angry that the burger giant evaded paying benefits and overtime by classifying all its workers as part-time and temporary. After almost three years of protest, McDonald's Korea announced, early in 2017, that it would hire full-time workers. In April, the corporation recognized the fast-food workers' Korean Arbeit Workers Union and began contract negotiations. "We are human too," Korean fast-food workers had chanted. Finally, said one worker, they were being treated that way.[10]

Meanwhile in Brazil, striking port and oil workers paralyzed the country. In December 2016, CUT, the national union federation, declared a month of work stoppages, strikes, and rallies. They were protesting a "legislative coup" three months earlier that removed Worker Party president Dilma Rousseff, her successor Michel Temer's announcement of a twenty-year freeze on public services budgets, and plans to privatize the country's oil reserves and allow oil drilling by multinational corporations.[11]

As turmoil built, fast-food workers took Arcos Dorados, the McDonald's Brazilian affiliate, to court. Reviewing evidence that the company had repeatedly violated Brazilian labor law, judges levied large fines. Fast-food workers also poured into Brussels as 2016 came to an end, demanding that the European Parliament investigate McDonald's for violating minimum wage laws, operating unsafe workplaces, and punishing employees who tried to unionize. Bleu Rainer and a delegation of American fast-food workers came to support their European counterparts.

At the same moment, Nepali migrant workers in Kuala Lumpur charged McDonald's with enabling labor slavery and human trafficking. The Nepalis told reporters they had been brought to Malaysia so that McDonald's could evade that country's labor laws, working them longer and paying them less than they could legally pay Malaysians. Their passports had been confiscated. They were billed for transportation and uniforms and forced to work for free until they had paid those costs. Since all Malaysian McDonald's are owned by the transnational corporation rather than franchisees, the workers hoped to embarrass executives into giving them their back pay and sending them home.

Corporate leaders seemed at first unmoved, insisting that these workers were not McDonald's employees but instead worked for the labor contractor who had brought them to Malaysia. It was a brave gambit, stateless migrants going up against the world's second-largest private employer. It seemed unlikely to work, but enough bad press did the trick. Six months later, McDonald's admitted complicity in slave labor and announced that it was cutting ties with unethical labor brokers in Malaysia.[12]

The European protests made an impression as well. The French government hit McDonald's with a bill for back taxes. The UK Labour Party cut ties with McDonald's. New Zealand's Parliament made zero-hours contracts illegal nationwide. In April 2017, McDonald's began offering UK employees fixed-hour contracts. On Labor Day 2017, UK McDonald's workers struck for the first time in four decades. After decades of worsening conditions, the needle seemed finally to be moving in a different direction.[13]

CHAPTER 15

THE NEW CIVIL RIGHTS MOVEMENT

EVEN SO, THE STRUGGLE GETS WEARYING. "It's been over one hundred fifty years since we abolished slavery," says Virginia home-care worker Lauralyn Clark, "but we still have slave-wage jobs where we're not paid enough to survive." Clark does not believe it is a coincidence that so many low-wage workers are people of color.[1]

Nor do Tampa fast-food worker-activists Reika Mack and Bleu Rainer. They feel they are standard-bearers for a "new civil rights movement." Stretch Sanders says that it is his job to teach the younger generation about the "freedom fighters on whose shoulders we stand."[2]

In 2015, Mack, then twenty-six, got to meet some of them. She was one of five hundred Fight for $15 activists from ten states who traveled to the Ebenezer Baptist Church in Atlanta, where Martin Luther King Jr. was once pastor. There, the young workers were tutored by some of the sanitation strikers who marched with King in Memphis in 1968. "Dr. King was supporting a labor action on the day he was killed," Mack learned. "Civil rights and labor rights have always been part of the same struggle." Forty-seven years later, white-haired Memphis activists led young fast-food workers as they marched to a McDonald's on a traffic-clogged Atlanta avenue. There they sat down and sang "We Shall Overcome."

Echoes of the 1960s black freedom struggle suffused the protest. Marchers carried signs that said: "I Am a Man," as the sanitation workers had in 1968. They also had "I Am a Woman" signs because most fast-food workers are. "It was a beautiful thing," Mack says, "to know that we were marching for the same cause as they did so many years ago. For our humanity, for our rights." She was impressed that the Memphis 1968 veterans, men in their seventies, seemed to fully grasp the anger of young women workers in the twenty-first century. It moved her to be part of a struggle begun in her grandparents' generation.

"One of the things the Memphis strikers told me was that it was fine to get mad, but to get mad enough to fight back. Politically. Channel it, they told us." She nods as she speaks. "Well, we're mad enough now. We're fed up and we can't take it anymore. We don't have any other weapons but to get mad and fight back for what's right."[3]

When Long Beach, California, McDonald's worker Maia Montcrief first came out to protest for $15 and a union, it was the day before her eighteenth birthday and the day after she took her last high school US history exam. "My role models are the protesters at civil rights sit-ins," she says. A child of Haitian immigrants, Montcrief shares a two-bedroom apartment with her mom and four siblings. Her mother is a postal worker. It's crowded and Maia would like to move to her own place, but she is saving to pay tuition at Long Beach City College. "I want to study psychology and minor in brain science so I can be a brain surgeon," she says confidently.

Montcrief joined the living-wage fight out of a sense of responsibility to her neighbors, she says. "I was born in Long Beach, raised in Long Beach, and I will fight for its survival." Besides, organizing feels natural to her. "I talk to my friends at McDonald's. I talk to my friends at Burger King. We are going to push for this—march, testify—until we get our rights."

Learning history has given her courage. "My heroes are Malcolm X, Rosa Parks," she says. "Rosa was strong. I want to be like that." She pulls herself up to her full height of five feet two, then pumps her fist in the air. "I want to be like our conductor of the Underground Railroad, Harriet Tubman. I want to meet the president." She recently learned that Tubman met Abe Lincoln. "I would like to meet President Obama," she says with a shy smile.

"And I want to see a woman president." (She had hoped it would be Hillary Clinton.) "I will tell her to support our feminist needs. Females make less than guys. Even if we have the same hours, the guys always end up making more. That's not right." And when something is not right, Maia says, "I make that my fight. And I will stand out there at the front until the fight is won."[4]

Stretch Sanders says he is carrying the torch for his aunt, Carolyn "Polly" Beach, a pioneering Black Panther youth organizer. He is also inspired by the women of the Las Vegas welfare rights movement who shut down the Strip in the 1970s to protest cuts in benefits to poor families. "It is cruel to tell a person with no shoes to pull herself up by her bootstraps," their leader Ruby Duncan used to say. Sanders agrees. And yet he feels that living-wage activists are doing that: picking themselves up by their bare, naked feet. Like the fast-food activists of Manila, Sanders is a radical Christian. He believes that God is on the side of the poor. "The struggle for freedom is a struggle for justice. And God will deliver justice." He pauses. "If we work for it."[5]

"Change is starting to come," says Bleu Rainer. "We've had wins across the board with fast food. We've had wins in Seattle. San Francisco. New York. LA. The McDonald's CEO resigned. We've had support from our friends in other countries. That only comes from workers standing up and applying pressure. Me and my colleagues here, we're going to stand up and fight back and we're going to keep fighting until they give us what we want."

Stretch Sanders credits worker protest for Carl's Jr. CEO Andrew Puzder's decision to withdraw from consideration to be Trump's secretary of labor. "The people have the power and ability to run fast-food companies better than he does. And to run the world. And I believe, I really do, that one day we will."[6]

CHAPTER 16

COUNTING VICTORIES, GIRDING FOR AN UPHILL STRUGGLE

ACTIVISTS IN THE LOW-WAGE workers' struggle are rightly proud of what they achieved between 2012 and 2016. Twenty-one states plus the District of Columbia raised the minimum wage. Thirty states passed wages higher than the federal minimum. By 2017, forty localities enacted minimum wages that were higher than the minimum wages in their states.[1]

In the spring of 2016, the movement won its most significant US victories when California and New York—the country's largest labor markets—both approved a $15 state wage. New York and California are very expensive places. Fifteen dollars an hour, phased in over several years, will not give workers enough to support families. Still, these are noteworthy victories, raising wages for tens of millions of workers after decades of wage stagnation.[2]

As important, the movement shifted public opinion, convincing most Americans that all workers deserve a living wage. By 2016, six in ten Americans supported a $15 hourly minimum. A few years earlier, the idea of more than doubling the federal minimum seemed delusional. And that belief crossed party lines. Even in Republican-wave elections, even in red states, voters approved wage raises. On the same night that Donald Trump was elected president, voters in five states raised the minimum wage.

Healthcare workers won increases in both public and private institutions. Hospital workers in five states won $15, as did home-care workers in Massachusetts and Washington. Community care workers in Canada won Sweet $16. And the University of Pittsburgh hospital system, the largest private employer in Pennsylvania, commenced paying $15.

Large banks, insurance companies, and high-tech corporations also raised wages: Aetna, Facebook, Amalgamated Bank, Wells Fargo, JPMorgan Chase, and the Bank of America adopted minimums of $15 or more. Many smaller companies have too. The usually intransigent retail sector moved a little: Target, Gap, IKEA, T. J. Maxx, and Costco raised their minimum. Even Walmart and McDonald's gestured at change. McDonald's raised wages for corporate employees (just ninety thousand of its workforce of over two million). And Walmart raised its minimum to $10, but then cut hours and benefits and closed stores.[3]

Activists also saw progress in their battle to guarantee a right to paid time off. In 2015, 36 percent of US workers, forty-one million people, were ineligible for even one sick day per year. In fast food, 86 percent of women workers had no sick leave and almost three-quarters admitted handling food at work while sick. In 2016, seven states and the District of Columbia passed paid sick-leave bills, as did New York, Los Angeles, San Francisco, Washington, DC, Seattle, Philadelphia, and other cities. In some city and county elections, voters approved paid "safe days" as well, allowing workers time off to recover from battering and sexual assault. There is a long way to go until paid time off is universal or even the norm in the US, but activists believe that the tide is turning.[4]

The period of 2016–17 even brought a new influx into labor unions, especially among airport workers. Baggage handlers in Los Angeles and airport workers in Minneapolis signed union contracts in November, seventeen years after they began living-wage protests. A month later, eight thousand New York City and New Jersey airport workers won union recognition. These victories proved that unions can win even in environments where workers are employed by many different subcontractors.[5]

UNITE HERE won union contracts across Indiana for Aramark food services workers. Hospital workers in Seattle formed a union in the spring of 2017, while Amazon security guards demanded that right. Facebook's cafeteria workers unionized in the summer of 2017. Graduate students and adjunct faculty were forming unions across the country. And autoworkers began ramping up efforts to unionize, fighting automakers' increasing use of short-term contracts to limit the number of workers eligible to join. The low-wage workers' movement was criticized by some for not focusing on bringing workers into unions, but by 2017 that was no longer true.

Airport workers Prince Jackson and Canute Drayton say they were inspired by fast-food activists. Jackson is a baggage handler, Drayton a security guard at JFK. Both are in their forties and have lived through other social justice struggles. This feels different. "We could feel that the movement was really growing," Jackson says. "We knew that there were thousands of underpaid service workers in New York City who don't get benefits for doing jobs that are vital to the life of the city. Most of us have a friend or relative who works or did work in fast food. We know how hard they work, what a tough job they have, and that the pay they get is ludicrous."

Jackson and Drayton were thrilled when President Obama signed an executive order in 2014 raising minimum salaries for workers under federal contract. As leaders in the fight, they were invited to the White House. "I went to Washington, DC, when the president signed the order giving federal workers $10.10 an hour," Jackson says. "It was an incredible feeling, standing with the president. Something I can tell my grandkids."

This wasn't a big raise, Drayton says, but a humanizing act. "It felt so encouraging to see Obama's response to workers' organizing. We in security play a key role in keeping the city and the airports safe. We should be recognized for that. We should be treated with respect."

Drayton gets emotional as he speaks. "The subcontractors, my bosses, treat us like garbage. It's wrong. You have to respect the work financially, but also change the way you treat people. Sure, we need a benefits package. We need safety precautions. But we also have to let them know that we're not garbage." He pauses, angry, collects himself. "We're human beings. We are the backbone of airport operations. We do our jobs well."[6]

After two years of organizing, the victory was sweet. Jackson and Drayton were elected to the New York/New Jersey Airport Workers Bargaining Committee for SEIU Local 32BJ. One newly unionized JFK worker echoed Drayton's sentiments. "It's all about respect," she said as she did a victory lap around the airport.

Since 2016, workers have struck at Dulles and Reagan in Washington, DC, as well as airports in Philadelphia and Denver. And Airport Workers United, a new national labor organization, has reached out to airport unions internationally. "The airline industry is global," organizers said. "So are we." Because, they insist, "Poverty Wages Don't Fly."[7]

Though $15 an hour is hardly a princely sum, it adds up. Between 2012 and 2016, living-wage activism earned $61.5 billion in raises for 19 million workers, twelve times what Congress gave workers when it last raised the federal minimum wage in 2007; 11.8 million workers in twenty-five states, cities, and counties won raises in 2016. On January 1, 2017, twenty-one states, twenty-two cities, four counties, and one region increased wages. After decades of stagnation, wages for the bottom 40 percent of American workers were finally starting to rise. That is a real victory.[8]

Workers know this is just a first step, says Laphonza Butler, president of California's hospital and home-healthcare workers' union and co-chair of the Los Angeles living-wage coalition. "Fifteen dollars an hour is only $31,000 a year. Nobody's going to Vegas on $31,000 a year. It's just enough to get by, to get the basics, but we think it is an incredible accomplishment."[9]

Even small economic victories pay big psychological dividends, she says. "When you're in communities that have been economically strangled, you see people who are broken, people who are so distracted by their everyday struggles that they are hopeless. We felt the living-wage campaign could be a ray of hope, something that could unite people around winning something for themselves, for their families. No one else did it for them."

Pausing to savor victories is essential for activists facing a long, uphill battle. The US political landscape changed dramatically after 2008. Democrats controlled most of the country's governors' mansions and state legislatures when Barack Obama became president. Most were relatively union-friendly. By 2017, anti-union GOP politicians controlled thirty-three statehouses and had majorities in thirty-two state legislatures. Freshly empowered, they began a fierce war on labor. Their primary weapons: "right-to-work" bills limiting workers' ability to form unions, and state "preemption" bills that nullified local living-wage and paid-time-off ordinances.

Right-to-work bills were first introduced amid the anti-Communist fervor of the 1950s and 1960s. For decades, they remained limited to the South and a few Rocky Mountain states. Where they became law, union membership plunged, poverty rates rose, gaps between men and women grew. In the 2010s, "right-to-work" returned with a vengeance, courtesy of the American Legislative Exchange Council (ALEC), a consortium of business leaders and conservative politicians that, by 2011, included one-quarter of the country's state legislators and eighty-five members of Congress. Their goal was to roll back the tide of wage increases and strip local governments of the right to lift wage floors or guarantee paid time off. ALEC generated model right-to-work and preemption bills. Between 2011 and 2016, they were introduced into state legislatures a thousand times.[10]

By 2017, twenty-five states had passed preemption laws. And right-to-work bills passed in states that had long been union bastions: Michigan, home of the United Auto Workers; Wisconsin, birthplace of public sector unions; and West Virginia, stronghold of the United Mine Workers. In January 2017, the US Congress introduced the first nationwide right-to-work bill. Trade unionists called the bill a possible "extinction-level event for American labor."[11]

Then winds seemed to shift ever so slightly. The national bill stalled, and in February 2017, a GOP-controlled New Hampshire legislature killed a state right-to-work bill, citing fierce labor protest. Perhaps public opinion on worker organizing was shifting. If so, at least some credit was due those who continued to wage intense local battles. Leading the way, changing hearts and minds, were some of the country's poorest and hungriest workers.[12]

CHAPTER 17

HUELGA DE HAMBRE

Hunger and Hunger Strikes Rising

AS SPRING CAME TO Rhode Island in 2014, Dominican hotel house-keeper Santa Brito and fellow hotel workers Ylleny Ferraris, Mirjaam Parada, and Mariano Cruz were gathering signatures for a Providence $15 wage initiative. "We had to divide up," says state representative Shelby Maldonado. "We asked: Who speaks the best Spanish? The best Creole?" Maldonado, a child of Guatemalan immigrants and a former UNITE HERE organizer, says that Rhode Island's immigrant workforce viscerally understood the issues at stake.

They delivered their petitions. The city council put their living-wage initiative on the November ballot. When they convened a public hearing, a hundred hotel workers came to watch. Twenty-two registered to testify. They took time off, found babysitters, and wrote their testimonies. Then, at the last minute, the hearing was canceled.[1]

Brito was angry. She believed city officials had been pressured by the Procaccianti Group, a hotel management and construction company that donates heavily to Rhode Island political campaigns. "The Procacciantis," she said, made her clean eighteen rooms daily, made her work till the day she gave birth. Then "the hotel told me they couldn't guarantee me a job. I was fired for speaking out. I know it." She shakes her head, disgusted. "I used to be afraid, but I've lost my fear. What else can they do to me?"[2]

"I have the power, the will, and the strength to fight and take a stand," she says. "I have a right to create a union in my workplace and fight to correct grievances. It's very important to be united at work, to be able to confront the injustices we face."

Her fellow organizer Mariano Cruz was also fired. He suffered a heart attack at thirty-five that he feels was caused by overwork and stress. Since it was illegal for his employer to fire him for organizing, he says, they invented reasons, told stories about him. Police served him a restraining order while he was lying in a hospital bed, legally forbidding him to speak with workers at his old workplace—the Renaissance.

What really irked his managers, Cruz thought, was his research into strange rashes on hotel housekeepers' limbs. Workers believed it was from exposure to toxic cleansers. There was "an epidemic of women's bodies just giving out with permanent injuries," he says.[3]

It seemed for a while that the workers were winning, that the $15 wage would become law in Providence, that worker safety issues would finally be addressed. Then state legislators introduced a preemption bill, banning local governments from enacting a wage higher than the Rhode Island minimum, which was only $8 an hour. Brito was outraged. "I have to borrow money from my brothers and cousins just to pay off my bills," she said.

The Rhode Island legislature was majority Democratic, but hotel and restaurant owners lobbied hard. They paid $100,000 to lobbyists to push the bill. "House leadership is moving to jail us in poverty," said Brito.

Brito and Ferraris announced a life-or-death fight for Rhode Island's working families. Seventy-three percent of jobs in the state paid too little to live on. The state's workforce—Dominican, Guatemalan, South American, Haitian, and Cape Verdean immigrants—lived in poverty, says Maldonado, unable to feed their children decently. So Brito and Ferraris, hotel chef Mirjaam Parada, and Maldonado decided to stage a *huelga de hambre*—a hunger strike. Setting up camp on the steps of the state capitol, the women told reporters they were giving up food so that the state's children might have enough to eat.

"I want to be able to buy more food for my children," Ferraris said. Maldonado saw the strike as educational. "We had hotel workers out door-knocking. They educated other hotel workers." And they "schooled" politicians, "who ended up being supportive because they found they had so many constituents living in poverty."

For UNITE HERE organizer and former housekeeper Heather Nichols, the hunger strike made the invisible visible. "If legislators were going to vote for a bill taking away workers' right to a living wage, we wanted them to walk past Santa and her child sitting there hungry on the State House steps before they voted." Photographs of the four women, and of Brito's young son, circulated widely. It wasn't enough. A majority voted for preemption.[4]

That was a wake-up call, Maldonado says. Rhode Island living-wage activists began running for state and local office. Maldonado became the first Guatemalan-American state legislator in Rhode Island. Nellie Gorbea became secretary of state, the first Latina to win statewide office in New England. Across Rhode Island, Latinx activists won elections, promising to attend to the needs of workers and immigrants. The difference was quickly obvious. The first successful bill sponsored by Maldonado was a ban on pregnancy discrimination in the workplace. She thought of Brito, and of her own mom, when the bill passed.

"This has to be a path for the new labor movement," the energetic young legislator says. "It gives us a voice that we must have." Maldonado became co-chair of the state black and Latino caucus. In 2017, she sponsored successful legislation forbidding Rhode Island state police from assisting federal ICE agents seeking to arrest undocumented immigrant workers.[5]

Brito continued Cruz's investigation of hotel workers' injury rates. In 2015, they released a study called *Providence's Pain Problem*, showing that housekeepers in hotels run by the Procaccianti Group had injury rates from 69 to 85 percent higher than the national hotel average. More than three-quarters worked in pain and had to take pain medication to perform their jobs. Brito testified: "I have difficulty using my arms and suffer from nearly constant pain in my neck, arms and hands." Ninety-five percent of workers she surveyed worried that they would never be free of pain again.[6]

Brito helped organize "End Our Pain, *No Más Dolor*" rallies that drew hotel workers from across the region. Housekeepers showed up at city council hearings when the Procaccianti Group sought permits to construct new buildings. In October 2015, when workers at the Renaissance voted to unionize, Brito felt victorious. She still struggles with pain, but life is now getting better, she says. Union housekeepers clean fewer rooms and have more time to finish their work, so they no longer feel like cleaning machines. Union organizing has also made Brito feel more human, she says. She enjoys speaking at rallies, bargaining, helping other workers give their children a brighter future.

By 2017, with Rhode Island's minimum still only $9.60 an hour, service workers seeking raises began reaching out to sympathetic business owners. Jeremiah Tolbert, owner of Jerry's Beauty Salon in Providence, became a spokesperson. He upped his workers' wages to $15, then invited the press to explain why. When small businesses pay more, local workers have money in their pockets to spend. For Tolbert, raising wages has been "a win-win." He has urged other local businesses to follow suit.[7]

Mirjaam Parada agrees that organizing on many fronts at once is the only way forward. She does face-to-face work for UNITE HERE and uses social media to talk with worker-activists around the world, sharing news, debating strategy. Parada says she's also writing an annotated English-Spanish translation of Karl Marx's *Communist Manifesto*. "Workers still need it," she argues. "Communist dictators and capitalist politicians have so distorted and misrepresented Marx. But I think his interpretation of history is correct and I want to explain Marx so that workers can understand."[8]

Nine months later and three thousand miles away, another group of hunger strikers from Walmart battled for a living wage. Los Angeles mayor Eric Garcetti had long insisted that he would only support raising the city wage to $13.25, says Denise Barlage. In April 2015, she and seven other women workers sat down outside LA City Hall. They sat there for two weeks, consuming only tea and water. Though temperatures hovered in the 60s, Barlage felt cold by the sixth day without food. Her blood pressure was low. She donned a hat and gloves to keep it from falling further.

"We were ready to be arrested," she recalls. "We were going to handcuff ourselves to the building." Then they saw the mayor walking toward them. They held up their sign: "Women Fast for $15." The mayor stopped. He looked at them, leaned down. "Then he told us he was on board with 15," Barlage remembers. Weak from days of fasting, some of the women began to cry.[9]

Before breaking their fast, the hunger strikers testified before the city council at a minimum wage hearing. The strikers were mothers and grandmothers who worked two or three jobs to survive, Barlage says, but still had to choose "whether to feed their children or themselves. That's just wrong." The women spoke of their fears of eviction and homelessness. They told of kids who didn't have decent clothes for school or bus fare to get there.

"I am Mary Carmen Farfan, mother of four. I work at Burger King," one woman began. "I decided to make a fast for my kids, for my family, for my coworkers. These are single mothers. We have struggled to pay rent, to feed our kids. . . . I can't . . . because I have only $9 for a minimum wage." No one can afford to live in LA on less than $15 an hour, Mary said. She also told city officials how she shared a home with nineteen people from three families who earned between $9 and $13 an hour. By hearing's end, LA's City Council had voted for the $15 wage, says Barlage. "What that felt like, I can't describe."[10]

Barlage is one among many living-wage activists for whom hunger strikes have become a way of life, a potent weapon because it crystallizes the moral bottom line of this struggle. "So many workers today are used to being hungry," Barlage says. "Hunger doesn't scare us. It only scares people who aren't used to it."

Seven months after their successful fast in LA, Walmart workers fasted for ten days on Manhattan's most famously wealthy boulevard, Park Avenue. They chose the Thanksgiving holiday—a ritualized celebration of American overindulgence—to highlight hunger among Walmart workers. Barlage came. So did workers from Florida, Virginia, Minnesota, and Maryland, their neon-green OUR Walmart shirts glowing in the gray November chill as they sat outside Walmart heiress Alice Walton's penthouse. Walton sits on a personal fortune north of $33 billion, and her apartment was rumored to have cost $25 million.

Sacramento activist Tyfani Faulkner says she came because "people don't realize that many Walmart workers are starving." She says it galls her that her colleagues are hungry. "You're working at this huge grocery store and workers are living off ramen noodles and chips because they can't afford to eat better. I thought fasting was a great way to show that and to be in solidarity with those who aren't eating, not because they don't want to but because they don't earn enough to eat well."[11]

"We didn't see Alice Walton the whole week," she says. The doorman told Barlage that Walton had groceries delivered rather than walk past the hunger strikers. "He told us she was up there drinking Scotch and smoking cigarettes, rather than talk to us." Meanwhile, the protesters lived on donated broth and tea. "I stayed and fasted for ten days," Barlage says, "because I didn't have a job to go back to. Walmart had closed our store.

They said it was plumbing problems but it was because we were too loud and strong."

The Park Avenue hunger strike was part of a nationwide "Fast for $15." A thousand people across the US forswore food for two weeks leading up to the shopping frenzy that is Black Friday. Some fasted in front of the Carmel, California, mansion of Walmart chairman Greg Penner. Bleu Rainer fasted in front of a Tampa Walmart. Fasting workers could be seen outside many Walmart stores. Finding a thousand people to fast might have been hard except that hunger is a condition that low-wage workers know too well. "I have had to rely on food stamps to get a good meal," Rainer says. "And when those food stamps run out, it's back to square one, which is nothing at all."[12]

Millions of workers are hungry in today's world. In Asia, labor activists say they know garment workers who consume just 150 calories daily. That's why some Cambodian and Bangladeshi union leaders have redefined the idea of a living wage to mean pay sufficient to purchase 2,500 calories of food daily for a worker and two children. That is the minimum required to sustain life.

Hunger is also widespread in the US. In 2016, more than sixty million Americans qualified for food aid. That's nearly 20 percent of citizens in the richest country in the history of the world. Forty-five million Americans that year received assistance through SNAP (Supplemental Nutrition Assistance Program), the federal program that used to be called Food Stamps. (Most people who receive it still do call it that.)

But in some US counties, as many as two-thirds of hungry citizens do not receive aid. Toward the end of George W. Bush's presidency and at the beginning of Barack Obama's, expansions in federal food aid cut the numbers of hungry Americans significantly. But then, Congress and state legislatures slashed budgets and tightened eligibility. And the number of hungry Americans rose again. Many of the hungriest are children.[13]

Hunger is endemic in places you'd least expect, in affluent states like New York and California, and even more so in the nation's most expensive cities and suburbs. Forty-two percent of students in the University of California system did not have enough to eat in 2016. Forty-five percent of UC employees said they were frequently hungry. Twenty-five percent ate substandard food because they could not afford better. Seventy percent skipped meals to save money.

And these are the winners: students and employees at one of the world's great university systems. Fifty-eight percent of surveyed employees held bachelor's degrees or higher. Ninety-six percent worked full-time and were the primary earners for their families. Clearly, they represent just the tip of the iceberg of hunger in America.[14]

"The thing that so many Americans just don't seem to get," says Barlage, "is that Walmart workers and McDonald's workers and so many other working people in this country are really, actually hungry all the time." OUR Walmart activists ask workers who bring lunch to "pool what we have so everyone can get a little—chips, some sandwich. Otherwise a lot of people won't have anything to eat. We take Walmart's line about how we're all family seriously—even if they don't." Pooling food has become part of what the movement does. "That's why we do hunger strikes. Two weeks without food. I might feel a little cold. My blood pressure might drop a little. But I can do it. Hunger doesn't scare me."[15]

The practice of fasting to protest injustice is very old. Hunger strikes appear in pre-Christian Irish and ancient Hindu texts. In both traditions, hunger strikers often fasted outside the door of the person they felt had cheated them. If the hunger strikers died before winning their due, the person at whose door the fast took place was dishonored before the community. Walmart workers' fasts at the homes of Walton family members and CEOs fit that ancient frame.

Women used hunger strikes in early twentieth-century Britain and the United States to demand the right to vote. Mahatma Gandhi completed seventeen fasts during the Indian independence struggle. Irish Republican Army activists launched prison fasts in the 1970s and early 1980s. (IRA leader Bobby Sands starved himself to death in 1981.) Since 2000, detainees at Guantanamo have gone on hunger strikes to protest violations of their human rights, as have Palestinian prisoners in Israel and women detainees at immigration prisons in Arizona and Texas.[16]

Maria Elena Durazo and UNITE HERE have long mounted hunger strikes. Partly, they were an homage to United Farm Workers leader Cesar Chavez, who staged a month-long hunger strike in 1968 to draw attention to violence against farmworkers. Durazo says she and other

UNITE HERE and SEIU leaders learned their craft in the UFW. "They knew how to build a movement," she insists.

Hunger strikes garner sympathy. Civil disobedience draws media coverage. Durazo has strategically used both. In 1994, she led hotel workers blocking traffic in downtown Los Angeles to protest the opening of nonunion hotels. In 1999, she joined baggage handlers as they blocked access to Los Angeles International airport to demand union recognition. That same year, she fasted for eleven days to support cafeteria workers and janitors at the University of Southern California who were trying to keep their jobs as the university brought in more temporary nonunion workers.[17]

Since 2010, hunger strikes have grown increasingly common. After a two-year battle to prevent Disney from cutting healthcare benefits, eight Disneyland workers fasted for a week in 2010 outside "the cathedral of happy." Standing where frolickers in the Never Land swimming pool could hear, fasting workers told reporters: "If they could whip us like in the old days they would." It took two more years, and they didn't win all they hoped for, but they did get a new contract and preserved benefits. Hunger strikes are, as they always have been, a desperate act.[18]

In the spring of 2012, workers at the Station Casinos in Las Vegas struck the city's third-largest employer, an anti-union boss in a resolutely union town. Hunger striker Norma Flores knew that union workers made 30 percent more than she did and paid nothing for health insurance. By contrast, Station employees paid $55 per week. This was a lot for Flores, a single mother of six. Station managers also threatened activist workers, she said. Flores knew she had a legal right to organize and she was determined that managers not stop her from exercising it.

So, she and sixteen colleagues went on hunger strike. They pitched tents outside the Palace Station, where they sat in 100-degree desert heat. For a week, they consumed only water as they explained to passing tourists why they were fasting.

The press described the protesters as a cross between Occupy Wall Street, Cesar Chavez, and Mahatma Gandhi. Casino managers called the hunger strikers union terrorists. Not until March 2017, after numerous protests and an NLRB suit, did the Station Casinos agree to let their workers unionize. In March 2017, Norma Flores signed her first union contract.[19]

One month later, amid festivities for accepted students, Yale University graduate research and teaching assistants began a hunger strike in front of the office of university president Peter Salovey. They joined thousands of graduate students and adjunct professors across the US who were no longer willing to provide free (and underpaid) labor to wealthy colleges and universities. In 2016, their lawsuits and activism had won an NLRB ruling that students are also workers and have a legal right to unionize.

Graduate teachers in eight Yale departments voted to form a union. They wanted medical and dental coverage, child care stipends, spousal insurance, and an end to sexual harassment.

On April 5, 2017, they delivered a petition signed by twelve thousand faculty, students, New Haven residents, and elected officials calling on the university to negotiate. Messages of support came in from New Haven's mayor, both of Connecticut's US senators, numerous state representatives, and 2016 presidential candidate Bernie Sanders. Yale appealed the NLRB decision, bargaining that board members appointed by Trump would reverse the ruling.[20]

Comparative literature student Julia Powers refused to budge. "As contingent and replaceable workers . . . we're very vulnerable," she said. She was fasting to show that this was a communal struggle. They were standing for graduate student workers everywhere.

Union co-chair Aaron Greenberg said the fasters saw themselves as part of an honorable tradition of hunger strikes for worker justice. Yale dean Amy Hungerford replied in a *Chronicle of Higher Education* essay that these students were too privileged to rightfully compare themselves to Chavez or Gandhi. Ignoring the vast power imbalance between students and the university, Hungerford insisted that "what is starved in this fast is the commitment to principled disagreement."[21]

Yale was not alone. Across the country universities had begun spending vast sums on law firms that specialized in breaking campus unions. Yale's students were leading an important struggle, said UFW cofounder and many-time hunger striker Dolores Huerta. Her protégée, Maria Elena Durazo, wrote to the students: "Those in power always want the rest of us to wait. Your brave actions speak louder than all of Yale's noise."[22]

Yale reacted defensively. Prospective students and their parents received a letter from Yale in the spring of 2017 explaining away the hunger strike. Graduate assistants had no reason to protest, the letter soothed. They were treated very well.

Fasting student Julia Powers disagreed. "We're really at the origin of something new," she said, "a new possibility, not just for resistance but for actually building something." From Providence to Los Angeles, Las Vegas to New Haven, vulnerable workers are reclaiming a millennia-old weapon for justice. And in the process they are staking out the moral high ground and holding their own in dramatically unequal fights.

CHAPTER 18

SOCIAL MOVEMENT UNIONISM AND
THE SOULS OF WORKERS

MARIA ELENA DURAZO believes that "there is a transformation in workers when they organize and fight that is far more important than the increase in wages or health care, all of which is very important. The soul feels great—fulfilled and powerful. The workers know they've changed. They've become more powerful, not just as a group but individually. And that matters."[1]

"I'm talking about social movement unionism," Durazo says, a broad vision of change. "We are not just trying to protect institutions. We are a movement—with all that entails." Durazo is no stranger to institution-building. She was president of her union local for seventeen years and led the Los Angeles Federation of Labor for eight, representing three hundred unions and eight hundred thousand workers. She has been a vice president of the Democratic National Committee and is running for the California Senate in 2018. But face-to-face organizing is what she loves best. "It is how workers' lives are transformed, how they learn, how they get power."

Rusty Hicks, the young Afghanistan war veteran elected in 2014 to lead the Los Angeles Federation, believes that social movement unionism empowers workers economically and psychologically. It's about more than wage negotiations. It is about social justice.

In many countries, social movement unionism has sought fundamental transformations. COSATU, the South African trade union federation, brought labor into the struggle to end apartheid. Brazil's MST, Landless Workers' Movement, occupies vacant land and builds new communities. For Josua Mata and his Philippine Alliance of Progressive Labor, it's about unions making workers' whole lives better by organizing inside and outside the workplace, in communities and schools as well as factories, offices, and hotels. And, he says, in an era with ever-fewer formal sector jobs, the definitions of worker and union have changed. He sees students, street vendors, and squatters as workers and believes unions must reach out to them.

In the US, social movement unionism has brought workers together with a range of progressive groups: seeking environmental and racial justice, LGBT rights and women's rights. Cleve Jones, the creator of the AIDS Memorial Quilt, went on to organize for UNITE HERE, building strong alliances between union hotel workers and gay rights activists. North Carolina minister William Barber and other progressive clergy have linked racial justice to the living-wage campaign. Barber and other clergy fasted with Denise Barlage and Tyfani Faulkner in front of Alice Walton's building. CLUE (Clergy & Laity United for Economic Justice) have energetically supported Walmart workers' organizing. Fight for $15 and Black Lives Matter have been thoroughly intertwined. These broad coalitions are a hallmark of twenty-first-century worker justice struggles, distinguishing them from what Durazo calls "institutional unionism."[2]

Some argue that social movement unionism is a product of Asian, African, and Latin American labor struggles, but US activists believe that the idea is just as strongly rooted in American labor history. Durazo, who grew up as the seventh of eleven children in a family of farmworkers, says her politics were honed in the farmworkers' struggle. She sees the UFW as a paradigmatic social movement union.

"Farmworkers were the original contract workers," she says. "No job security, negotiating for pennies. To the bosses, those pennies were business. To my family, it was food on the table." Bert Corona, known to farmworkers as "El Viejo," taught her that organizers need to grasp workers' whole lives: hunger, homelessness, immigration status. Corona and UFW cofounder Dolores Huerta schooled her in movement-building, Durazo says.

"There's no doubt of the impact that the farmworkers' movement had, because the UFW was not a traditional union," says Durazo. "It was much broader in its vision. It had its problems for sure, but it never was the kind of stale institution that so many old-line unions became." Not surprisingly, veterans of the United Farm Workers are key strategists both in UNITE HERE and SEIU—prime drivers of the low-wage workers' struggle in the US. The UFW was always a racial and immigrant justice movement as much as a workers' struggle, Durazo says. It had to be.

Durazo believes this was also true of the other union where she learned about social movement unionism—the International Ladies' Garment Workers' Union (now part of UNITE HERE), which she joined in 1983. Its roots in the labor socialism of early twentieth-century Jewish and Italian immigrant communities mattered, she says. The ILGWU was the "one union in Los Angeles in the 1970s that was aggressively organizing immigrant garment workers" into a multicultural labor movement. They didn't "look at immigrants as union busters, but rather as union leaders."

Even so, many male ILGWU leaders were myopic about the political potential of women and immigrant workers, Durazo says, especially Latinas. In 1987, Durazo led a drive to change that. There was resistance from old-timers, and in 1989 she unseated them, becoming president of her local—a post she held for seventeen years. "If we want to tap this vast unorganized immigrant workforce, we've got to be bold," she believes. "We've got to be creative. It's not just that immigrants need a labor movement. If we want to grow as a labor movement, we need immigrants and women."

Many different political streams came together to create the twenty-first-century low-wage workers' movement, Durazo says. "It lent itself to a convergence. Women's rights, LGBT issues became part of labor's struggle." You can't separate identity and redistributive politics, Bleu Rainer argues. "All these issues are about who we are. They affect our lives. We can't ignore any of them."

Tyfani Faulkner thinks that this fusion makes the new labor movement difficult to categorize. "I am interested to see how this activism will be labeled," she says, "because the Walmart workers' movement is a women's movement and a labor movement. But it's also a racial thing. Black Lives Matter, Fight for $15, and the Walmart movement are different but also not. It's all the same idea—more equality."[3]

In the age of ALEC and an ascendant right wing, unions have engaged in broad coalition-building as a survival strategy. How could low-wage workers build momentum and gain political power? Labor leaders tried different approaches. Durazo and her late husband (former LA Federation of Labor head Miguel Contreras) organized immigrant workers to vote and run for office. Mary Kay Henry, the gifted and controversial organizer who became president of SEIU in 2010, sought ways to organize low-wage workers who were not, and might never be, union members, in order to build a national consensus that wages must rise. Both of these strategies have brought real change.

The germ of what would become Fight for $15 was planted in the winter of 2011. Newly elected Wisconsin governor Scott Walker pushed the state to cut salaries and benefits. An ALEC bill was introduced to take away collective bargaining rights from public employees. Protests erupted at the state capitol in Madison.

In a surprisingly strong response, eighty thousand people participated. Members of conservative police and firefighters' unions joined more traditionally progressive nurses' and teachers' unions. Social media spread images of the protests worldwide. Arab Spring protesters sent pizza. European unions sent messages of support. In the end, Wisconsin's unions lost. The bill passed. But, unexpectedly, they had sparked a much larger uprising. A few months later, Occupy Wall Street began. Fight for $15 soon followed.[4]

Labor leaders knew that this was a turning point. Walker, Governor John Kasich of Ohio, and other rising Republican stars were commanding the media spotlight as anti-union warriors. Unless they could channel the kind of energy manifest in the Wisconsin protests, unions in America might actually disappear. Hoping to shift the national conversation as the country geared up for the 2012 elections, SEIU launched Fight for a Fair Economy. Instead of focusing on calls for austerity and budget cuts, they wanted people to start talking about rising inequality and wage stagnation. Their tactic worked.

Despite devoting millions to Obama's campaign and to Senate Democrats in 2008, organized labor had been unable to pass its top priority, the Employee Free Choice Act, a bill that would have made it easier for unions to organize. It was time for a new strategy, a new kind of labor movement, Mary Kay Henry announced. "We're taking risks in building a movement that's going to birth the next form of worker power."[5]

In the lead-up to the 2012 election, fifteen hundred SEIU staffers knocked on more than three million doors in seventeen cities. A majority were not union members. It would be a drawn-out struggle, they knew, to win union elections in retail or fast food, with its millions of workers. So SEIU began organizing workers to wage legislative and public relations battles. Fight for $15 was born, and was more successful than anyone expected.

"This is our John L. Lewis moment," says Seattle SEIU officer David Rolf, comparing Fight for $15 to the 1935 decision by the United Mine Workers leader to leave the American Federation of Labor and create the Congress of Industrial Organizations. With a mass-organizing ethos and a vision that embraced skilled and unskilled workers, men and women, whites and people of color, the CIO catalyzed an era of mass strikes nationwide. Workers of all kinds flooded into unions. Rolf believes that Fight for $15 is the biggest success that labor has had in a generation and its best hope for building power in the future.[6]

Low-wage workers across the globe share that optimism. Philippine labor activist Joanna Coronacion believes that, in a workforce that is increasingly young and contingent, "social movement unionism is catching on like fire," and changing the meanings of worker and workplace. "We don't organize just in factories," she says. "We organize in communities and schools. We organize young people, even children. We believe that children are the future of workers' movements. And we know that many children are already workers. They need unions."

Josua Mata, cofounder of the progressive Philippine union federation SENTRO, says that social movement unionism is also defined by its global reach. "Right at the beginning of the neoliberal era—globalization, the forces that started the collapse for workers—we had a protest and we raised this huge banner. It said 'Down with Privatization. No to Liberalization.' We were just starting to grasp what was happening, that global organizing was essential."

Mata, then a hotel worker, says global union federations educated him. The Geneva-based IUF was crucial. Its longtime general secretary, Dan Gallin, was one of the first to realize how important it was, as capital globalized, to build a truly global labor movement. "Globalization wasn't yet a buzzword in the labor movement," Mata says. "But the IUF was talking about globalization. It captured our imaginations."

Democratic socialists began to think about how trade unionism could be simultaneously global in its vision and grassroots in its practice, Mata says. "We began educating, cultivating, and mobilizing people and popularizing the idea of social movement unionism. The strategy was to teach workers to organize and educate other workers. That's real trade union work." And it is the only way, he says, to bring a paradigm shift toward a world in which workers govern their workplaces, their schools, and their lives. That will take nothing less than a global uprising.[7]

CHAPTER 19

"CONTRACTUALIZATION"

ON A GREEN SIDE STREET in Quezon City, a buzz of conversations emanates from the cheerful yellow cinder-block building that Finnish unionists helped build for the Philippine labor federation SENTRO. Downstairs Josua Mata and the elders are strategizing. Upstairs, activists in the RESPECT Fast Food Workers Alliance talk about their lives. Thirty-year-old Benedict Murillo is explaining to younger workers the concept of contractualization.

"You sign on for four months at a McDonald's. When four months is up they move you to another. You never get to stay in one place. You never get to be a regular worker. That's contractualization. It was seven years of four months here and five months there, and I didn't even know anything was wrong until I heard RESPECT people shouting for their rights. Now I'm in the streets shouting too."

Sister Nice Coronacion nods as Murillo speaks. She has worked in fast food too. So many young Filipinas do. Fast food is a big part of life in modern Manila. Middle-class people take their children to McDonald's or Kentucky Fried Chicken to show others how well they're doing. As for the poor, fast food feeds them in two ways. Young people work at McDonald's or KFC or the Philippine fast-food chain Jollibees. Children and old people scavenge fast-food waste from Dumpsters so it can be recooked and sold as *pagpag* in slum restaurants. The poor are the original recyclers, Coronacion says. They reuse and repurpose everything.

That's one reason why wage theft has become the galvanizing issue for low-wage workers in the Philippines. Manila fast-food managers call it "charity work," says Em Atienza. Workers must put in hours for which they are not paid. It is the price of having a job, says Joshua Noquit. At his McDonald's, "we work for six hours. Then we're told to punch out. After punching out, we work for an hour more, but unpaid. That is wage theft." Noquit says he didn't even understand that until he met Coronacion and the members of RESPECT. "We all have the same experience in fast food," he says. "Our wages are not paid on time. Every time we ask for our salary there is a dispute."[1]

Wage theft goes hand in hand with contractualization, Atienza explains. "Contractualization" makes it difficult for workers to turn to the government for help, because labor laws protect only "full-time, permanent" employees. Most workers in fast food and at call centers (another big employer of Filipinos under thirty) are classified as "temporary" or "contract" labor. This is true even if they have worked for the same company for years. RESPECT and SENTRO are fighting hard for legislation to guarantee predictable schedules, and long-term security for all Filipino workers. "After a certain length of time on the job, the worker should be considered a permanent employee," says Coronacion. Worker-activists are fighting for this worldwide.

Contract labor is a hallmark of the twenty-first-century global economy. An ever-diminishing percentage of workers are full-time employees, whether at a college, a hospital, a restaurant, a hotel, or a factory. Fight for $15 leader David Rolf estimates that half of US jobs created since 2008 are part-time. We all know, or are, freelancers, home workers, service providers, car service/ride-sharing drivers, adjunct professors pulling together brief contract jobs to make ends meet. Most don't earn enough to pay their bills. In 2016, more than 127,000 people slept in New York City homeless shelters. Many were working people and their kids.[2]

The cheerful pictures painted by Amazon, Uber, and McDonald's are lies. Precarious workers are not plucky free agents creatively making their way in the "gig economy." They are victims of what should be considered a vast criminal conspiracy. The Economic Policy Institute estimates that in 2016 alone, US workers were robbed of $50 billion in wages. Meanwhile, wealthy companies around the world were systematically denying precarious workers their rightful earnings—in fast-food restaurants, factories, nursing homes, and farms.[3]

McDonald's is infamous for the practice. Kwanza Brooks and Lukia Williams, now Fight for $15 activists, say that they have worked as managers in multiple McDonald's where they were ordered to "adjust" time sheets to make it appear that employees had worked fewer hours than they did. "That is the worst," says Brooks. "Because they did the work.

They were there. They deserve to get paid for what they did. It's a job. It's not right."[4]

McDonald's managers are also pressured to rewrite time sheets to avoid paying overtime rates for work beyond an eight-hour day. Employees are forced to "literally clock out . . . because they are going into overtime," Brooks says. Then they are ordered to continue working.

The two activists have seen other kinds of wage theft as well. For "a uniform or a name tag or a meal. They deduct and take it out of your pay," says Williams. She sees those deductions as taking food out of children's mouths. "Being a mother and seeing other mothers treated this way, it hurts me," she says. "They can't afford to pay their bills. I feel that McDonald's is stealing from their workers. The corporation as a whole is so greedy."[5]

Fast-food jobs also steal workers' sense of self, says Coronacion, crushing them with stress and anxiety. She remembers slipping on sauce, staining her clothes, bruising her hip. But she wouldn't let herself cry because she feared losing her job, or being reprimanded in front of customers. Running a cash register terrified her, because, "at the end of the day, if anyone was short ten pesos [less than a quarter], we had to pay it back. But when I paid it back, I had to walk home because I didn't have money for the bus. It was a seven-kilometer walk. And I didn't have a cell phone to call my mother."

She felt liberated from bondage when she became "involved in the movement. I thought, if only I had known about this when I was suffering all that stuff, I would have been more assertive. Everything started from there. My whole life started again."

CHAPTER 20

"STAND UP, LIVE BETTER"

Organizing for Respect at Walmart

GIRSHRIELA GREEN FELT a weight lift from her shoulders when she founded Respect the Bump, an advocacy group for pregnant Walmart workers. "We used to blame ourselves and blame each other for everything," she says. "Once we got educated, we knew that something needed to be done. Because this was not a give-and-take relationship with Walmart. It was just take."[1]

Venanzi Luna, leader of the 2012 Pico Rivera strike, felt a rush of power "being part of OUR Walmart. I learned what retaliation is, what intimidation is, what rights workers have. I would never have imagined in my life that I have so many rights at work. Walmart likes to say that the union puts words in my mouth. I say: Nobody speaks for me. This organization gives me the knowledge I need so I can speak for myself."[2]

At first, recalls Green—a forty-eight-year-old mother of seven—getting a job at the Crenshaw Walmart in South Central LA was a tremendous boost. "I got the job through welfare-to-work," she says. "I knew absolutely nothing. I was a loyal Walmart employee, dedicated to my job and my employer. I was told at orientation that I could have a career at Walmart. That was a dream come true for someone like me. So I fought for that career."

Green says she was a model employee. She "exceeded expectations" during employee evaluations and was promoted "a couple of times." Within three years, Green had become a department manager for health and beauty products. It was a great feeling. "Then I started to realize that something was really wrong."

For starters, the promotion brought her only a 20-cent raise—to $9.80 an hour. Then there was the pressure. Store managers are constantly pushed to cut staff, Green says, to come in under the "preferred labor budget" determined by corporate executives. Green never had enough workers in her department to do everything her store manager wanted. The stress was killing her.

Walmart is the world's largest private employer—with two million employees in 11,695 stores in 28 countries, under 69 corporate banners. It imports more products from China than any other US company. By some estimates, those imports cost four hundred thousand American workers their jobs. Walmart's managerial culture has been adapted in stores worldwide. In China, a hundred thousand associates work in an environment that employs the cult-like aspects of Sam Walton's business vision within hierarchical structures of Chinese Communism. The result has been called "Wal-Maoism."[3]

It's not much better in the US, says Green. Surveillance of low-wage workers has been growing worse for years. "This call may be monitored for quality assurance." We've all heard that so many times, we never think about what that means for workers. It's just as bad in person, say Amazon and Walmart workers. Computers monitor how many items a cashier scans per hour, says OUR Walmart activist Cantare Davunt. Everyone is expected to meet quotas. "It's gotten so bad, associates are afraid to go to the bathroom."

Surveillance, speed, stress, and understaffing are why so many Walmart workers get hurt on the job. Ever cost-conscious, Walmart fights hard to avoid paying compensation or providing medical care. The company has waged a long campaign to allow employers to opt out of paying into the federal Workers' Compensation program. As of 2015, only Texas and Oklahoma permit that. Still, Walmart cuts costs by self-insuring. All settlements with injured workers come from company coffers, so Walmart contests every worker claim vigorously.[4]

Girshriela Green believes she got hurt because "we were severely understaffed. I was doing the work of five people and I developed a repetitive injury in my arm. Since management told me to keep on working, I compensated with the rest of my body and ended up with a bone spur in my throat." Injury on the job is an all-too-common story at Walmart.

"I was given twenty-four hours to return to work or quit," Green says. "But after I was injured, I was treated so badly at work." She shakes a little, remembering. "After all the work I had put in, that was heartbreaking to me. But I had kids. I couldn't afford not to work."

Walmart tries to avoid firing workers, she says, because "corporate" does not like to pay unemployment. Instead, they make life so unbearable that workers quit. This has been especially true for pregnant workers, Green believes.

"I didn't tell my boss at first when I returned to work that I was pregnant. I was terrified. I knew the odds were already against me because of my injury. Then I came in with a release from my doctor saying I shouldn't do heavy lifting." Her manager was furious and things deteriorated quickly. Before long, Green's injuries became debilitating.

She was sitting at home in a neck brace, warned by a doctor not to move too much, when the phone rang. It was a group she had never heard of: Organization United for Respect at Walmart. She wanted nothing to do with them, afraid she'd lose her job. Then a close friend was fired without warning after twenty years. "That was it for me. I knew then that we weren't the problem. They were." She and her friend joined OUR Walmart together.

Green wanted to take OUR Walmart in a new direction, organizing pregnant workers. She began by using the OUR Walmart Facebook page to link workers in different stores. Meanwhile, she studied the 1978 Pregnancy Discrimination Act to learn what accommodations pregnant workers could legally request.

At first, pregnant Walmart associates only "met" online. Then Green started traveling for face-to-face encounters. The United Food and Commercial Workers funded her journeys. Green recalls meeting a Texan named Chrissy Creech whose manager had refused to give her bathroom breaks. Creech's mother patted her daughter's pregnant belly and said to Green: "They need to respect this bump." The name stuck.

A new kind of labor organization was born, dressed in fuchsia maternity smocks. Green was amazed at how many women wanted to join Respect the Bump. Maryland Walmart associate Tiffany Beroid received nine hundred responses when she posted stories about her experiences of discrimination. Latavia Johnson in Chicago had a similar experience.[5]

"A lot of women started speaking out about their hardships," Green says, "about being retaliated against, discriminated against, being pushed out early, not given accommodations, being told that they had to lift a certain amount or they needed to leave." Respect the Bump called on Walmart to change its policy of not accommodating pregnant workers.

They announced plans for a pregnant women's protest at the 2014 Walmart sharcholders' meeting. Corporate caved before the meeting, Green says, smiling, and for the first time agreed to accommodate pregnant workers. "They smelled a lawsuit coming."[6]

Green was pleased with the victory, but the policy change mostly helped women with "high-risk pregnancies," she says. All pregnant workers needed accommodations to be safe at work. Thelma Moore was hit by a falling television set at the Chatham, Illinois, store. Ordered back to work, she refused and was fired. Moore came to Respect the Bump for help. "I'm here to stand up for myself, and other pregnant women all over the world," Moore said.

Respect the Bump gathered an army of angry pregnant Walmart workers at its first national conference in Chicago in September 2014. Delegates demanded that Walmart comply with the 1978 Pregnancy Discrimination Act. They also announced a campaign to press for a more expansive bill, the Pregnant Workers' Fairness Act. State versions of the bill have since passed in twenty-one states, and in 2017 it was reintroduced in Congress.[7]

Attorneys from the National Women's Law Center and A Healthy Balance (a law practice dedicated to improving working conditions for pregnant employees and workers with small children) helped Thelma Moore and other pregnant associates file suit against Walmart. Respect the Bump picketed the store where Moore had worked. Among the protesters was Bene't Holmes, who miscarried in a Walmart bathroom after her manager forced her to lift fifty-pound boxes containing bleach and other toxic chemicals.[8]

"They don't even follow their own policies," says Denise Barlage. "The rule is 'two for a lift of fifty or more.'" When the store manager came out to ask the protesters to leave, Holmes handed him a water bottle and a stool. These two "little things," she told him, can prevent miscarriages at work.[9]

In the spring of 2015, the US Supreme Court ruled that pregnant workers have a right to workplace accommodations. Respect the Bump was a party to the pregnancy discrimination case brought by United Parcel Service worker Peggy Young. Interestingly, the Young decision, like the 1978 Pregnancy Discrimination Act on which it was based, was supported by conservative as well as feminist groups, working-class and middle-class women, pro-choice and pro-life organizations. Pregnancy discrimination was clearly an issue that transcended traditional political divisions, and the court's conservative justices concurred.

Four years earlier, the Supreme Court had rejected a sex discrimination lawsuit filed on behalf of Walmart's 1.4 million women workers. Originally brought by a fifty-two-year-old African American woman named Betty Dukes, the suit claimed that Walmart managers discriminated against women. Plaintiffs pointed to a workforce that was 72 percent female, and a managerial team that was more than two-thirds male.

Lawyers for Dukes showed that Walmart corporate had, at every turn, prevented women from building the kinds of careers that Girshriela Green had been promised. But in the Dukes case, the justices split along partisan lines, with conservatives ruling that lawyers for the plaintiffs had not proven their case for sex discrimination. Women's right to pursue careers free from sex discrimination remained controversial even in the twenty-first century. But in the 2015 Young case, joined by Respect the Bump, the court affirmed women's right to remain safe at work through a pregnancy. Some said the victory belonged more to babies than their moms. Still, it was a victory, and a significant one.[10]

Unfortunately for Green, by the time it came, she had been fired by Walmart. "I knew they were aware of my organizing. I was doing a lot of speaking out in public at that time." Still, she thinks she crossed a line when she was quoted in the *Los Angeles Times*. "I hope to send a direct message that we will not take the abuse, the disrespect, the impoverished wages, the neglect of communities, associates and small businesses any longer," she told reporters. The movement to hold Walmart accountable was growing, and that heartened Green. "My voice is louder with each and every one of these voices."[11]

Respect the Bump continued to organize and Green remained at the forefront. The group began to "take on issues of single parents too, especially not having a regular work schedule that will let parents maintain a healthy environment for their children." Walmart's insistence that workers come in whenever managers call has gotten some single parents in trouble with Child Protective Services, Green says. They don't always have time to get a sitter. Fearful of losing their jobs, they leave their children alone. "It doesn't matter if they are eleven-year or nine-year or just two-year associates," she says. "Walmart expects them to jump the minute they call."

And usually they go, says former deli manager Venanzi Luna, until the day something breaks inside. Then, says Luna, "you know you won't jump, even one more time. There is only so long you can live in fear." The corrosive disrespect builds up scar tissue that becomes ever more inflamed. Her floor manager yelled at her in front of customers many times before she finally exploded. Called into the store manager's office to explain, she seethed: "How dare he? I am not his daughter. He is not my dad."

Denise Barlage remembers the moment she reached her limit. "I told my manager: 'My husband knows better than to talk to me like that. Who do you think you are?' He said: 'Denise, sit down.' I said, 'No, this is done.' I told him I knew my rights and walked out."

Learning their legal rights has been transformative, Luna and Barlage say. They throw around the phrase "unfair labor practice" (ULP) whenever managers bully them. "I will always have to fight," says Barlage. "I understand that. But the constant intimidation gets you down. When you just want to do your job and you are constantly getting 'coached.'"

"One time a manager pulled me over, physically you know, and he said: 'You just took a twenty-two-minute break.'" Barlage shot back: "'Are you counting my bathroom time?' I had to pull out my wallet and show him my card, which shows my right to take a break. 'I know how to file a ULP,' I said. 'This is getting old, guys.' And it was."

Walmart specializes in intimidation and retaliation, OUR Walmart workers say (and the National Labor Relations Board has affirmed this repeatedly since 2010). "As soon as they found out that I was part of OUR Walmart," Luna says, "it all started. They gave me a verbal, a write-up, and my last warning all in one week. That was unheard of."

When managers ordered Luna to write a statement explaining why she wanted to keep her job, she replied: "You're not going to get that from me. You never asked me how many times I didn't take a lunch. How many times I never took a break! How many times you asked me to fix the time clock so that it shows I took a break when I didn't, so it says I took a lunch when I didn't. I'll show you who Venanzi is.' That same day I filed a ULP."

Salvadoran immigrant and eleven-year Walmart associate Evelin Cruz came to the boiling point after years of watching managers and corporate executives be gratuitously cruel to workers. Cruz was treated well. But she grew ever more horrified watching managers demean grown women and men.

At daily morning meetings, she recalled, "it was drilled into all of us how replaceable we were." Cruz felt that Walmart intentionally made "predatory hires: single mothers, felons, people they knew would keep quiet just because of their situation, because they're the sole supporters of their families or because they have a record and are not able to get better employment." She burned watching. "It was just so wrong."

The final straw for Cruz was when her store manager denied leave to a coworker whose daughter was dying of cancer. Under the Family Medical Leave Act, Cruz told the manager, the woman had a right to take time with her daughter. The manager refused. "How dare they?" Cruz was incredulous. "It's hard enough to have a child who's dying. But to not be able to take care of that child because you have to work? To worry about putting food on the table and a roof over your children's heads at such a time? To worry about not having medication for your child to survive a little longer or to lessen her pain? I couldn't stand it. What I saw in that one instant opened my eyes. That's when I became an activist."[12]

Jenny Mills says she became an activist when her son was injured on the job and Walmart "gave him the runaround." She had been working at Walmart for nine years before his accident. Looking back, she can't believe it took her so long to open her eyes.

She told me her story on a hot September day in 2015, over a breakfast of banana and smoothie at the Denny's where she washes up each morning after sleeping in her car. Mills was wearing the green OUR Walmart T-shirt with thumb and forefinger forming an O and three fingers pointing upward. That was the signal activists would use to silently connect inside the stores. Managers listened for any talk of unionizing. So activists created a hand sign.

Jenny Mills was not one of those pioneers. "I was afraid," Mills says. "I had never done anything like this before, so I was nervous about what the repercussions would be." But a friend said that it was her responsibility as a mother to fight for young people. OUR Walmart probably won't save middle-aged workers, her friend said. "But we need to help the next generation."[13]

Mills's son was a night-shift worker. In small towns like Pico Rivera where Walmart contributes 10 percent of all tax revenue, it is common for multiple family members to work at the same store. Working and living together, pooling income to pay the bills, they can get by on Walmart salaries—until something happens.

The men who steam-clean the floors each night at Pico usually put rugs down to prevent workers from slipping, Mills says. One night they forgot. "My son was pushing a cart when his feet went right out from under him. He landed on his back and elbows. After that, he was in such pain it was ridiculous." The company delayed sending him to the doctor, she says. Meanwhile, they told him to return to work or lose his job.

Finally, he got to see a Walmart doctor who said he would have to live with the pain. Jenny insisted he get a second opinion. "That doc told us my son's tailbone was hanging on by a thread. He needed surgery, and soon." Three years later, Walmart was still refusing to pay.

The injury would not have been so debilitating, Mills says, if Walmart had given him time to recover. Instead, they had him "lifting and twisting and doing all the things he could not do" until he was completely incapacitated. Since then, he has been unable to work.

At the time her son was injured, Mills still had her job at the Pico store. The two lived together. Then her son lost his job and the landlord raised the rent from $1,000 to $1,400. "I lost my apartment because I wasn't getting paid enough to keep it on my own. I was making more than $13 an hour. It took me nine years to get to that wage and I couldn't afford my apartment. New people come in making $9 an hour and they don't get to work full-time. Come on!" She raises her voice. Heads turn. "Who can rent an apartment in California on $9 an hour part-time?"

When I met Jenny, she was living in a small hatchback with her husband and cat. And she wasn't the only homeless employee at the Pico Rivera store. "There were at least three others," she says.

For a few months, her manager let her park (and sleep) in the store parking lot. But after she joined in a protest when Walmart board members were meeting the prime minister of Japan, she was evicted. "A guard came and told my husband that corporate had seen my name in the newspaper and we couldn't park our car there anymore."

The owners of Party City, a nearby store, told the couple they could park and sleep in one of their parking spaces. It was right across from Walmart. Her old boss could see her get out of her car every morning and walk deliberately to Denny's to brush her teeth and wash her face.

Walmart closed the Pico store in April 2015 and Mills lost her only income. The UFCW gave her husband a part-time job but it didn't pay enough for them to put together first and last month's rent on a new place. At fifty-three years old, Mills applied for and received a Pell grant to study computer science at a nearby community college. She is hoping an associate's degree will help her find a job that pays enough that she can rent an apartment, or at least a mobile home. Meanwhile, she says, being active in OUR Walmart keeps her spirits up.

"I'm very enthused about the movement. I think we have a lot to gain," she says. "It's empowering to stand up. Maybe we won't benefit right away. But I'm really doing it at this point for future generations. It's for them that I keep telling the story of what happened to me. I'm going to stay active in the movement no matter what. We need to help people get better jobs."

Though it is illegal under the National Labor Relations Act to fire workers for organizing, every OUR Walmart activist I interviewed had been fired. One large wave of firings came after the 2013 Ride for Respect, which brought a hundred associates from across the country to Walmart headquarters in Bentonville, Arkansas. Girshriela Green recalls the meeting.

"They wouldn't let us in. The senior VP for Labor Relations and Human Resources came out and we stood in the parking lot with her for an hour. The workers kept saying to her: 'You need to respect your associates.' All of us were underpaid, so for associates to insist on respect before talking about a fair wage should have let them know how wrong things were.

"She assured us she had no idea we were being treated badly and no one else in corporate did either. We told her we were in fear for our jobs when we got back." Green shakes her head. "She said she would not tolerate retaliation from any manager. Of course, as soon as we got back, the firings started."

The next time activist protesters traveled to Walmart headquarters, Green says, "we were met in the parking lot with dogs. Yeah. Police dogs and private police were blocking us and telling us we were not welcome as associates in our own home office. So we said to them: 'We are the heartbeat of the company. How dare you treat a vital part of your body like that?'"

Barbara Collins remembers it too. She had worked in the Placerville, California, store for seven years before she joined the second Ride for Respect. She was fired three weeks after she came back to work. She joined other fired workers filing suit with the NLRB.

The NLRB ruled that their rights had been violated. Walmart protesters won NLRB suits in 2014, 2015, and 2016. Denise Barlage believes that this was because the corporation's behavior was so egregious and so obviously illegal. The NLRB had no choice, she says. In January 2014, the NLRB ruled that Walmart had illegally disciplined and fired sixty workers in twenty-four states for participating in Black Friday protests. Eleven months later, the NLRB ruled that managers at two California stores had broken the law by threatening to fire workers and close stores if employees organized. That's how Barbara Collins got her job back.

In January 2016, the NLRB ordered Walmart to rehire sixteen laid-off workers, including Evelin Cruz, and to compensate them "for any loss of earning and other benefits suffered as a result of the discrimination." Walmart appealed. In May 2016, the NLRB ruled again that Walmart was guilty of illegal retaliation against workers. In an extraordinary punishment, it ordered store managers in ten states to read aloud to workers the statutes affirming their right to organize.[14]

Collins was excited to return to her store. "It takes a long time for anything to happen through the government," she says, "but I wanted to go back (at a higher wage of course) and just smile at the manager who fired me." In the midst of her ebullience she grows serious. "There are still a lot of people who are just consumed by fear. I want to be an example. You can win."

For some, victory took too long. Evelin Cruz, who suffered from chronic heart disease, died before she could enjoy her victory. Barlage will never forget the night Cruz called her, crying, to the hospital. "I told her things were going to be OK but she just shook her head and said: 'Promise me you'll keep with the program.'" Barlage told her friend to calm down and rest. But Cruz was anxious and insistent. "Promise me!" she said as tears rolled down her face. Barlage did.[15]

Barbara Collins returned to her job at the Placerville Walmart but she says she was a different person than when she was fired. The movement had changed her. "I learned about the economy. I registered to vote. I was forty years old and I had never registered to vote. I didn't think my voice mattered. OUR Walmart taught me that our voices do matter." Collins learned she was good at lobbying. When California passed the paid-sick-leave bill she had worked on, Collins was invited to stand with Governor Jerry Brown when he signed it. Barlage stood beside Brown when he signed the $15 living-wage bill.

"Besides the historic stuff," says Collins, "protesting is fun." Gleefully, she boasts that she has been arrested eight times. She was among forty-two Walmart employees who shut down Park Avenue in November 2014, sitting in the street atop a giant OUR Walmart blanket. Facing Alice Walton's building, they chanted: "Didn't your mother teach you to share?" Collins was also part of a group that blocked the doors to Walmart's lobbying firm in Washington, DC. To celebrate her daughter's high school graduation, the two plan to get arrested together.

Tyfani Faulkner was fired on a spurious charge but she has no intention of giving up the fight for Walmart workers. She now works as a home-health aide, caring for fragile, elderly patients. She likes the work. It feels meaningful and the hours are flexible. She works back-to-back twenty-four-hour shifts. "That leaves me plenty of time for OUR Walmart," she says.

Faulkner, Green, Luna, Barlage, and other OUR Walmart leaders are in for the long haul. But they know well that the stakes are high and victories hard-won. "Everyone in OUR Walmart has suffered a lot," Luna says. The Pico women, widely known for their courage and militancy, were badly shaken in April 2015 when Walmart closed their store. In a husky, whispery voice, Luna notes that 533 families "lost their breadwinner." And it wasn't just Pico. Five stores in four states were closed, 2,200 workers laid off without warning.

Luna came to work that day and found the doors locked. Full-time workers and a few part-time employees received sixty days' severance. Many got nothing. Walmart claimed that workers who wanted transfers to other stores were given them. Luna says that is not true and that no activists were offered transfers.

Management claimed the stores were shut down to repair plumbing problems. OUR Walmart and allies in the UFCW say it was punishment. Walmart had warned workers they would shut down stores to punish organizing, says Barbara Collins. When meat cutters in a Texas store voted to unionize, Walmart moved to prepackaged meats. It's how they respond, workers say, swiftly and with imperial coldness.

When the Pico store reopened, not one OUR Walmart activist was rehired. "I was suicidal for a while," Luna admits. "People came to me and said: 'If it wasn't for you, we would still have our jobs.'" For a moment, she rests her forehead on her arms, then resumes. Court injunctions prevent OUR Walmart activists from entering Walmart stores, except to shop. Even that is denied her, says Luna. When she walked into the reopened Pico store to shop, someone recognized her. She was escorted out by security.

Deep friendships are the gift that compensates for many losses. "It's all her fault." Barlage nudges her younger friend. "She's the one that signed me up. When I first started doing this, there was so much negative feedback from everybody else. You know: 'If you don't like what you're doing, get another job'? I was ready to say, 'Venanzi, I'm out. I can't do this. It's too negative.' But she said: 'It's OK, mom. We're going to change things.'"

Over a long Mexican lunch, they reminisce about their high times. They begin with the first walkout at a US Walmart, back in 2012. Barlage lets out a hearty laugh. "Venanzi said to me, 'Mama, we're going to strike over our ULP.' I didn't even know what a ULP was then. She said, 'Just be there. Tomorrow. We're going to strike.' I thought, 'Oh, crap.'" Barlage pressed herself against the back wall, hoping Luna might miss her. "But she took my hand and said, 'Come on, mama. Let's do this.'"

Luna says, "I didn't know if the associates would really walk out." But she and Barlage and Cruz had done their jobs well: Luna organized the fresh-food workers; Evelin, health and beauty; and Barlage, the night shift. The night workers liked the idea of striking, Barlage says, because they were the ones most frequently injured. "Everyone is scared to leave their position to ask for help so they lift heavy boxes alone, and they get hurt." After a quick visit to the "No Care" clinic, she says, "they are given an aspirin and sent back to work. So when I said, 'Let's get together, let's make a change,' they were receptive. You bet."

Still, the workers were nervous, says Luna. "They kept asking me, 'Can we get fired?' And I said, 'No, we cannot get fired. We will file a ULP for you.' I tried to hide how scared I was." Luna's manager glared as she walked the strikers out the front door. "They were on the phone with corporate as I said: 'Clock out everyone. The strike begins now!' And people were like, 'Oh, my God. Walmart workers just went on strike to protest retaliation.'"

It wasn't until she was outside, Luna says, that it hit her. "Oh, my God! We are on strike!" She heard management tell reporters that the strikers were not Walmart workers, that they were outside agitators, union organizers. Luna laughs. "I told them, 'Come see me inside at the deli where I work.'"

Support came from across the globe. The best was the busload of unionized Walmart workers from Uruguay, South Africa, Italy, and elsewhere, who came to walk them back in. When she saw the parade of foreign workers marching behind her, Luna says: "I got goose bumps. I felt like the president of the United States walking into the store with all of them behind us, dancing and singing. When the store manager tried to throw them out, they said, 'We're Walmart workers. We have a right to be here.'"

Luna heard workers whispering that the strikers were going to be fired. She didn't think so. It felt "so good having that support from everywhere. I said: 'No. This is what happens when you actually believe in something.' Our emotions went wild that day."

Barlage nudges Luna in the shoulder. "She's an emotional girl." She tells of the time they shut down Cesar Chavez Avenue in downtown Los Angeles. They were all there: Evelin Cruz, Tyfani Faulkner, Girshriela Green, and a raft of supporters from organized labor and from Clergy & Laity United for Economic Justice.

"The day was so hot," Barlage remembers, "and we were all nervous. I looked at Venanzi and she was on her knees hyperventilating. She wouldn't look at me. The cops were coming down the line, reading people their rights. I was three people down from Venanzi. There was this young guy next to her and I said: 'I need you to put your hand on Venanzi's back because she looks like she's going to pass out.' He looked at me funny. But he did it. And then I said, 'Now rub her back.' He did, and I saw Venanzi start to breathe again."

Luna had not told her parents that she was going to be arrested. "I didn't want them to see me on TV," she says. "They would be: 'Oh, my God, what are you doing?' I was OK once we were arrested. But those few moments, in the streets waiting, I was nerve-racked."

In prison, Rabbi Jonathan Klein of CLUE relaxed them by getting everyone to sing: old civil rights and labor songs, even Motown. "In one cell were the women," Luna and Barlage recall. "On the other side of a brick wall were the men." They heard Rabbi Klein start singing. "He said, 'Come on, everybody. Let's sing.'" Luna laughs. "It was like a party in jail." Luna says she started to joke with the police. "I told them I didn't like my mug shot. They needed to let me get my lipstick, let me fix my hair, and take it again."

The pleasures of protest, the rush of feeling a part of history. When Barlage, Luna, Faulkner, and twenty-five others shut down the Crenshaw store in November 2014, they made the national news. It was the first retail sit-down strike since saleswomen occupied Woolworth's in Detroit and New York in 1937.

"We shut down the store for almost two hours," Luna says with glee. "Corporate was freaking out." They taped their mouths shut to protest Walmart's attempts to silence workers, wrote the word "strike" in thick black letters on the tape. Leaning against the display cases cross-legged, they held up black-and-white pictures of the Woolworth strikers—role models, allies from another time. Barlage and Luna grin, remembering. "We enjoyed that."

That same night, Cruz led hundreds of protesters in Pico singing "We Shall Not Be Moved." Then, tweaking Walmart's slogan "Pay Less, Live Better," they sat down in traffic holding hand-lettered signs that said: "Sit Down, Live Better."

"But maybe the best times, and the scariest," Luna says, were their trips to Walmart shareholders' meetings. They've all gone several times. Faulkner went four years in a row. "It can be shocking the first time you go," she says, "because they hold it in a basketball stadium. And when you think of how the workers live and you see this extravagant concert and show that they call a shareholders' meeting, it can feel very overwhelming."

"Walmart Moms" came one year to speak about their children's needs for clothing, food, and medical care. Another year, the fired Pico strikers demanded their jobs back. The protesters cornered Walmart's CEO and spoke directly to him. "Doug McMillon was very polite to us," Barlage says. "He talked for about thirty minutes." Over the years, they have even gotten face-to-face meetings with Alice Walton.

In June 2013, two months after the Rana Plaza garment factory collapse in Dhaka, Bangladesh, Walmart workers helped bring Kalpona Akter to Bentonville. She spoke directly to the Walton family, asking why they would not spend even 1 percent of one year's personal dividends to save the lives of the workers who sew the clothing that has made them a fortune.

Venanzi Luna introduced a petition from the floor in 2012 asking CEO Rob Walton to step aside. She spoke again in 2015, demanding to know why the Pico store had been closed and hundreds of workers laid off. "I get really nervous speaking in front of people.," she says. "This was thousands of associates and Walmart corporate. And the family. My hands were shaking. If you look at the video you can see my entire body was shaking." A working-class hero is something to be. But Luna will let you know that her fierceness is just covering her fear.

Since the 2016 election, Tyfani Faulkner has been trying to heal rifts in the movement, reaching out to Walmart workers who voted for Donald Trump. Though she voted for Clinton, she says she understands those who didn't. "They wanted to believe in what Trump said he'd do: bring back manufacturing jobs. Then they wouldn't have to work at Walmart anymore. That excited them." Faulkner says she's trying to "reunite us around the goals we all share. If you voted for Trump because he said he'd help workers, then hold him to it."[16]

Luna has been through a lot since the 2012 strike. She's lost her job, lost Evelin, lost her mom, whom she nursed through it all. "It's not easy," she says. "Everybody who is part of this movement has suffered. But without that suffering we wouldn't be where we are."

I ask her where she thinks they are. She says, "The ladies that made a revolution at Walmart, we literally started a chain reaction. First it was the Walmart workers, then the fast-food workers, the car washeros. . . . It's still going on. We did that! We started it.

"People never expected Walmart workers to take a stand against the world's biggest company. But you know what? If we can change Walmart, we can change everything. People don't realize how much power they have as workers. But if you put your little bit of rights on the line and go from that, you can change anything in the world."

PART III

GARMENT WORKERS' ORGANIZING IN THE AGE OF FAST FASHION

CHAPTER 21

"IF PEOPLE WOULD THINK ABOUT US, WE WOULDN'T DIE"

Beautiful Clothes, Ugly Reality

SEPTEMBER 2013—FASHION WEEK in New York City, a time when the city's glamour shines bright as models, designers, and buyers from around the world flock to see the newest designs. Kalpona Akter stood near the fountain outside Lincoln Center, New York's iconic performance space. Five months after the Rana Plaza factory collapse, the worst disaster in the history of the garment trades, a group of top-tier models were picketing and chanting: "Nautica, Nautica, you can't hide. We can see your greedy side." Some carried photographs of injured Bangladeshi workers. "No one should die for fashion!" they shouted. "Nautica, don't throw workers overboard! End death traps now: Sign the Bangladesh Fire and Safety Accord."[1]

Factory disasters were nothing new in Bangladesh. There had been hundreds of fires during the twenty-first century, claiming thousands of lives. But the Rana Plaza building collapse on April 24, 2013, had changed the global discussion, when 1,134 workers were killed and 2,500 more injured. The scale of devastation—nearly ten times that of the Triangle Fire—had infused the fight for justice in the garment trades with fresh urgency.

As a result, eighty-six global clothing companies and retailers from twenty countries signed the accord in the first months after the disaster. Most of the signatories were Asian and European. It was a quantum leap in corporate accountability in the country that exports more garments than any except China. The accord allowed inspectors chosen by workers' associations to inspect any factory for fire and safety hazards. Signatories legally committed themselves to make all necessary repairs and, if they didn't, opened the door to lawsuits in their home countries.

American companies were slow to sign and some never did. Many would agree only to voluntary inspections and repairs. The Florida farmworkers' advocacy group Coalition of Immokalee Workers had done studies proving that inspections run by employers reveal little, that only worker-enforced safety codes like the accord substantively improve labor conditions. Still Walmart, Gap, and other American apparel companies resisted.

To increase pressure on them, activists decided to crash Fall Fashion Week—the time when big buyers decide which lines to carry that year, and when labels are especially sensitive to bad press. The target of the models' protest, VF Corporation, was among the biggest apparel companies in the world, and it had not signed the accord.

VF manufactures high-end sportswear for Nautica, Jansport, Timberland, Lee, Wrangler, Vans, the North Face, and Reef. It is not a fast-fashion producer. That was the point that Nautica's lead model, Sara Ziff, wanted to make when she organized the models' protest. Killing conditions are not restricted to factories making inexpensive clothing for mass distribution. They are endemic to twenty-first-century garment work.[2]

Ziff was radicalized by the Rana Plaza collapse. Afterward, she traveled to Bangladesh, met Akter, and interviewed survivors. "As the faces of the fashion industry," Ziff said, "models are in a unique and powerful position to promote decent working conditions not only for themselves but also for the women who make the clothes that we wear." Models picketing Fashion Week chanted: "Exploitation is not a good look."[3]

The scale of the carnage after the Rana Plaza collapse struck workers, consumers, and activists worldwide, evoking horror and sparking anger. Pressured by their customers, hundreds of companies soon signed the accord. Akter and survivors convinced President Barack Obama and the US Congress to end preferential trade status for Bangladesh. In February 2014, the Senate Foreign Relations Committee met to consider restoring Bangladesh to the status of preferred trading partner. Akter traveled to Washington to try to dissuade them, and to push for a bill requiring that clothing sold in the US be produced in safe factories with decent working conditions.[4]

Dressed in a handmade Bangladeshi sari, Akter told her story to the Senate. How she had started sewing clothing for the US market at twelve years old and earned $10 a month for 450 hours of labor. How as a teenage union activist, she had been beaten and teargassed. And how she had been arrested by the Bangladeshi government, charged with crimes she did not commit. In 2012, her friend and fellow organizer Aminul Islam was tortured and murdered—by police, Akter believes. Since that time, she and other garment union leaders have been under constant surveillance by Bangladeshi security forces.

The hearing room was silent as she spoke. Akter admitted that preferential trade status had been a big boon to the Bangladeshi apparel industry and to the global clothing brands who profited mightily from manufacturing in a country where workers were paid so little. And it was true that labor conditions had improved somewhat after Rana Plaza. But Akter urged the senators not to renew trade privileges until factories in Bangladesh were truly safe and garment workers free to organize without retribution. That was not yet the case.[5]

Reba Sikder, a slight eighteen-year-old survivor of Rana Plaza, testified next. She looked weary, a little dazed, and not a day over fourteen. Sikder wore a striped hoodie sweatshirt to ward off the chill of a damp DC winter. In 2013, she had worked fourteen-hour days for $49 a month. She couldn't afford to miss work, even for a day, she said, though she had noticed cracks spreading through the walls of the Savar building. And she knew that older workers were worried.

When Sikder arrived for work on April 24, 2013, she saw her colleagues milling outside, hesitant to enter. One worker pointed to rubble by the doors. The building foundation appeared to be dissolving. Then Sikder heard the boss yell: "You bloody people . . . if you don't go inside, you won't get your salary." Workers nervously filed in. Sitting at her sewing machine, Sikder could feel the building shake. But the bosses wouldn't let anyone leave. When the walls collapsed around her, Sikder was hit by debris and knocked unconscious.

The teen woke to the sound of people crying, but she could not see anything. She lay trapped under rubble for three days, scratching a tiny opening through which she called for help. Then rescuers' hands were on her, inching her toward the light. "I saw many injured and dead workers," she says. Many surgeries later, she still suffers daily pain. Her bones never healed properly. Nor has her heart or her mind. And yet she knows she is lucky.

Garment workers understand that their bosses in Bangladesh don't care if they are hurt or killed, Sikder said, looking members of the Senate Foreign Relations Committee in the eye. But she didn't think American consumers or corporations cared either. "I don't think they think about us," she said in English. "If people and brands would think about us, the people who are making their clothes, we would not die."

Some in the room had tears in their eyes. "You all wear clothes that were made in Bangladesh," she said. "Thousands shouldn't die just for coming to work. Please think about the workers who have lost their limbs, their feet, and their hands and about the families who have lost sons and daughters, wives and husbands." She took a breath. "Please think about their pain."[6]

Sikder's story touched California congressman George Miller, who asked to meet with her privately. Afterward, he released this statement: "The apparel industry has created millions of jobs for Bangladeshi women. But your job should not cost you your life. We must call out the clothing brands that manufacture irresponsibly in Bangladesh." Otherwise, he said, "their clothing labels may as well read: 'Made with Violence Against Women.'"[7]

On June 1, 2014, six months after a garment workers' protest in Phnom Penh ended in smoke and blood when police shot into the crowd, 150 Cambodian garment workers staged a fashion show. They advertised on wall posters around the city. Over pictures of the latest fashions, jagged words were splashed: "Beautiful Clothes, Ugly Reality."

Months after killing five garment workers and wounding forty, the ruling Cambodian People's Party had not lifted its ban on demonstrations. Before the crackdown, workers had been protesting by the hundreds of thousands for a living wage. But to do so now would be very dangerous. Garment worker–activists sidestepped the ban by announcing a fashion show. Performances did not require a permit. Police watched but did not intervene.[8]

On a rare day off, workers busied themselves assembling a catwalk at United Sisterhood Alliance, a feminist NGO active in Phnom Penh since the early 2000s. The large first floor opened onto a leafy street in the city's diplomatic quarter. The models—women in their twenties and thirties—applied dramatic makeup, fit their feet into killer heels, and donned clothes they never could have afforded if they'd had to pay market prices. American and European house music blared; pink and white lights pulsed.

The show opened with a piece called "Crackdown Hip-Hop." Four young male dancers performed a Cambodian version of an African American street dance known as "krumping." *Crack*. The sound of gunshots filled the air.

The stage darkened, then relit. Music throbbed. Women workers strutted defiantly to the Swedish hit "I Love It." The workers-turned-models posed in the dresses they spend their lives sewing. Logos for Old Navy, H&M, Gap, Nike, Levi's, and other companies were projected onto their faces and bodies. Each carried two-foot-long hundred-dollar bills.

As cameras flashed, the women stopped, then theatrically ripped up the hundred-dollar bills. Torn pieces floated into boxes labeled Rent, Electricity, Water, Medical Care, Food. At the final box, the women held up empty hands. Cambodian garment workers live on as little as 150 calories a day, says union leader Roth Minea. "Feeding themselves is the one expense they can cut," he said. "And they do, day after day."[9]

Some held placards displaying annual company profits: Gap—$6.2 billion; Old Navy (owned by Gap)—$6.6 billion; Nike—$30.6 billion. Others held cards showing CEO salaries: Ralph Lauren, $24 million; Walmart CEO Doug McMillon, $25.6 million; Nike CEO Mark Parker, $47.6 million. And finally, one displayed the net worth of Nike chairman Phil Knight: $22 billion.

Models in Puma, Nike, and Adidas sneakers that sell for over $100 in the US and Europe carried signs showing the minimum wage for garment workers in Cambodia: $140 a month—under $2,000 a year. Workers had fought for years for that wage. Some had died.

Sok Thareth said she organized the show to illustrate the vast profits that multinationals make on the sweat of garment workers. Their gains should be shared more equitably with the women who make their products, she said. H&M announced before the show that it would pay suppliers more so they could raise Cambodian workers' wages. Sok scoffed. "They have yet to deliver."[10]

The show changed scenes fast. Women rushed onstage, wearing red head scarves, white T-shirts, and jeans. Their signs decried the injustices they'd endured: "Job Insecurity." "Poor Ventilation." "Sexual Harassment." "Pregnancy Discrimination." More women ran out, circling anxiously. Their headbands said only "$160." Garment workers had died six months earlier wearing the same: a simple statement of the monthly minimum wage they were demanding.

Then came men carrying toy guns. The music stopped. The women turned to face the men. They raised their fists. Red and white lights flashed. Gunfire sounded and workers fell to the ground. The room went dark.

When the lights came back on, women workers stood behind the podium wearing orange or pink T-shirts that said in Khmer and English "People Before Profit." They laid on the ground hand-lettered signs with their demands: "Dignity." "Safer Conditions." "A Living Wage."

Twenty-three-year-old worker Hil Chandy spoke to the media. "Our unity will create a better path and society so that our children and our children's children may be free from oppression, exploitation, and inhumane treatment. The arrests, bans, threats, and killing of our activists cannot prevent a workers' movement. We still demand all buyers take responsibility to find a solution."[11]

Then it was over. The women changed their clothes, piled two, three, and four onto motorcycles, scooters, and bicycles, and rode back to tiny rooms they share near the factory districts. That night, as they do every night, they cooked whatever food they had that day on grills and propane burners in the open-air pathways between their cramped lodgings. They talked excitedly about their show and went to bed early. Everyone had work the next morning.

Cambodia and Bangladesh have been central to the rise of "fast fashion"—the endless river of flimsy, colorful clothing that has flooded our planet since the 1990s. They have also been the sites of higher-end production—sneakers, designer labels. Fashion has made a lot of people rich in the twenty-first century, in affluent countries and poor. In Bangladesh, garments account for 70 to 90 percent of exports annually. In Cambodia, still rebuilding its economy after a quarter century of civil war, garments constitute up to 85 percent of exports. In 2015, while other nations reported losses, the garment sectors in Cambodia and Bangladesh grew lustily.

Garment workers in those countries therefore have economic leverage. They understand that and it gives them courage to organize and strike. They know that foreign investors seek cheap labor. But they also know how badly their governments want to keep the river of export clothes flowing. When they protest, they are heard.

Through nearly ceaseless organizing, workers in both countries have won shorter hours and safer conditions. Cambodian garment workers have almost tripled their wages since 2010. Bangladeshi workers have increased their wages twenty-five-fold since the 1980s, and tripled them since 2006. In 2017, they sought to triple them again.[12]

The Bangladesh Fire and Safety Accord has improved conditions for millions of workers, says activist Nazma Akhter. By 2016, 220 apparel companies had signed on. But enforcing the accord has required constant worker vigilance, she says. Companies "speak a good line" but are slow to make repairs. Even worse, Walmart, Gap, and the US military have never signed. The bottom line, though, says Kalpona Akter, is that since the signing of the accord, the death toll for Bangladeshi garment workers has plummeted.[13]

Ongoing pressure from garment unions and consumer and student groups such as Clean Clothes Campaign, International Labor Rights Forum and United Students Against Sweatshops has also moved US and European authorities to act. In 2016, the US Congress passed, and President Obama signed, the Trade Facilitation and Trade Enforcement Act. The bill banned importation to the US of goods made with slave labor or under life-threatening conditions.

The law is weak and doesn't guarantee workers' right to unionize. Nor does it address widespread use of prison labor in the United States. But it placed Department of Homeland Security officers in forty-six countries to monitor manufacture of goods bound for US markets. With Donald Trump in the White House and Ivanka Trump sourcing her clothing line from low-wage sweatshops in China, Bangladesh, Indonesia, Uruguay, Peru, and Ethiopia, enforcement of the law has grown weaker. But unless it is repealed, it establishes a floor for human rights in the garment industry. That will literally save lives. It already has.[14]

CHAPTER 22

HOW THE RAG TRADE WENT GLOBAL

IN THE TWENTY-FIRST CENTURY, almost all clothing sold in the United States and Europe is sewn abroad, far from once-thriving garment districts in New York and Los Angeles, London and Paris. Encouraged by global trade agreements, garment manufacturers decamped from the industry's historic centers and moved to countries where labor costs were low, unions weak, and laws protecting workers largely ignored. Kalpona Akter always asks audiences in the United States and Europe to check the labels on their shirts or jackets. The room buzzes as people read aloud. Made in Bangladesh, Cambodia, China, the Philippines, Vietnam, Indonesia, Mexico, Honduras, Haiti, the Dominican Republic, and, increasingly since 2014, Ethiopia.

Between 1994 and 2004, the US garment industry lost eight hundred thousand jobs, mostly as a result of an international trade pact called the Multi-Fiber Agreement that limited how much clothing any one country could export to the United States. Though the agreement was supposed to protect a declining US garment trade, the result was the opposite. Low-end stores and high-fashion brands alike began to source clothing from many different countries, creating a fragmented, truly global garment industry.

Global lenders—especially the International Monetary Fund and World Bank—fueled the spread of the garment trade, buying up the debts of poor countries or forgiving them in exchange for policies making it easier, cheaper, and more profitable for foreign companies to invest. In 2005, World Trade Organization negotiations brought an end to the Multi-Fiber Agreement. With quotas lifted, countries where labor was cheap, unions weak, and labor laws few quickly came to dominate the clothing trade.

China, India, Vietnam, Bangladesh, and Cambodia became engines of a "fast-fashion" revolution, eroding wages and working conditions in countries and regions that once had strong labor movements: the Philippines, Mexico, Central America, and the United States. Garment workers speak of "a global race to the bottom," says Filipina organizer Asuncion Binos. "We in the Philippines have come a long way down." By the 2010s, countries with decent wage and labor protections could only compete if they established export zones where strikes were banned and labor regulations suspended. Global lenders offered rewards for creating "special economic zones."

The garment workers' musical group the Messenger Band sings about the process as it unfolded in Cambodia. "Donors give aid loans but with conditions attached. The debt ties the hands of our government. This is not a destiny. Many countries have suffered. . . . The loans look good but they are chains around our necks. We must stand up for freedom."[1]

One condition global lenders imposed was that countries privatize their healthcare, energy, education, and even water systems. The effects were harsh. In a song called "Suffer from Privatization," Vun Em sings: "The private sector now controls everything. Services are expensive, so how can we survive? Hospitals, electricity, and roads. The government gave everything away. The prices increase constantly." Private companies "pay our wages, determine our hours, and charge us for the places we sleep, the water we drink, and pollute the air we breathe." In a music video to accompany that song, Vun Em wears a headband inscribed with the Khmer word for "freedom." At concerts, audiences sometimes stand and sing: "We must stand up for freedom."[2]

Garment workers in Cambodia, Bangladesh, China, and Vietnam understand that they are small pieces in a global game. The garment industry tripled in size and value between 2005 and 2015. Certain brands became visible markers of success, worn proudly by affluent women and men worldwide.

To meet rising demand, US, European, and Asian labels opened more and more factories, and garment manufacturers became the largest employers of Cambodian and Bangladeshi women and among the largest employers of women in Vietnam, China, Mexico, Honduras, Myanmar, and India. In 2000, there were twenty million workers worldwide making clothing. By 2016, there were between sixty and seventy-five million. The vast majority are women.

The twenty-first-century fashion revolution has caused environmental disaster. Bioengineered cotton seeds and pesticides have salted the earth, especially in Asia. Manufacturers use staggering amounts of water in a drought-racked world: 2,700 liters (more than 700 gallons) to produce a T-shirt; 9,982 (more than 2,600) for a pair of jeans. Textile and leather dyes have poisoned rivers. Discarded clothing has left mountains of waste. Fast fashion is the second-dirtiest industry on earth. Only oil is worse.[3]

For workers, it has been deadly. As manufacturers rush to establish factories, they set up shop in structurally unsound buildings without adequate ventilation, water, or fire exits. Three of the biggest disasters in the history of the garment industry have happened since 2010. More will likely happen before you read this book.[4]

The rapid proliferation of export-processing zones (EPZs) around the world has intensified the danger to workers and sped the loss in wages and labor power. Since 2000, 130 countries have created EPZs. That includes the United States. By 2015, there were 4,300 export zones worldwide, employing more than sixty-six million people. That's nearly twice the population of Canada, more than half that of Mexico. In most of those zones, workers are forbidden to unionize or strike. Government inspectors ignore safety violations, forced overtime, beatings, and sexual violence.

Many export-zone workers migrate from rural areas, forced off their lands by corporate developers or government leases to foreign mining and agribusiness companies. Migrants hope that the money they send home will keep their families afloat. Sometimes it does. In China alone, between 1996 and 2008, 130 million people moved to find work—many of them landing in export zones. Shenzhen, site of China's first export-processing zone and of five other "special economic zones," grew from a town of thirty thousand in 1980 to a city of twelve million by 2015—eighteen million if you count its vast suburbs. By 2012, Guangdong province had sixty thousand factories. It produced one-third of the world's textiles, shoes, and toys.[5]

Opinion on these zones is sharply divided. The World Bank considers them essential to reducing global poverty. The International Labour Organization says they have eroded wage and safety standards globally, and limited workers' ability to unionize.[6]

Governments that set up export zones understand that foreign investors are looking for cheap, compliant labor. The Bangladesh Export Processing Zone Authority advertises a "congenial investment climate free from cumbersome procedures." It offers foreign companies tax abatements, marketing funds, and freedom from labor, safety, and environmental regulations.[7]

Since the late 1990s, garment manufacturers have flocked to these zones, using them to fill European and American stores with clothing that seems to drop in price every year. Besides Walmart, Gap, JC Penney, and Kohl's, fast fashion has made new titans. The Spanish company Inditex (owners of Zara) became the world's largest clothing retailer by pioneering fast-fashion production techniques. The Swedish company H&M became the world's second-largest retail clothing chain and the largest producer of clothing in Bangladesh and Cambodia. And Gap, the world's third-largest chain, drove its explosive growth by producing heavily in Asia.[8]

The flood of low-cost clothing from China, Bangladesh, Cambodia, and elsewhere has generated incredible profits. In 2015, annual profits in global apparel and textile production were $1.2 trillion, the total net worth of the industry, $4.4 trillion. As oil prices dropped and global oil profits fell, the garment industry continued to boom. Like consumer electronics, which also employs millions of migrant women, fast fashion is one of the main drivers of the new global economy.[9]

That new economy relies heavily on forced labor. In 2015, unfree and child labor was found in garment factories in Argentina, Bangladesh, Brazil, Cambodia, China, Vietnam, Thailand, India, Nepal, and Ethiopia. Sexual violence is endemic in garment shops. So are beatings. In 2014, 90 percent of garment workers surveyed by the AFL-CIO said they had been physically punished for making errors or for not meeting quotas. In 2016, Bangladeshi workers told Human Rights Watch that foremen beat them with iron bars.

And rather than protect workers, governments that depend on garment exports to drive their economies have been quick to deploy troops and police to keep workers in line. Protesting Cambodian garment workers were shot in 2014. Hundreds of protesting Bangladeshi garment workers were arrested in 2017.[10]

Less violent, but perennially troubling to garment workers, are "run-away shops" an age-old problem in the rag trade. Always on the lookout for cheaper workers, garment manufacturers close up and move to other countries at the drop of a hat. Millions have been left jobless and homeless.

In boomtowns like Guangzhou, in southern China, where nearly 40 percent of the city's population is migrant, citizens have grown accustomed to the site of stranded men and women dragging their belongings in garbage bags after their factories closed suddenly. They sleep in the city's train stations and huddle around fires in squatter camps. Since few garment manufacturers pay employees when they shut down operations, workers are left with nothing, not even enough for a suitcase or a train ticket home. Chinese workers, who make 15 percent of the world's clothing, have been particularly hard-hit. But migrant workers abandoned by mobile employers can be found from Cape Town to Sinaloa.[11]

Fast fashion may be a revolution that cannot be undone. It has transformed purchasing patterns across the affluent world. Hypnotized by ever-lower prices, shoppers are lured to buy, wear, discard, and buy again. We are now addicted to five-dollar shirts, ten-dollar skirts. Shopping has been a popular form of recreation since ready-to-wear appeared in large-city stores during the late nineteenth century. But in the twenty-first century, it became a habit-forming, dirt-cheap high. And, as with any addiction, the stakes have risen quickly. We always need something new, something more.

Garment production can barely keep pace with the frenzied purchasing. In the United Kingdom, clothing purchases rose nearly 40 percent from 2001 to 2005. Americans are the largest buyers of clothing in the world. In 2010, we purchased five times the amount of clothing we bought in 1980. Worldwide, clothing sales quadrupled from 1995 to 2015. Will this growth stop or even slow? Who knows? We stand with our feet in the water, as the river of fast fashion roars along.[12]

CHAPTER 23

"THE GIRL EFFECT"

CLOTHING COMPANIES ARGUE that global garment production has been good for women and girls. (And the World Bank has commissioned studies to prove it.) If not for jobs created by Nike or Gap, the argument goes, rural women would languish in isolated villages, pulling plows like oxen. Or, worse, they might be sold into sex slavery. Since "the Nike Foundation first began investing in girls," the corporate-funded foundation says, "we've spent thousands of hours . . . to fully understand . . . their hopes, dreams, opportunities and challenges."[1]

Nike, the world's largest shoe company, started pushing the idea of a "girl effect" in the mid-1990s. Coincidentally, this was just when activists had begun to focus on the company's sweatshops in Asia, where millions of girls and women worked under horrendous conditions. Unions and students threatened a global boycott if things did not improve. Nike's slogan, "Just Do It," became the rallying cry "Just Don't Do It."

To sell the idea that garment work was liberating for Asian women, the Portland sneaker company brought in the former president of Smith College, well-known feminist historian Jill Ker Conway. She promised an investigation of working conditions in Nike's Asian plants. If abuses were found, she swore, they would be fixed. Conway hired Asian women academics to visit plants and interview workers. Meanwhile, she toured college campuses in the United States, making the case that global garment manufacturers like Nike were educating the world's poorest women and rescuing them from a life of poverty.[2]

By 2008, Nike had succeeded in rebranding itself as a champion of global feminism. The company launched a campaign called the "Girl Effect" that promised to make girls "aware of their economic potential" and to "prepare them to work." Nike insisted it was giving girls in poor countries "control over their future . . . many for the first time."

The Girl Effect became an independent foundation in 2015. Its website opens with this statement: "We exist to create a new normal with and for girls." Girl Effect has won praise and funding from the World Economic Forum (a global consortium of business and political leaders), USAID (the foreign aid arm of the US government), and the Clinton Global Initiative. The foundation partners with the United Nations and NGOs throughout the world and is seen by many as promoting a successful strategy for women's economic empowerment.[3]

Asian garment workers are skeptical. The Messenger Band paints a picture of garment work that is not so uplifting. "This is the life of garment workers. We dare not take a day off because they will never allow it. We work though we are ill because if we dare to take leave, they will reduce our salaries. Oh. My tears please stop falling down because it solves nothing. As women, we have to be strong and overcome our hardship."[4]

Sok Thareth of United Sisterhood Alliance says Cambodian garment factories are run in ways that intentionally undermine women workers' solidarity. Women must work on teams, required to finish as many as 1,000 shirts a day. (Or, in Bangladesh, says Kalpona Akter, 1,200 pairs of jeans.) As a result, "workers cannot even go to the toilet," says Sok. "They cannot dream at their machines. They cannot talk to each other. They cannot even make friends because the team as a whole is responsible for the job. So if one woman cannot complete her part on time, she is blamed by her coworkers."

Pressure to fill quotas causes repetitive stress injuries, bladder infections, and hemorrhoids, says Sok. Women sit for eight or ten hours without standing. Slower workers worry they will get their entire team fired. "It's incredibly stressful physically and mentally."[5]

In a song called "Fate of Garment Workers," Vun Em summarizes the stories women clothing makers have told her: "We are insulted by society. There is no pity for garment workers like us. We work from early in the morning till the dark of night. We work very hard to earn a few US dollars." Workers tell her they like that song, Vun says, because "it validates their feelings, their weariness, their frustration."[6]

Nike is not completely wrong, Sok and Vun admit. Garment manufacturing jobs provide higher incomes than women could have earned working on family farms. But many garment workers do not leave their farms voluntarily. They are violently evicted.

In the music video "Land and Life," Vun stands in a boat as images of struggle are projected onto her face: Women fighting men in uniform. Thatch-roofed homes set aflame by soldiers. Rice paddies uprooted by bulldozers. For anyone over fifty, the images call to mind news footage of the Vietnam War. Young Cambodians see it as a war too.

"Because of dollars, we have lost our homes and lands," Vun sings. "With a war of words, we have been evicted, beaten, and abused. Dollars are the weapons." Images of police with truncheons raised, flash on her face. Bloodied protesters lie on the ground by her feet. "Using all means, they confiscate our land where we used to live peacefully." Images of women cooking for children in squatter camps. "The land must be returned to the people."[7]

Hundreds of thousands of rural women like Em have been forced from their ancestral lands since the 1990s. Leaving children, parents, and spouses, they move to Phnom Penh where they pay exorbitant rents for a spot on a mattress in a dark room with other workers. Em lived in a dormitory with forty other garment workers when she first moved to the city in 2004. Sending money home to her family, she was left with little for herself. She sings: "We are away from our parents and friends; we struggle to work even though our hearts suffer; all so that the lives of our families will be peaceful." Even so, says Vun, sometimes whole families are forced to move.[8]

In Vietnam, Nike employs a million-plus workers, most of them women. The corporation boasts that these women are "the first in their families to work in the formal economy." While it is true that garment work has given many of them an independent income for the first time, a 2016 investigation found that Nike workers in Vietnam earned just a quarter of what they need to feed, clothe, and shelter their families. City life is strained and poor.[9]

In Philippine export zones, where Ann Taylor and Ralph Lauren clothes are made, garment workers can't afford more than a few spoonfuls a day of powdered Nestlé drinks to feed their children, says Asuncion Binos. And Kalpona Akter says that many women garment workers in

Bangladesh are expected to turn wages over to parents, husbands, and brothers. "Liberation?" Akter laughs aloud. "I would like to ask anyone to try to live for a while as a garment worker in my country. Then she can tell me if that is liberation." And yet, workers "need the jobs," says Akter. "Of course. We just don't want to die for them."

Thai worker Noi Supalai insists that if Nike really wanted to empower women it would let its workers form unions. The company has been celebrated for turning around its image as an exploitative employer. But Noi, who toured US colleges in 2016, says that Nike continues to close factories when workers try to organize. She wants to see UN oversight to hold transnational companies accountable. Otherwise, she thinks the abuse will continue. In 2016, her factory was shut down, and Noi burned a pile of Nike sneakers in front of the closed shop in protest. "Nike says that it has humanity, that it has morality." Noi scoffs. "That's not true."[10]

What is true is that almost no garment workers earn a living wage. In China and Indonesia, they make one-third of what is needed to feed, clothe and house their families. In Vietnam, they earn less than one-quarter. In Bangladesh, the women, girls and men who make clothes for American and European consumers earn just 14 percent of what they need. Indeed, as profits exploded in fashion, wages have fallen. In Cambodia, Mexico, and the Dominican Republic, all major apparel exporters, wages declined by almost one-third between 2003 and 2013.[11]

The rising tide of fast fashion has lifted only yachts. Workers' small boats are sinking. As demand for cheap clothing has grown, dramatically enriching top executives and shareholders, fierce competition for market share has caused regular price slashing. This delights consumers. But it has squeezed small cotton growers and manufacturers. And what it has done to workers is far worse: nothing short of mass murder.[12]

CHAPTER 24

"MADE WITH LOVE IN BANGLADESH"

BETWEEN 1980 AND 2000, more than 150 garment firms from around the world moved to Bangladesh. The poverty-stricken country—still reeling from a horrific war of independence and repeated coups—was making a name for itself as a rising star in the global garment trade. Regulations were lax, child labor common. And there seemed to be an inexhaustible supply of women, children, and young men ready to work. The industry boomed, fueling an annual economic growth rate that sometimes reached 6 percent. By 2010, four million workers were making clothing in Bangladesh. Local elites and global corporations reaped huge profits.[1]

Twelve-year-old Kalpona Akter and her ten-year-old brother began working at the end of the 1980s. After their parents fell ill, they had to find ways to put food on the table for five siblings. Shifts at their Dhaka garment factory often lasted twenty hours, Akter recalls, and when there were large orders, they worked around the clock, sleeping on the factory floor. Once they worked for three straight weeks. Brief bathroom and food breaks were their only relief.

After the bloody 1970 war for independence from Pakistan, government structures in the new country were designed to benefit people who had invested in the garment trade. Clothing manufacturers dominated both major political parties, Akter says. So, although power shifted back and forth between them, garment workers found few friends in government at any time. Trade union leaders were arrested, imprisoned, kidnapped, tortured, and even murdered because Bangladesh had a special position to preserve: as the cheapest place on earth to produce clothing.[2]

Bangladeshi garment workers earned less than one-third the wages of their Indian and Pakistani counterparts, one-fifth of what Chinese workers earned, and less than a tenth of what some garment workers were paid in Thailand. Bangladesh has, since the 1980s, been the threat that hangs over the heads of garment workers the world over, says Cambodian union leader Ath Thorn. "If you keep asking for a higher wage, the factory will close and move to Bangladesh," his members have been told anytime they ask for raises.[3]

It took an unbearable tragedy, a twenty-first-century Triangle Shirtwaist Factory fire, to make Bangladeshi workers finally, painfully, visible to the world. On April 24, 2013, the twenty-first-century garment industry was literally shaken to the ground when vibrations from a thousand sewing machines opened cracks in the Savar building in Dhaka and it collapsed, killing 1,134 workers. Families lost loved ones—often their only breadwinners. Thousands of survivors suffered life-changing injuries.[4]

Photos of bodies wrapped in cloth and dazed survivors staggering from the rubble were beamed round the world. Young workers lost arms and legs. Crushed spines left many paralyzed. Traumatic memories of being caught under the rubble haunted survivors who came out otherwise intact. The garment workers of Bangladesh had finally captured the attention of the world.

As she watched, Kalpona Akter said: "I don't care if it's direct contract or subcontract or whatever excuse you want to make. If I find your label there, it's your responsibility. That's my word and I will make you pay."[5]

Akter was in Washington, DC, when Rana Plaza collapsed, but she hurried home. A few days later, she stood with her feet buried by dust in a vast rubble field. Scraps of brightly colored fabric shivered in the hot wind: purples, blues, and pinks, shreds of the beautiful traditional clothing worn by Bangladeshi women. "I had to go," she whispers. "I couldn't resist my need."

She found it difficult to breathe, both because the air was still filled with grit from the collapse and because she felt her heart swelling in her chest. Still, Akter did what she always does after a disaster takes the lives of garment workers. She sorted through the debris to try to find labels. "This is how we figure out and disclose the supply chain," she says. "Otherwise, it is so complicated that you don't even know who is buying the clothes made at each factory."[6]

Akter plunged her fingers into the pulverized brick and chalky dust, feeling around until she found a package of labels a few inches down. "I was pulling a label up and then I saw that it said 'Made with Love.'" She is silent for a moment as she tells this story. Then anger twists her voice. "It says "Made with Love' and thousands died under that building." In a bitter irony, the labels she found were for children's clothes. The biggest buyer at Rana Plaza was the American chain the Children's Place.

"This Children's Place for a long time denied any compensation to the workers," she says. So Akter traveled to its corporate headquarters in New Jersey to demand reparations for the injured and for the families of workers who were killed. She brought several survivors. No executive would meet with them. Instead, she says, "they arrested me and the Rana Plaza survivors who were with us."

When the Savar building fell, Akter says, she was still suffering nightmares and other symptoms of post-traumatic stress from witnessing a terrible fire at Dhaka's Tazreen factory, five months earlier. That fire erupted on November 24, 2012. As at Triangle, as always, the doors were locked, she says bitterly, "to prevent workers from stealing."

When Akter arrived on the scene, she saw "thousands of people crying and screaming." The fire trucks ran out of water and she watched people dragging full buckets from their homes, which they threw, futilely, at the flames. Dhaka's garment factories are built at the center of worker neighborhoods, Akter explains. So "parents and siblings knew right away and they started running. I had to hold one mother. She was crying. She wanted to jump into the fire and find her daughter."

As the flames weakened and the night cooled, Akter moved closer to the building where she "met another mom." She drops her eyes. Her voice grows soft. "This mom lost her only son there. His name was Kolash. He was eighteen or twenty."

Kolash had called his mom as soon as the fire started, Akter says. Though they lived outside the city, the mother quickly found a bus and rode through the night toward her son. From the moment Kolash called, his mom never let him off the phone. "The whole time she was on the bus," Akter says, "the whole time she stood outside the burning factory."

The grieving mother recounted the conversation to Akter:

"Son, try your best to find the places where people are escaping."

"OK, Mom, I'm trying but I can't find any place."

"Find a window. Break the window and jump."

"Mom, I can't find any way out. It's dark. There's smoke. There's fire in the building."

"Go to the bathroom, wet your shirt in the sink. Bury your face in the wet cloth so you can breathe. I am coming to you."

The son made his way to the bathroom but there was no water. "The last call, the son said, 'Mom, there is no way I can survive. I am opening my shirt and tying it around my waist. You can find my body seeing this." When light broke the next morning, Akter says, "mom was crying in front of me. She found the body just the way her son said." Akter's eyes fill with tears as she tells the story. "So this is basically the pain, these tears. It's hard to live with these memories."

Akter went home briefly at 2:30 a.m. that night to surf the Internet and try to figure out which company owned Tazreen. When morning came, she returned to the factory, armed with the knowledge that it was run by a company called the Tuba Group. "They own many garment factories," she says. "Tazreen was just one."

Akter stood in the smoky dawn light, watching as 112 bodies were carried out and laid in rows. "The area was surrounded by police and army, security and intelligence." She told them she was a journalist. "They weren't letting people get close to the site, but I forced my way in. There was so much pain in the air. People were looking at the bodies. And you could smell the burnt flesh. The families were crying. They were looking for their beloved ones. But they could not find them because many of the bodies had burned to ash." Some had no faces. "So families were trying to recognize their beloveds looking for bangles or a nose pin. Whatever was left."

When the police recognized Akter, they asked her to make a statement, to tell the crowd that the fire was over, to give them a definite death toll. She refused. She didn't yet know for sure how many had died and she would not pretend that she did. Akter had no interest in calming anyone. She felt choked by her own grief and anger.

Akter ran to the factory with a camera and forced her way inside. The aisles were piled high with fabric that had fed the fire and blocked exits. "There was still flame I could feel on my face," she said. She started rummaging through the ruins for labels. "That was why I was on the inside. I wanted to make sure there were no bodies. And I wanted to find out what brands were being sewn there." She found labels for Walmart, Sears, and a German brand called KiK.

Akter tried to tear labels from fabric but she didn't have the strength. Furiously, she looked for a scissor, then started cutting out labels and stuffing them in her pockets. She took pictures of clothing. She searched the office and found paperwork and invoices, evidence of who the buyers were. "So at least these brands had no legitimacy when they denied that they were there." On the fifth floor, she found baby shirts and Disney labels and broke down.

In the office, she found pamphlets from the organization she leads—the Bangladesh Center for Worker Solidarity. "That means these workers had at some point come to our center and picked these up or another worker gave them out trying to organize. Management must have found out and took them away."

By a shattered plate-glass window, Akter says, she saw hundreds of sandals. "Workers had broken the glass and jumped." She thought of the sound bodies make when they hit pavement after a fall. Then she saw a door open to the roof. She climbed up. Below her lay the building's bamboo scaffolding, hanging broken and limp. Some had made it down before the scaffolding came apart. Akter walked through the building again, taking pictures of everything: the locked doors on the sewing and cutting floors, the piled sandals, the ruptured scaffolding. Then she went home and tried to escape the nightmare images.

Soon after, Akter sent Walmart executives the labels she had found in the embers of Tazreen, demanding compensation for families of the dead and wounded. Walmart would not budge. "Even after we sent the labels, they told us, 'We were not there.' Then we sent pictures of their products and documents showing that they were the buyers. They said, 'We weren't there.' When we sent a picture of me and the labels together, standing with ashes in my hand, they said, 'Well, we were there but it was a subcontractor. It's not our responsibility.' Go to hell! My workers are making clothes for you to sell. You make the profit. That's all we need to know."

Fire has been omnipresent in the lives of Bangladeshi garment workers. They are haunted by it. Almost every garment worker has had personal experience with a factory fire or knows someone who was burned. Factories operate without water, working fire extinguishers, or fire escapes. Doors are locked, exits blocked by piles of fabric. In some factories, barred, sealed windows prevent workers from taking even a breath of air.[7]

There were twenty-five garment factory fires in Bangladesh in 2012, the year of Tazreen. There were sixty more between 2013 and the spring of 2015, Akter says, causing thirty-one deaths and nine hundred injuries. And since worker neighborhoods ring garment factories, many of these

McDonald's worker and Fight for $15 activist Bleu Rainer, showing burns on his arms. Similar burns can be found on the arms of fast-food workers around the world.

Chhim Sitthar, president of the NagaWorld casino hotel workers' union (L), with union vice president Pao Chhumony, Phnom Penh, Cambodia.

All photos © Liz Cooke.

Kalpona Akter, executive director of the Bangladesh Center for Worker Solidarity, seen here in Montreal after addressing the 2016 World Social Forum.

Maria Elena Durazo grew up as a migrant farmworker, learned organizing in the United Farm Workers, and for thirty years has been organizing hotel workers and building labor-community coalitions.

Joanna "Sister Nice" Coronacion in the headquarters of the Alliance of Progressive Labor beside a portrait of the Philippine revolutionary Andres Bonifacio.

New York's unionized home-care and hospital workers at the Fight for $15 march on April 15, 2015, when low-wage workers walked, struck, and marched in 250 US cities and 40 countries on 6 continents.

Brooklyn fast-food workers rally for respect, April 15, 2015.

Activist fast-food workers take pleasure in subverting expensive corporate advertising. They have taken as their slogan a riff on McDonald's "I'm Lovin' It" jingle, which the corporate giant paid Justin Timberlake $6 million to sing in a global branding campaign.

Lei Catamin, organizer and choreographer for singing and dancing flash-mob protests staged by the RESPECT Fast Food Workers Alliance, Manila.

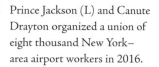

Prince Jackson (L) and Canute Drayton organized a union of eight thousand New York–area airport workers in 2016.

OUR Walmart activists Denise Barlage (L) and Venanzi Luna. In 2012, Luna led the first strike against a US Walmart, and in 2015, Barlage led a hunger strike in front of the Manhattan apartment of Walmart heiress Alice Walton.

OUR Walmart activist Jenny Mills has been living in her car for more than two years. Many twenty-first-century low-wage workers are homeless.

Sreypon, a local garment union president in Phnom Penh, often conducts union meetings in the dark, overcrowded worker dormitories where thousands of Cambodia's garment workers live.

Hotel workers' union meeting, Phnom Penh.

Chea Mony, longtime president of Cambodia's largest garment union, bears a jagged scar on his forehead from a beating. Many Cambodian garment union leaders have the same scar.

Thareth Sok (L) and Vun Em, organizers for United Sisterhood Alliance, Phnom Penh. Em is a founding member and lead singer of the garment workers' group Messenger Band.

Asuncion Binos, a former garment worker and longtime union leader, bravely organizes workers in the Cavite Export Processing Zone—work that could cost her her life.

Arcenio Lopez, director of MICOP, the Mixteco Indigeno Community Organizing Project, and his mother, Anastasia Lopez. Three generations of their family crossed the border to pick fruits and vegetables in California.

Mixteco strawberry picker and United Farm Workers organizer Bernadino Martinez was beaten and tasered for organizing indigenous migrant pickers to strike in Oxnard, California, in 2012. When Martinez was fired, he took growers to court and won.

Since the 1990s, more than 750,000 Cambodian farmers have lost their land to foreign sugar, rubber, and lumber leases. This displaced farmer now sells produce in Phnom Penh.

fires have spread to the tin, straw, and cardboard shanties where workers live, destroying homes, leaving thousands homeless, burning their few belongings—clothing, photographs, or worse—pets and loved ones. Akter herself lived through a factory fire when she was fourteen—with eight hundred workers behind locked doors. "I still have nightmares," she says, "maybe because I've seen it again and again."[8]

Kalpona Akter is done with excuses. She has been blacklisted by factory owners and arrested by her own government, charged with a murder she most certainly did not commit. (Only international pressure won her vindication and release.) She has been held for a week in handcuffs underneath a desk in Dhaka's eighteenth-century Central Jail. And she lost her friend and fellow organizer Aminul Islam to police torture.

She has felt the flames, smelled wet smoke, and breathed in the scent of fire and death. She has held sobbing mothers in her arms and tracked down damning evidence. She knows who is responsible for the regularly occurring factory disasters that have taken the lives of thousands of young Bangladeshi workers, and she is no longer willing to let them hide behind their complex and fragmented global value chains. "We don't want to know how complicated your supply chain is," she says. "There's a worker and a clothing company. I don't want to know who is in between."

Multinational clothing corporations must be held accountable, Akter believes. There's a moral bottom line—life and death, burned and crushed limbs. She intends to draw that moral red line on our clothes by traveling the world, speaking out, fighting for safer workplace conditions, and sparking pangs of consumer conscience until everybody understands.

The women Akter represents are as angry as she is. By 2017, Bangladeshi garment workers had been fighting for twelve years. Their rebellion began after a 2005 garment factory collapse that trapped 450 workers, killing 64 and injuring 80 more. Over the next year, waves of strikes spread from the Ashulia factory district across the country's production zones.

Despite a fiercely patriarchal culture, hundreds of thousands of young women took to the streets, refusing to listen to elders and imams who urged them to stay indoors. They chained factory doors shut. They sat in. They blocked highways and ports. And in bursts of anger, some women poured gasoline over factory floors and burned their workplaces.

Kalpona Akter and Nazma Akhter condemned these burnings. "We never condone vandalism. Never." But there was a catharsis some found in setting fires, turning the element that has caused garment workers so much pain back on the products that bring profit to their bosses.[9]

They made themselves heard. European and US consumers and unions pressed the Bangladeshi government and global clothing brands to fix building foundations and equip factories with fire exits, clean drinking water, and proper ventilation. The Bangladeshi government increased the minimum wage in 2006 and again in 2010 and 2013. Increases came again in 2017. A few negligent factory owners were indicted. Bangladeshi officials, on the defensive after Rana Plaza, swore they would make their factories safe.

Two hundred and twenty clothing brands and retailers, holding contracts with 1,600 Bangladeshi factories employing two million workers, signed the Accord on Fire and Building Safety in Bangladesh. Bangladeshi activists agree that it has saved an unknowable number of lives, and could do more if all the hazards identified in inspections were repaired. Still, the accord was only a paper agreement. To enforce it, and to extend it beyond 2018, there would have to be continued pressure. And there was.[10]

CHAPTER 25

"WE ARE NOT A POCKET REVOLUTION"

Bangladeshi Garment Workers Since Rana Plaza

IN THE MONTHS aFTER RANA PLAZA, Bangladesh garment workers continued to push for victim compensation and a living wage. Fifty thousand workers led by Nazma Akhter shut down six hundred factories, demanding a raise from $38 to $100 per month. They had not had a raise in three years. "We are not asking for mercy," said Akhter. "Our labor moves this economy." They also demanded compensation for Rana Plaza and Tazreen victims, and criminal charges against their owners. In an export zone outside Dhaka, ten thousand women went rogue and vandalized factories.[1]

In December 2013, the government conceded, raising the minimum wage from $34 to $68 per month. For the first time in the era of fast fashion, Bangladesh was no longer at the bottom. Some reports put Sri Lanka and the Philippines lower. Two months later, Tazreen's owner, Delwar Hossain, was arrested and jailed.[2]

The taste of victory quickly turned sour, however, when Tuba stopped paying its employees. Months dragged on with no one receiving pay. As it grew closer to the Eid holiday, the workers ran out of patience. Eid marks the end of Ramadan—a month of daytime fasting for observant Muslims. It is also a flash point for labor unrest in Bangladesh. To help them pay for expensive holiday feasts, employers traditionally give workers Eid bonuses. The previous year, Tuba failed to do that. Angry workers stormed Tuba's offices, holding the boss hostage for eighteen hours until he promised to pay bonuses to nine hundred workers.

As Eid 2014 approached, things were worse. Never mind bonuses. Tuba workers had not been paid in months. Desperate, they turned to Moshrefa Mishu, president of the Garment Workers Unity Forum and a well-known figure in Dhaka radical politics for thirty-five years. The

workers liked her fierceness. "The government, the owners, the corporations, they are serious, sure," she said. "But we are fighting for our lives."[3]

Mishu's dissident career began when she was a sixteen-year-old university student protesting military dictators and Islamic fundamental-
ism. "I fought at the same time *for* women's emancipation, a democratic
society, and against fascist religious forces," she says. Still, "my heart
belongs to the garment workers. I had been with them for twenty years"
when the Tuba workers came calling. "They knew they could trust me,"
she says.

Mishu's decades of activism had earned her the enmity of leaders in
both of Bangladesh's major political parties—the Awami League and the
Islamist Bangladesh National Party. She was even more reviled by the Bangladesh Garment Manufacturers and Exporters Association (BGMEA).
As a result, Mishu had been arrested and imprisoned numerous times.

In 2011, she was held for five months after leading a massive garment
workers' protest. "They came to arrest me at midnight," she says. "They
were very aggressive. I live with my mother. She was seventy-five and
she was crying. 'Why are you arresting my daughter?' They said: 'She is
troubling us. She instigates the workers.'

"It was December. It was freezing and I didn't have a warm coat, so I
became sick." Mishu is asthmatic. She told them, "I need inhalers." They
denied her request and she says she almost died. She was given medical
care only after international supporters in Korea, England, and Germany
pressed the Bangladeshi government.

While she was in the hospital, Mishu's captors tried to buy her off,
she says. A representative of government came to visit. "'Why are you
involved with poor workers?' he asked. 'Why are you wasting your life?
Why don't you join the government? We don't want to see you in the
streets,' they told me. 'We want to see you in Parliament.'" Her inter-
rogator leaned in close. "'It's a long time you are fighting for these poor
garment workers. Don't you get tired? You are a big dignitary from
Dhaka University. Why don't you do something serious? You could have
a nice quiet life.'"

Mishu was unrepentant. "I told them, I don't like this government.
It is corrupt, not for workers, and not democratic." Her visitor shifted
from cajoling to threats. "If you don't stop, it will be tough for you. The

government is very angry with you. You are working to increase wages, but these are ignorant people. You are wasting your time." They began to beat her.

She was again saved by foreign intervention, this time by Korean labor and human rights groups.

Mishu has never backed down. She says she can't. "I see the distress of workers and I cannot tolerate it. I feel too sad. I fight for justice because I am thinking not just of their humanity but my own. I fight for the empowerment of women and workers because that is my commitment to my country."[4]

In the summer of 2014, Mishu and the Tuba workers fought hard. But the Tuba Group refused to pay anything while their chief languished in prison. The standoff left the workers "very unsafe," Mishu says. "Landlords were angry. They told the workers if you don't pay before Eid we will kick you out."

So the protests ratcheted up. On July 9, 2014, five hundred workers blocked roads leading to Dhaka's largest garment factories. Crowds of women in blue, pink, yellow, and fuchsia saris formed human chains, refusing to move, even when company truck drivers threatened to run them down. Police used water cannons. Ten women suffered broken bones and injury to internal organs. Company guards threatened to rape the women right there in the street.

The workers had to strike, Mishu says. It was their only weapon. The demands were clear: they wanted Delwar Hossain tried for negligent homicide, three months of back pay with overtime, compensation for families of those killed and injured at Tazreen, psychological care for survivors, and an end to short-term employment contracts. They wanted to be regular employees with benefits. Tuba refused.

Hundreds of workers marched to the garment manufacturers' association and demanded their wages—immediately. BGMEA officers promised that workers would be paid. When Eid began, no money had come. So 1,300 women and 30 male Tuba employees occupied their factory. And they took a hostage: Delwar Hossain's mother-in-law, who was in the building when they locked its doors.

Mishu offered to negotiate with government officials and factory owners but talks quickly broke down. The workers settled in. "The occupation was very peaceful," Mishu recalls, "but nothing changed. So, we realized, we had no choice. We had to go on hunger strike." On July 28, 2014, sixteen hundred workers began a "*satyagrahic* [soul force] fast."

After just two days without food, 112 workers fell ill; 14 were hospitalized. These were not people who ever had a lot to eat, Mishu explains. They were too poor. And they were hungrier than usual because many had been living on one meal a day during Ramadan. They physically could not afford to fast, but still they did. No one wanted to give in.

Worried that the state and employers would soon unleash violence, Mishu reached out to middle-class women's and student groups, faculty at Dhaka University, progressive lawyers, and human rights activists. "So many people expressed their solidarity with us," Mishu recalls. "The teachers marched. They staged a hunger strike in the street." Women's groups linked arms to block entrance to the city's press club. Lawyers formed a human chain on the steps of the Bangladesh High Court. Garment workers from across the city sat in at BGMEA headquarters.

When police beat protesting workers, Mishu reached out to international groups: Clean Clothes Campaign, United Students Against Sweatshops, and Asia Floor Wage. Front Line Defenders sent observers to report human rights violations. Across Dhaka, red and white posters of Delawar Hossain were plastered on walls. "The Butcher of Bangladesh Garment Workers," the posters called him, alluding to Hossain's namesake, the infamous "Butcher of Hindus," then on trial for slaughtering Bangladeshi civilians during the 1970 war of independence.

On the third day of the fast, the garment manufacturers association promised workers two months' back pay within ten days. The workers were not in a compromising mood. The hunger strike would continue, Mishu told Bangladeshi authorities, until "all workers of the Tuba Group get their wages, bonuses, overtime, and allowances."

The inevitable crackdown came a few days later. Hossain was released on bail, and almost immediately the fasting workers were locked inside the factory. On August 6, police stormed in, attacking weakened hunger strikers with batons and tear gas. Two hundred workers were driven into the street. Mishu and other strike leaders were arrested. The cry went up for a national strike. International supporters protested and Mishu was released. But police cut off water to the occupiers and shot rubber bullets into the factory windows. It was only a matter of time.

Surprising everyone, Tuba announced defeat and said workers would be paid back wages *and* overtime. The occupation ended. A week later, the Tuba Group closed all five of its factories. One thousand workers lost their jobs. Protests began again. Workers marched to demand reinstatement. They sued in court and won, but the factories remained closed.

In the summer of 2015, Mishu and thousands of garment workers were still marching for a living wage. Like their counterparts around the world, the women were also protesting land expropriations and the polluting of waterways around Dhaka by foreign corporations. Mishu explained in her speeches how these issues are intertwined. It was too much for the government.

In July, police stopped Mishu as she was addressing a rally and placed her under house arrest so she could no longer "inflame workers." She refused their orders to remain silent. "I tell workers: The garment owners are united. They are the owners of the media. They are the owners of the banks. They are the government. So if you, the workers, are not united, you cannot change anything. You will not even get your regular pay."

Mishu does not expect the danger to abate anytime soon. When I first interviewed her in the fall of 2015, she was nursing a broken arm, smashed by police clubs—the price, she says, of being a revolutionary. In 2016, Human Rights Watch declared a crisis in Bangladesh. Government forces were kidnapping, torturing, and imprisoning scores of dissidents. Mishu shrugs. "That's a given."

On September 10, 2016, a fire at the Tampico Foils Company took the lives of thirty-four workers. Yet again the streets of Dhaka were filled with protesters. They demanded indictment of the factory owners and compensation from the global corporations they supplied.

"The government, owners, and corporations don't like democratic people," Mishu says. "They don't like militant people. Courageous people, they really don't like. They want them to be quiet. And they want workers' leaders to be pocket leaders. They like their pocket leaders. They like pocket organizations. But we are not pocket leaders and this is not a pocket revolution. We will continue to fight."

We spoke by phone while she was under house arrest. The line went dead, clicked, then reconnected. Mishu said: "I am sure the government is listening." She paused. I asked if she was frightened, if she was being careful. "Sure, sure," she said hoarsely. "Ha. Ha."

. . .

Kalpona Akter has no intention of stopping, either. She has too many new projects. One is teaching workers how to organize using social media. Many garment workers have smartphones, Akter says. "We are poor, but we are close to China so smartphones are not expensive." The Bangladesh Center for Worker Solidarity is showing them how to use those phones to learn their legal rights and track garment union struggles globally. Organizers also show workers how to set up Facebook pages to draw workers into new unions.

Akter also has a team researching how many calories a day Bangladeshi garment workers consume. People can argue about what constitutes a living wage, she says, but everyone knows that people need about 2,000–2,500 calories a day to live in good health. "People with jobs shouldn't be hungry," she says. From the Philippines to Pasadena, I heard the same.

Rampant hunger among Bangladeshi garment workers may help explain a rash of ghost sightings, says Akter. Workers have been fainting in factories. When awakened, they say they were haunted by dead friends or family. Akter believes that malnutrition and post-traumatic stress disorder are what really haunts Bangladeshi factories. Workers have seen so much death and destruction, she says sadly. They need treatment. So Bangladeshi unions are demanding that employers and labels pay for trauma counseling.

Another reason for the faintings, she believes, may be exposure to toxic chemicals used in making clothing, especially sneakers. "There are tons of chemicals that don't have any visibility or smell. In a factory without fresh air, that can be very dangerous. If a chemical reaction happens and workers are fainting, they may think they saw a ghost. But what they don't see is the most harmful." Akter describes garment workers' exposure to toxic dyes, glues, and fumes as "silent killing." To fight that, she and her colleagues are "researching the long-term effects of breathing and touching and maybe drinking chemicals in factory water."

Her last project is fighting violence against women. Bangladeshi women workers are faced with violence at every turn, Akter says. There is "violence when women try to organize and become leaders. They get beaten inside the factory and outside by hired goons." Then there is state violence, "when they make a human chain to block the factory and get beaten by police."

The most widespread kind of violence is the most difficult to tackle, says Akter, because of the social stigma. "There is a huge incidence of sexual violence but nobody talks about it because it is a cultural taboo. We've been taught not to talk about it. If you get raped or touched inappropriately by men, don't talk about it or you are the bad one."

So Akter and her colleagues have created drop-in centers across Dhaka and eight-week discussion groups for women workers. From New York to Dhaka, Phnom Penh to Cape Town, the new global labor movement has revived consciousness-raising groups. "Even with all these new very strong women leaders in our movement," Akter says, "it is not easy to talk about gender-based violence. Even the leaders are not comfortable talking about it."

The discussion groups really help, Akter says. After long weeks in the factory, workers want company, solidarity, a little bit of fun. Food. Music. Only after they unwind, says Akter, do they begin to feel comfortable enough to talk.

"The first meeting, everybody says they haven't heard of any sexual violence. In the second meeting, they are still shy. At the third meeting, someone might say, 'OK, I heard this happened to my coworker.' By the fourth meeting, finally one of the workers is brave. And she says: 'I was raped on the shop floor by a foreman or an owner or the owner's son who says I can't keep my job if I don't give in.' We are now breaking the ice. Once we have evidence, we will try to pass a bill that makes sexual harassment at work a crime." Rape is already illegal in Bangladesh, she says, but most women workers are afraid to file charges.

Akter is part of a group of women unionists around the world pressuring major clothing labels to write "zero tolerance for sexual violence or sexual harassment in the workplace" into their codes of conduct. And they are working to pass an ILO convention banning gender-based workplace violence. If it passes the ILO, garment workers will press the Bangladeshi Parliament to ratify it. "It's a huge chunk of work. And it will take a huge chunk of money," Akter says. That's one reason she travels incessantly. Financial support comes mostly from abroad. Canada's public sector unions have been particularly generous.

By the beginning of 2017, a decade of activism had pushed some companies who make clothing in Bangladesh to weigh in on the side of workers. Dhaka garment workers were again demanding a wage increase—to $201 a month, an amount they say would allow them a decent subsistence. The manufacturers refused to talk, instead shutting down fifty-five factories, laying off fifteen hundred people. Protesters again filled the streets. Seven hundred workers were arrested.

Fourteen were detained for months. H&M led accord signatories in sending a joint letter to Prime Minister Sheikh Hasina, urging their release and calling on her to create a tripartite wage board through which workers, government officials, and manufacturers could negotiate. The letter embarrassed the Bangladeshi leader. On January 17, she addressed the World Economic Forum in Switzerland, assuring the gathered bankers, heads of state, and corporate leaders that her government was "committed to ensure . . . labor rights, workplace safety, and environmental standards in the [garment] industry." Perhaps the wheel was finally turning.

All of this has taken decades of work. "I am like an alcoholic for work," Akter says. "I can never stop." Fortunately, she sees younger women picking up the torch. "Many women say that I'm an inspiration to them but I know there are many more inspiring women out there." She hopes the new workers' centers will give women "safe space to find and inspire each other."

CHAPTER 26

"A KHMER WOULD RATHER WORK FOR FREE
THAN WORK WITHOUT DIGNITY"

ON THE DAY BEFORE CHRISTMAS 2013, hundreds of thousands of Cambodian garment workers filled the streets. Vast protests stretched from one end of the country to the other. One of the organizers was a lean, thoughtful thirty-year-old named Khloek Outrok.

Khloek had worked at the FY garment factory in Phnom Penh since 2003. He says he saw "many of the worst conditions you can think of. Workers had to work twelve-hour shifts at least." And management would "always find ways to delay payment." So he organized his coworkers into the Free Trade Union of Workers of the Kingdom of Cambodia (FTU). "We started to educate, to advocate, to improve workers' rights."[1]

They won some quick victories: convincing management to stop firing workers without cause and limiting the overtime labor they required of workers. Before they formed a union, Khloek says, workers at his shop were sometimes asked to work all night. Now the limit was two hours. And management agreed to pay workers one and a half times their normal wage for overtime, double if they worked on national holidays.

Like many in the new global labor movement, Khloek believes in applying pressure to the top of the supply chain. That's the best strategy for Cambodian garment workers, he says. Pressure global brands: H&M, Puma, Nike, Adidas. In turn, they push factories to raise wages and improve conditions. The big companies are squirrely at first, he says. "They tell us it's the factory owners who are exploiting us. But we know all the power is with them."

First, he has to figure out who he is working for. Like Kalpona Akter, Khloek is obsessed with collecting labels. "Workers are kept from knowing who the buyers are," he says. "So we started collecting labels wherever we could find them." Sometimes he would spot a label on the floor and pick it up. Other times, he would dig around in the factory office. But even when he found labels, they did not always indicate which major corporation was paying the bills. "If we are not sure," says Khloek, "we bring labels to the union office. They help us figure it out. Then we contact the buyers and push them."

The unions help shop-floor organizers like Khloek research and translate into Khmer the corporate codes of conduct for each buyer. "Workers benefit when they report violations by factory owners. It embarrasses the brand," says Khloek. Then the brand demands improvements. "Factory owners are afraid of the international brands," he says. The Cambodian government is too. Without them, the booming garment trade on which Cambodia's new prosperity has been built would disappear. The workers know this and keep on pressing.

At the end of 2013, the minimum monthly wage for garment workers in Cambodia was $80. Renting a room cost $35 monthly without running water, $50 with a toilet and shower. The cost was prohibitive. But because most garment workers leave their families behind in the countryside, they share a room with three or four other workers—a windowless, dank, eight-foot-square room with one bed and ceilings so low that even small women crouch to come inside.

The Cambodian Labor Department responded to the nationwide protests by offering to raise the monthly wage to $95. The response was powerful: across the country garment workers marched in silence, wearing headbands that said "$160," the bare minimum necessary to sustain a decent life. Opposition leaders in the Cambodia National Rescue Party (CNRP) called for a general strike. Protesters chanted for Prime Minister Hun Sen to step down. Once garment workers' protests threatened the regime, the ruling Cambodian People's Party grew impatient.

Riot police clashed with striking garment workers in the capital. Seven were arrested. To defuse tensions, the government upped its offer to $100. Riding the momentum of their vast crowds, the protesters held firm at $160. The crackdown was bloody.

On January 3, 2014, military police opened fire on workers blocking a road to a garment production zone. According to multiple reports, four workers were killed and dozens wounded. Some disappeared that day, never to be seen again.

With some success, the workers tried to draw in global brands. H&M, the country's largest buyer, wrote to Cambodian officials, arguing that workers have a right to ask for a living wage. But Sweden's retail behemoth insisted it had to tread carefully, lest it alienate Cambodian officials. Khloek doesn't buy it. "The government of Cambodia respects H&M more than they do the leaders of most other countries," he says. "And they need H&M."

Khloek believes that international condemnation of the shootings forced the Cambodian regime to forgo further repression, and that he benefited directly. He was arrested after the January 3 protests, but after H&M's letter, he was freed. "I was lucky," he says quietly. "They didn't do anything to me then, even though they knew I was one of the protest organizers."

Emboldened, Khloek continued his work. On January 3, 2015, one year after the massacre, he "mobilized workers to hold a few minutes of silence outside of the National Assembly. I didn't know the workers they killed the previous year, but I wanted us to take a moment to honor their courage." Khloek was arrested for protesting without a permit. In prison, police pressed him to give them names of other protest organizers. "I was lucky again."

The Cambodian human rights organization LICADHO (the Cambodian League for the Promotion and Defense of Human Rights) sent lawyers. Khloek vividly remembers what it felt like to walk out of prison a second time. He has not been arrested since, but he knows he could be at any time. Many labor organizers in Phnom Penh have charges hanging over them—reminders that they can be jailed in a moment. The murder of human rights activist Kem Lay in the summer of 2016 made clear to every Cambodian activist how high the stakes are for dissidents. Since that time, leaders of the CNRP have been arrested and charged with treason. Newspapers have been shut down. Pressure is increasing on all fronts.

Still, governments are not the only ones who violate human rights, Khloek says. In March 2015, Human Rights Watch (HRW) charged H&M, Gap, Adidas, Marks & Spencer, and Armani with condoning widespread labor abuses in their Cambodian factories. When the brands denied the charges, HRW called on them to release a list of their suppliers and to open factories to inspections. Marks & Spencer had never released the names of its Cambodian contractors before but promised to. H&M sent its list to labor leaders and encouraged Cambodian officials to fine factory owners who were abusing workers. Adidas created a process for workers to report abuses. Gap, long opposed to any agreement that is legally binding, promised to investigate.[2]

Several months later, following more protests in the capital, the Cambodian Department of Labor raised the monthly minimum for garment workers to $140. It was not enough to live on, but it was a major victory. Bangladeshi workers took note and took heart. The big raise made news worldwide. And it gave Cambodian workers the courage to fight for more.

When I visited Phnom Penh in December 2015, many buildings were swathed in banners bearing corporate logos: H&M, Gap, Adidas, Puma, and Walmart. In English and Khmer, the banners said "End Corporate Greed. Pay Workers a Living Wage." Walls across the city were plastered with green circular stickers showing a clenched fist and the newest monthly wage demand—$177. "Even that is not enough," workers told me. To live decently in Cambodia, a parent needs well over $200 a month, they said. "Maybe $210 to $215 would work."

Asia Floor Wage, an international coalition of workers, academics, and activists that calculates a living wage for every country in Asia, estimated in 2016 that Cambodian workers needed $283 a month to survive. This "floor wage" would not move anyone into the middle class, they said. But it would allow workers to shelter and clothe themselves and two children, provide food and basic medical care, and have 10 percent left to save or spend on recreation. In 2016, workers offered a compromise: $180 per month minimum. The international brands insisted they couldn't afford that much. The government raised the minimum to $151.

Ath Thorn, leader of one of Cambodia's largest garment unions, insists that, as much as wages, this struggle is about dignity. "We Khmer need our dignity and our respect," he says. "If you respect us, we will respect you. If you look down on us, we won't take your money. A Khmer worker would rather work for free than work without dignity."

CHAPTER 27

"AFTER POL POT, WE NEED A GOOD LIFE"

DARK, NARROW STAIRS lead up to the offices of the Free Trade Union of Workers of the Kingdom of Cambodia (FTU). The country's largest federation of garment workers, it has more than sixty thousand members, most of them women. The long room is lined with metal filing cabinets flanking a scarred wooden conference table. The only English words in the room are on a wall banner that says: "Social Justice Is the Foundation of Peace."

There are no lights on. The atmosphere is murky. Immediately to the right of the door are video monitors that show the stairs, the office, and the streets below. Why would a labor union office have surveillance cameras? Chea Mony, a slight, dark man with abundant hair, a soft, high voice, and a worried face, says he is not paranoid. In his life, state violence has been very real.

"Government people come here often to investigate us or observe us. In case there are any 'accidents,' we have evidence to reconstruct and document what happened. And we will have video to show who committed the crime."[1]

Three officers in Chea Mony's union have been assassinated—two in front of factories where they were organizing, one on a busy boulevard in the middle of Phnom Penh. One of them was his brother. Thirty-seven members of his union have been imprisoned. Chea Mony faces six federal charges. He could be arrested without warning.

On his forehead the veteran organizer wears a jagged diagonal scar that extends from his hairline across his forehead. He has been beaten by police clubs and rock-wielding company guards. He describes the men who beat him as goons; the English word jumps out from his long Khmer sentences. The goons, he says, were sometimes hired by garment manufacturers, other times by the government.

Every year on January 22, Chea Mony ignores warnings from the ruling Cambodian People's Party and leads a march by union workers to the site where his brother, Chea Vichea, was gunned down on a busy Phnom Penh street in 2004. Chea Vichea was a cofounder of the Free Trade Union and of the Cambodian National Rescue Party, fierce opponents of the ruling Hun Sen regime. CNRP was deeply involved in the December 2013–January 2014 garment worker protests. Their prominence was one reason the government unleashed violence.

Educated in the Soviet Union in the bracing atmosphere of 1980s "Perestroika," (reconstruction), Chea Vichea was one of the most important early leaders of a Cambodian garment workers' movement that is admired worldwide for its courage. As he bought his morning paper on January 22, 2004, Vichea was shot in the head and chest by unmasked men on motorcycles. Six months later, Mony left his job teaching chemistry at the University of Phnom Penh to take over as president of the union his brother had founded. Between them, the brothers Chea ran the Free Trade Union for twenty years.

The Chea brothers are not uncontroversial in Phnom Penh. Some objected to middle-class intellectuals leading a working-class movement. Others believed, and continue to, that garment union leaders should stay out of party politics. They feel that garment workers cannot afford to lose the support of Hun Sen's government. Finally, since most of Cambodia's 750,000 garment workers are female, many believe that its garment unions should be run by women.

Despite all this, Chea Mony has long stood as a symbol of resistance to factory owners and the repressive ruling party. And he is admired for that. Under his leadership, the minimum wage for garment workers grew fivefold. And he is beloved by shop-floor activists, many of whom he has mentored. In 2016, a woman was finally elected to lead the FTU. Fifty-three-year-old Touch Seou rose from the shop floor under the tutelage of Chea Mony.

On a hot November afternoon, Chea Mony leans his forehead against his hand. Thoughtfully he lays out his goals for Cambodian workers: decent wages, full legal enforcement of Cambodian labor laws, freedom of association, and government reform to ensure transparency and democracy. Though garment workers' wages have gone up steadily, he admits, his larger goals—respect, freedom of speech and assembly, and labor law reform—remain unfulfilled.

Chea Mony and other members of the FTU have survived horrific violence. At a minimum wage rally in 1997, someone threw four grenades into the crowd, killing sixteen and wounding more than a hundred, including an official of the US Republican Party. (An FBI investigation found that the grenades were likely thrown by Hun Sen's bodyguards.) Sixteen years later, in January 2014, FTU members were among the protesters killed and wounded when police shot into the crowd.

"We are willing to risk our lives for the worker," Chea Mony says softly and without bombast. "After the Pol Pot regime, we need a good life, a truly democratic society. We deserve that. We've earned it. I don't see that violence has or ever can stop our workers from joining strikes and demonstrations. I have never seen our workers afraid."

Wim Conklin, Solidarity Center director in Phnom Penh, says he is in awe of the courage of Cambodian garment workers. Conklin has worked in the Philippines, Malaysia, Thailand, and Myanmar. He met brave labor activists in all those places, he says. "But there is something different about the Cambodians. I have watched them stand their ground facing an employer who they know has a gun in his desk. They don't flinch. They don't give way."[2]

That is certainly true of Ath Thorn, the robust, gregarious former garment worker who leads the Cambodian Coalition of Apparel Workers Democratic Union (CCAWDU), a progressive federation with over fifty thousand members. Thorn has a scar on his forehead that looks just like the one Chea Mony has. Thorn got his back in 1999 when he was a shop-floor worker and grassroots organizer.

"We were educating workers and advocating with bosses to improve working conditions," he says. "We won an agreement at the bargaining table." Thorn thought he had negotiated a clean victory. "When we finished, we came out to find guys holding big rocks. They hit me in the head." Thorn shows a deep scar that runs from his scalp line to the middle of his forehead. He points it out as a badge of pride, a combat ribbon in the war for workers' rights.

They couldn't frighten him, Thorn says, so government and business leaders tried another tack. In 2006, they offered him a $750,000 bribe if he would quiet his union, stop making so much noise and so much trouble. Global corporations and their government allies bribe labor leaders around the world to try to subvert militant unions, he says. Thorn calls these men "yellow." He shakes his head in disgust.

It is dangerous to say no to a bribe in Cambodia, but Thorn did. "They tried to buy me, but they can't," he says. "So they tried to kill me. Gangsters on motorbikes began chasing me, shooting. I lived only because I was lucky. When they almost had me, I was able to hop on a ferry and cross the river. They missed the boat so I lived. Another minute—I would have died."[3]

Ath Thorn agrees with Chea Mony that the relentless violence directed against Cambodian labor activists has only strengthened their resolve. "Workers understand that employers and the government collaborate to hurt the worker so they need to stand together. The violence and repression makes them become more militant. They're committed to the growth of the labor movement precisely because employers and some people in government use gangsters to attack any worker who is willing to form a union. They will not be made fools."

CCAWDU's membership is 95 percent female and its members combat violence against women by employers and government, by police, and by men they know—in the workplace and at home. Collectively, the members of CCAWDU won the 2012 Arthur Svensson International Prize, an honor given those who do the most each year to promote workers' rights. They used the $80,000 prize to upgrade their building. It was a good investment, they say.

On the day I visited, there were local union meetings under way, counseling sessions for laid-off workers, and healthcare referrals. Thorn's office is in an open loft visible to everyone who comes in. The Svensson prize hangs in a glass box over the main room. The bright Phnom Penh sun glints off it and casts rainbow light on floors and walls, and on the green and white signs showing silhouettes of pregnant women. These signs explain to workers that women have a right to paid maternity leave with no loss of seniority.

The union supports the programs of United Sisterhood Alliance, the Messenger Band, and the Worker Information Centers. Thorn is conscious that his constituents are mostly women; he does his best to be a feminist labor leader. Though 85 percent of Cambodian garment workers are women, there are few women union leaders.

Yang Sophorn, president of the Cambodian Alliance of Trade Unions, is one of the few. A veteran of the garment shop floor, she now leads an alliance of garment workers, teachers, and construction workers. Late for a meeting, she speeds to her office, a long narrow room squeezed above a Phnom Penh alleyway. She rides a motorcycle, wears a black leather jacket and a black helmet bearing a white sticker with a green fist that says "$177." That was the wage she was fighting for in 2015.

When Yang takes off her helmet, her hair rides up to reveal the same jagged white line on her forehead. Yang has been beaten many times. It never mattered that she is a woman, she says. That never stopped the violence, against her or anyone else.[4]

Yang rose in the labor movement because she came to the attention of Chea Vichea and because everyone admired her fierceness. A highly successful piece worker, Yang made more money than most, because she could sew so fast and well. But when her employer offered to make her shop supervisor, she refused. "People who get that position become part of the oppression," she said. "And my dream was to make things better."

In 1999, Yang helped organize Cambodia's first nationwide minimum wage protests. Afterward, she led a negotiating team that won workers at her factory extra money for daily meals, an end to mandatory overtime, time-and-a-half pay for additional work hours, and maternity leave. The national movement was still trying to achieve those goals seventeen years later.

As a rare woman union leader, Yang began to attract attention both from men in the labor movement and from leaders in business and government. Not all of it was welcome. One day in the early 2000s, she says, armed men came up behind her, pinioned her arms, and started to drag her out of her factory.

Furious, she whispered to them: "'You decide who you want trouble with. If you don't do this, I suppose you will have trouble with your boss. But I promise you, if you do this, you will have trouble from me.' They said, 'We're sorry. We have to do this because we are afraid of the owner.' I walked to the front of the factory and told the workers what was happening. They stopped work and walked out with me."

Yang's removal sparked a month-long strike, after which she nego-tiated wage increases, safety improvements, and reinstatement of all who had been fired. At age thirty, she was elected president of the ten-thousand-member Cambodian Alliance of Trade Unions. By 2016, she led a large union federation.

Yang's militancy has been her calling card. She believes that strikes are the best way to reduce violence, that workers must not be afraid to wield the only weapon they have. To stop the roaring rivers of fast fashion slows the flow of profits. That gets noticed.

In 2016, the National Assembly of Cambodia passed a law limiting the right to strike or even protest and making it more difficult to legally register a union. Bangladesh did the same. As garment worker protest built around the world, similar labor restrictions were proposed or passed in India, the Philippines, Mexico, Turkey, and elsewhere. While the Cam-bodian National Assembly debated the new trade union law, Yang called for a nationwide general strike to demonstrate worker power. The call fizzled. After the violent crackdowns in 2014, workers were too afraid.

But a similar call went out in India to protest proposed restrictive new labor laws. And on Labor Day 2016, close to 150 million workers struck across India. It was the largest strike in history, a high-water mark of twenty-first-century global labor unrest. If the new labor movement has not yet built lasting institutions, it has clearly demonstrated its ability to organize mass protest.

In Cambodia, Yang complains, union leaders are too divided and too scared to mount that kind of action. "If workers strike or don't strike de-pends on the union leaders themselves," she says. "If union leaders explain in detail the important issues that workers are facing, like losing their rights and freedom when the new union law is implemented, workers will strike."

Still, Yang's own experiences underline the rationality of Cambodian workers' caution. She was badly beaten by police in April 2016 protesting outside the national legislature. "We have no confidence in this govern-ment," she responded angrily. "The protest was peaceful. It did not even cause a traffic jam. So why did they do this to us?"

When Yang is not organizing marches to hold the Cambodian Labor Department accountable, she has begun—like Kalpona Akter—to tour the places where affluent consumers live and shop. In the spring of 2017,

Yang spoke at US college campuses and to union groups, then addressed the UN Conference on the Status of Women. She also led protests against Nike, her former employer.

Yang insists that the sneaker giant has gone too long without paying a living wage or allowing independent inspections of its factories. She encouraged United Students Against Sweatshops to apply pressure on their campuses for universities to suspend contracts with Nike until they do. Yang has revived the slogan "Just Don't Do It." Just don't do business with Nike until the company reforms. From Cornell to the University of Washington, she was greeted by students who promised to carry on that struggle.

On the 2017 anniversary of the Triangle Fire, Yang helped a group of students shut down Chicago's largest Nike store. "What is so crazy and saddening and shocking to me," Yang said, "is to go into stores like Nike and see that the price tag of one sneaker is almost equal to one month's salary for a woman worker, when she must produce hundreds and thousands of sneakers a month. And when they ask for higher wages, say $10 or a chair, or just better working conditions, they face abuse, threats, and restrictions."

Yang encourages low-wage workers and their allies to keep their eyes on history. "It is a long struggle and workers get tired. They cannot always fight. They feel despair." But they always revive again.

When Yang was beaten by "a group of gangsters, probably organized by the Ministry of Labor, the workers came to help me. They struggled with the gangsters." She looks intensely across her cluttered office table. "Workers will rise up. They will organize. They will strike—if they know what they are striking for." Then she is off to another meeting. She raises her fist, bows, and heads off on her motorcycle into the crowded city center.

CHAPTER 28

CONSCIOUSNESS-RAISING, CAMBODIA STYLE

IT'S SUNDAY AFTERNOON and Sok Thareth has called ahead to a United Sisterhood Alliance Worker Information Center to say that I will be coming to listen to their discussion. The Worker Information Center lies deep inside one of the half-hidden garment worker neighborhoods that ring Phnom Penh. We are driving out on Vathanak Serry Sim's motorcycle.

Sok explains the purpose of garment worker discussion groups. "We try to promote women's leadership. We want women to take over unions and workplaces. And we want them at the policy level, in government to make the decisions that affect women garment workers' lives."

Sundays are relatively quiet in downtown Phnom Penh—a stark contrast to the weekday chaos when a sea of motorcycles, open-air cabs known as tuk-tuks, and a few expensive cars choke the city's streets. They converge in chaotic mayhem on crossroads and grand traffic circles that seem to have no streetlights and no rules. It is said that Phnom Penh has three bus lines. But, as in many booming Global South cities, public transport is hard to find.

The city is crowded, polluted, and elegant in a gritty way—a mix of Buddhist temples, French colonial buildings and their modern variants, and gated garment factories set back from broad ceremonial avenues. Entire families pile onto motorcycles. Children without helmets stand between their parents, bracing themselves against potholes by placing their hands on adults' shoulders.

When shifts begin and end, women workers jam into open-air trucks for brief, dangerous rides. Many wear white surgical masks to screen out toxic fumes, protecting their faces from the dust and stones that fly up off the road. There are no seats, no seat belts, and accidents are common.

When drivers jam on the brakes, workers are thrown to the road, scraping skin off, breaking bones, sometimes dying.

With rural Cambodians being pushed off their lands by government concessions to logging, rubber, and sugar companies, there has been a rapid population shift from the countryside to the city. Between 2000 and 2015, Phnom Penh doubled in population, from nine hundred thousand to a sprawling boomtown of two million, home to one in eight of the country's citizens.

A big part of the city's growth has been in garment factory districts. Alongside gated factories rise gleaming glass and steel buildings that would not look out of place in Los Angeles. These are homes and offices for the factory managers sent by foreign companies to run the Cambodian garment industry. They come from China, Japan, Taiwan, Korea, Europe, and the United States. In these districts, you see signs in Chinese, Korean, Japanese, and English as often as in Khmer. Meanwhile, says Sok, Cambodian college graduates have a hard time finding work.

From the back of Vathanak's maroon motorcycle, the Sunday ride to the drop-in center is a little hair-raising. He points his bike into oncoming traffic, speeds through shortcuts and around sharp curves. No one looks twice. We ride a long way from ceremonial Phnom Penh: the confluence of the Tonlé Sap and Mekong Rivers, the Royal Palace, and national government offices. The road grows rougher, the buildings lower, trees fewer, potholes everywhere, filled with muddy water.

It is difficult to find the address we've been given. We ride up and down dirt alleyways between crowded apartment buildings. There are food vendors, smells of grilling meat, skinny stray cats. Vathanak is used to searching out the hidden refuges of his city's labor movement. Fluent in English and Khmer, adept in French, Chinese, and a smattering of other languages, he is the resource officer at Cambodia's Solidarity Center, nexus of the country's myriad and fragmented labor unions. He is also a child survivor of the Khmer Rouge death camps.

Vathanak's parents were from families well known for their mastery of traditional Cambodian music. They are among only a few artists to have survived the Khmer Rouge genocide. "It's because my father was the best fisherman in our camp," he says. "He was able to feed everyone. Plus, he and my mother entertained the guards, so they let them live." He swallows. "We were just lucky."

A toddler during the war years, Vathanak doesn't remember much. "And I don't like to ask my mother," he says. "She doesn't like to talk about it. She worries she might burden me." Most Cambodians are very young. The Khmer Rouge killed two million people between 1975 and 1979. And they continued killing civilians in some parts of the country, with the acquiescence of the US and the Chinese governments, into the late 1990s. Young people don't like to talk about it, says Vun Em. "We didn't live through what our parents did. It's their story, not ours."[1]

Suddenly, Vathanak points and my mind jumps back to the present. There is a tight cluster of women and girls in an open doorway, waving at us. "I guess this is the place," he says, turning off his engine. The young women lead us into a long, sunlit room where twenty garment workers sit in a circle on the floor. They are talking as we enter.

The walls are lined with hand-drawn diagrams of women's reproductive organs and the stages of gestation. There is a poster from the "Beautiful Clothes, Ugly Reality" fashion show. Some placards explain workers' rights under Cambodian law. Others describe the ILO workers' rights conventions that Cambodia has ratified.

Though they work six days a week, the women seem excited to be here. "Our work," says drop-in center coordinator Sok Thareth, is to "try to draw each worker from her rented room one afternoon a week to have a little enjoyment." There are eight drop-in centers around Phnom Penh run by United Sisterhood Alliance. Each has a paid facilitator. Dina runs the show here. She is a former garment worker who came to the attention of United Sisterhood when she led a successful campaign to win workers back pay from a "runaway" garment factory owner.[2]

Advocating for workers whose factories have fled is a specialty of United Sisterhood. They visit workers' homes, bring food and clothing, and help workers plan campaigns to get what they are owed. United Sisterhood tries to cultivate leaders from every factory, says Sok. Each brings other workers into the movement.

On the day I attended, the discussion group was packed and highly animated. "We have outreach activities at night and on Sundays," Sok explains. "Organizers go to the factories when workers are leaving, usually around 6 p.m. We try to engage the women to feel comfortable speaking out. Sometimes the organizer invites a worker to eat with her. At first, most workers are scared. We have to build trust. Sometimes it takes ten times of our organizers visiting before a worker will come to our center. It's challenging."

The workers are at first attracted by survival aid, Sok says—food, clothing, medicine. But United Sisterhood organizers offer much more. They help workers file sexual-harassment suits, help with child custody and domestic violence cases too. "The drop-in center is for workers who want to study, to learn about labor law and workers' rights," says Sok. "But we also help a worker with her problems—in the factory, or in the family."

United Sisterhood offers job and business training too. "Some of the women are highly skilled seamstresses who dream of opening small businesses," Sok says. United Sisterhood has helped a few women get started. Their businesses are models "that help others to dream."

Worker Information Centers are training grounds for new leaders and new strategies, says Vun Em. The Messenger Band got its start at one. Womyn's Agenda for Change founder Rosanna Barbero was leading a group that Vun was part of. "We were shy," Vun recalls. "Women didn't feel like they could speak. So Rosanna had us sing and that was easier." Soon Vun was interviewing garment workers and turning their stories into songs and plays. Now she is helping women "talk about domestic violence, violence against women, dropping out of school. We are part of the global Safe Cities for Women movement, so we perform our pieces in the streets during Safe Cities actions."

Dina says that issues of reproductive health and justice are also very compelling for women at her center. Workers want to know how to avoid getting pregnant, how to care for themselves while nursing, how to treat infections. Sitting for so many hours, garment workers get urinary tract infections, yeast infections, hemorrhoids, and repetitive stress injuries.

Since hospitals have been privatized in Cambodia, doctors are too expensive for most workers. So the center offers an herbal medicine course, says Dina, "how to cure reproductive organ problems with traditional Cambodian medicine. And we have the herbs right there we can give them." She also shows women what plants treat illnesses and where to find them.

Vun Em gathers leaves in the countryside that can be boiled into tea to treat fevers. The drop-in centers distribute those leaves when workers' children are sick. Dina also has leaves workers can soak in to calm skin infections and relieve aches. Few workers have access to bathtubs, but they still enjoy soaking in plastic or metal laundry tubs.

For mental health, United Sisterhood developed "what we call the Happy Happy program." They throw parties. The women "cook and eat together; they drink and have music—mini concerts or dances." They are lonely and isolated, far from family and friends in their villages, Sok says. Workers need community before they can stand up for themselves.

Finally, drop-in centers teach workers to understand global supply chains, says Sok. "We show them, this is the profit of Puma, Adidas, Walmart. This is what CEOs earn in a year. We take workers to other countries when we can, to meet people who make clothes there for the same companies. We take them window shopping to see the clothes and shoes they make. They learn what those cost in stores overseas compared to how much they make for sewing each item. They feel so hurt." But next come anger and ideas about how to bring change.

After a few weeks of Sunday afternoon discussions, the women in Dina's group are quite willing to engage with Vathanak and me. Sitting or crouching in a circle on the floor, they raise their hands. One after the other, they shout suggestions for making garment work safe and just.

"We propose that all of the brands, but especially Walmart, give us more wages because we cannot buy adequate, nutritious food for our families on what they pay us," one woman says firmly. "I propose that the brands must send someone down to each of their factories to check on conditions," says another. "You have a responsibility to enforce your code of conduct at the factories where you source your clothes. The suppliers violate our rights. We would like the brands to monitor compliance directly, with actual people coming to the shops."

Others wanted to speak to consumers: "I propose that consumers should not just buy clothes but they should ask, 'Are these clean clothes or not clean clothes?' You need to see the work behind the thing you buy. Is it a sweatshop behind your clothes? Let consumers check for that. That is how they can help us."

Dina has taught these women that the brands get 90 percent of the profits for every piece of clothing. The factory owners get 9 percent. Workers get just 1 percent. One woman raises her hand. "I would like to propose to the international brands that they take care of the worker by giving us $1 for every shirt, every pair of pants we make." Approving murmurs. "Do you all agree?" Dina asks. Everyone nods. Children at the outer edges of the circle look up from their toys and laugh.

At a similar gathering on the other side of the city, three local union presidents—Dany, Danu, and Sreypon*—tell me that, in their factories, pregnancy leave is the biggest concern of workers. Cambodian law mandates employer-paid maternity leave, says Dany, but "the employers don't give it. We help workers learn how to negotiate with the boss. And when they win they feel powerful. They have helped themselves."[3]

Sreypon's factory has seen mass faintings. They are endemic in Cambodia. "There were many cases of fainting," she says, "because the plant was narrow and hot, and the fabrics smelled bad. So did the glue for putting together sneakers." But Sreypon does not believe the fainting was a result only of exposure to toxic fumes. "There's too much overtime and not enough food," she says.

Like the workers of Bangladesh, these activists are beginning to organize around calories rather than wages: how many calories a worker can buy on what she earns. "Workers know from the 2012 ILO report that everyone needs two thousand calories a day," says union president Roth Minea. "In Phnom Penh, many can only afford around a hundred and fifty calories after they send money home and pay rent and water and electricity."

This is a problem that vexes garment workers around the world. So they are working through the ILO and UNI Global Union to enact global standards. Every human needs two thousand calories a day. "Everyone needs fresh air and water every day," says Sreypon. "Please tell the brands this," she says with a warm, broad smile. "Please tell consumers." Then she fits a gold motorcycle helmet over her long hair, straddles a purple motorcycle, and speeds off for an organizing meeting at a nearby garment worker dormitory.

---

* For worker safety, using first names only.

CHAPTER 29

FILIPINA GARMENT WORKERS

Organizing in the Zone

SIGNS OF COLONIALISM ARE EVERYWHERE IN MANILA—from the sixteenth-century Spanish buildings and gardens of Intramuros to the early twentieth-century Manila Hotel, an American icon on the harbor. Kentucky Fried Chicken and McDonald's dot the traffic-choked avenues, fronted by vendors selling hot peanuts, their mouths and noses masked in white to filter the smog. American R&B songs from the 1970s blare from car radios, restaurant loudspeakers, and brightly painted open-air "jeepneys"—Manila's version of city buses.

In Rizal Park at dawn, hundreds of women Zumba-dance to the beat of American pop icon Beyoncé. The music throbs above stone busts of indigenous leaders, most of whom died fighting the Spanish or the Americans. "The Americans did not just colonize my land," says labor activist Josua Mata. "They colonized our minds."[1]

Shadows of the 1940s Japanese occupation also hover over the lives of twenty-first-century Pinoys. Barbed-wire enclosures dot the Cavite and Bataan Peninsulas, the jaws of land that enclose Manila harbor. Where Japanese prisoner of war camps stood, there are now barracks of a different sort. Worker dormitories line the alleyways of the Mariveles and Cavite Export Processing Zones—semi-hidden, overcrowded, without light, privacy, and, often, even indoor plumbing.

The air in these zones is thick with fumes from factories owned by Japanese, Korean, Chinese, and Philippine corporations. The Spanish fast-fashion giant Inditex has factories here too. But most of the clothing made here is for American companies, says garment union organizer Asuncion Binos. High-end fashion is produced in the same ways as fast fashion. Ann Taylor and Ralph Lauren, JC Penney and Gap are all here.

The women workers sit at their sewing machines inside industrial zones patrolled by private armies.

"Organizing in Cavite Export Processing Zone, you see much harassment," Binos says. "You also might see a dead person floating in the river. If they see that you are an organizer, they can make you disappear. That's why most labor organizations don't even try to penetrate the export zones. It's too scary."[2]

It is the new colonialism, says Mata. And everyone who works here knows it. Filipino workers are torn, Mata says. "The Spanish were here for five hundred years. Still, no one thinks of themselves as Spanish. But America eats at us from the inside." There is the America whose musical rhythms reverberate in Filipino bodies and minds, the America where so many of their relatives live. (Much of Mata's family lives in New Jersey.) And then there is a reflexive revulsion toward American colonialism that is so deeply ingrained it feels like blood and bone. The Philippine labor movement is soaked in that feeling of resentment, Mata says.

In the twenty-first century, the struggle against colonialism has morphed. The old oppressors are still around. A few Filipino families, many of Chinese ancestry, control too much land, money, and power; they have for generations. So does the US military. After a twenty-five-year absence, American military bases reopened, provoking visceral negative responses from those who believe that the US has, for too long, poisoned these islands with hazardous waste and toxic male misbehavior. But there are new colonial overlords now. "Globalization is the same as the old colonialism," Mata says, "but it's also not. So what is a union today? What must our trade union strategy be? We are figuring that out. We are learning."

Asuncion Binos, who goes by the nickname Sion, has been thinking about that question since she began working in Manila garment shops in the 1970s. Conditions for Filipina garment workers have worsened since that time, she says, and opportunities have narrowed. A thin, tall woman with thick dark hair and a soft voice, Binos pulls up a chair in the Quezon City offices of the Alliance of Progressive Labor. She introduces herself as president of the United Voice and Strength of the Working Class, a garment workers' union. She also works for the International Trade Union Confederation—ITUC. Organizing workers has been her life passion. She's tired but not quite done.

Binos used to worry about how to unify fractious Philippine garment unions. Now she is thinking globally. She is touched when unions in Scandinavia and other affluent nations aid her financially strapped union. "They know they have to. We all do. Globalization. It is really my hope now that everyone working for the same labels in different countries can unite," she says.

Instead of myriad small shop-floor unions, Binos wants Filipina garment workers in one big union. But the struggle is bigger than that. "Labor needs to be organizing together all around the world." Her dream is that "eventually, we will be one, whether the workers are in the Philippines or Bangladesh. Those who produce clothing for the same company should work under one contract, maybe even for the same union. Then we can really help workers."

It's a twenty-first-century vision, but Binos says that her way of thinking has roots in the history of the Philippines as a global crossroads for trade. For five hundred years, the Port of Manila connected China with the Americas. The Spanish promoted trade between its colonies in Latin America and its crown jewel in Asia. Thinking globally only makes sense, Binos says. She would like to see her country once again a global nexus—this time not for profit or military might but for workers' rights and international solidarity.

Like so many in her city, Sion Binos first came to Manila from the countryside as a young girl looking for a brighter future. Her brother took a truck-driving job to pay for her to finish high school. Then the whole family moved. Her father became a street sweeper. Her grandmother sold bread. Her mother started a weaving workshop in their home—baskets, plates, and hats woven of palm fronds.

Binos got to attend college, but she had to work at the same time. She found a job in a garment shop. There were many in Manila in the 1970s. The big clothing companies were first fleeing the United States, Europe, and Japan then, relocating their factories to cheaper lands. Asia became the export powerhouse of the rag trade. The number of garment jobs in the Philippines tripled. Most workers were young women like Binos. For twenty years, she sewed in shops that were "right around the corner from my house."

Garment factories dotted Manila's working-class neighborhoods in the 1970s. Women walked or bicycled to work. Soon after Binos began sewing clothes for a living, union organizers came to speak with her. Being in a union was the norm for Manila workers then, she says. "When we first entered the shop, we had an orientation to teach us about workers' rights. The union was very present and happy to organize us. You could work in one shop for a long time, and make a living—not a lot but enough."

Excited by what she was learning, Binos became a union officer before she was out of her teens. When she asked her parents for their blessing, her father said that she was old enough to make her own decision. "He didn't know much about unions but he was willing to let me go my way. But my mother cried. She said, 'No. Please. Please, no.' She was frightened. And I understand why."

By the late 1970s, dictator Ferdinand Marcos had backed off somewhat from brutal assaults on labor organizers. But the violence never really ended, not in his administration nor in those of Corazon Aquino, General Fidel Ramos, or the country's twenty-first-century presidents, Gloria Macabal-Arroyo, Benigno Aquino, and Rodrigo Duterte. Thousands of Philippine labor activists and indigenous land rights activists have lost their lives.

From the 1960s through the 1980s, the rationale for the killings was that the activists were linked to armed Communist insurgents. Later, the murdered were said to be members of Islamic terrorist groups. Both do exist in the Philippines, but the wars against them have too often provided a pretext for murdering innocent people with impunity. The US has done little to stop the killing. Often, in the name of fighting Communists, Islamists, or drugs, it has provided the weapons.

Since Marcos's fall, the Philippines has been a dystopian democracy. There is a vigorous free press; there are labor and land rights laws, but too many union leaders, journalists, land rights activists, and the urban poor have paid the ultimate price for speaking out. Marcos killed an estimated three thousand people over his twenty-one-year reign. The most violent era was the early 1970s, after he declared martial law.

Then, in 1974, hoping to cultivate allies inside the labor movement and blunt the growing influence of Communist-affiliated unions, his Congress enacted a labor code that offered limited recognition of workers' rights to unionize, strike, and bargain collectively. There was now a power base for trade unionists willing to work with the government. Unions were tolerated so long as they were not anti-capitalist or anti-government. They were especially well treated if their leaders agreed to report on dissident organizers.

In the 1980s, the grass roots were aflame. The May First Movement, KMU, organized workers to resist sale of Philippine lands and resources to foreign companies. KMU grew eight-fold to four hundred thousand in less than a decade, winning respect among the poor by criticizing local elites along with the International Monetary Fund, the World Bank, and even the AFL-CIO, which it believed was cooperating with the Philippine military. (There is some evidence of this.)

Because of their purported ties to the Communist New People's Army, KMU was a target of government repression. A hundred KMU leaders were imprisoned. Its chair, Rolando Olalia, was assassinated in 1987, one year into Corazon Aquino's presidency. More than a million people lined the streets of Manila during his twelve-hour funeral march. They were mostly poor, clad in torn pants and rubber flip-flops, a world apart from the middle-class protesters in pressed jeans and yellow T-shirts who had propelled Aquino to power one year earlier.[3]

The stakes were high in the 1980s for those investing in the Philippines. Marcos had borrowed staggering amounts of money to keep his regime afloat, allegedly earmarked for infrastructure and economic development but mostly squirreled away in family accounts. His kleptocratic regime left the country hugely in debt—a crisis inherited by Aquino and Ramos.

They turned to the International Monetary Fund and the World Bank, which responded in the same way they had in scores of the world's poor countries during the 1980s and 1990s. They provided debt relief—but at a price. The Philippines would have to cut spending on public services and allow foreign corporations to purchase Philippine debt, land, and water rights. And a string of export-processing zones would be established—in Papanga, Batangas, Laguna, Cebu, and Cavite.[4]

Perhaps the most infamous was the Bataan Export Processing Zone (BEPZ) in Mariveles, on the tip of the Bataan Peninsula across the bay from Manila. It was there during World War II that American and Filipino soldiers began their infamous "death march." A small fishing community remained there into the 1970s, trolling the rich waters of Manila

Bay in dugout canoes. Then Asian Development Bank funds created a port for Japanese factory trawlers. They quickly depleted the fish supply.

In 1972, under the cover of martial law, Philippine soldiers bulldozed the homes of four thousand fishing families, forcing them to move twenty-seven miles inland. Fishermen were banned from crossing the zone to get to the bay. Without access to their fishing grounds, and with few people possessing enough land to plant, the cost of food in the area rose sharply.

Garment manufacturers flocked to the Bataan EPZ. By 1980, there were fifty-four global companies making clothing there. They employed twenty-six thousand women workers. Rents skyrocketed as people moved onto the peninsula. In 1975, there were twenty-five thousand people living near the zone. Two years later, there were forty-two thousand, either working in EPZ factories or providing services to those who did. Fishermen and farmers, too, lived in the shadow of the barbed wire.

A culture of resistance grew quickly among zone workers because conditions were so horrible, Binos says. In the city, close to their communities and to labor union offices, garment workers had full lives. They could eat and sleep at home; they had family and friends nearby. "In the zone," they were cut off from their children, husbands, and parents. They slept two and three to a bed in dark workers' dormitories.

The only food there was of poor quality and overpriced. They were forced to pay a premium for water as well. Lights were kept dim, causing eyestrain. Fabric dust filled the air, choking workers' lungs. "It's not really a life," says Binos. "The workers are very depressed. They want a way out."

In the twenty-first century, millions have moved overseas to get out of the zones. But in the 1980s, amid rising resistance to the Marcos regime, workers in the Bataan EPZ revolted. Low wages and unhealthy working conditions would soon become the norm in export zones around the world. But in that one place and time, fierce organizing mitigated the worst effects.

On January 4, 1982, twenty-six thousand Bataan EPZ garment workers launched the first general strike ever in a special export zone. Housed in dormitories inside the zone, the women were closely watched. Organizing had to be done in secret.

Marcos called in the military, insisting that it was illegal to strike in an EPZ. The soldiers turned powerful fire hoses on the women, beat them with truncheons, arrested hundreds. But they held out. And, remarkably, they won.

Workers fired for organizing were reinstated, wages were raised, and procedures were established to address sexual harassment in the factories. In an industry where most unions have just a few dozen or a few hundred members, the Bataan strikers proved that broad sector-wide organizing can work. That strike, says Binos, moved the country's labor movement forward.[5]

In its aftermath, KMU called *welgang bayan* (people's strikes) around the region. These *welgang* united workers with larger community groups. They shut factories, schools, and businesses, halted public transportation, and decried foreign corporations grabbing farmers' lands and fishermen's waters. In 1985, a people's strike shut down a Westinghouse nuclear power plant in Bataan (built in an earthquake zone near an active volcano). Thousands of export-processing zone workers lay down in the roads to block trucks and military transports to the plant.

After the 1986 People Power revolution, Corazon Aquino at first seemed to welcome labor organizing. But repeated coup attempts, complaints by global corporations and by her own family, which owned large investments in sugar and other export crops, moved her to take a different tack. One year after Aquino took power, police opened fire on workers and farmers seeking an end to evictions and demanding the breakup of plantations and the return of expropriated lands to their rightful owners. Thirteen farmer-activists were killed. Thirty-nine more were wounded in what became known as the Mendiola massacre.[6]

For the next twenty years, Philippine presidents banned protests and memorials at the site. It was a time, Josua Mata says, "when we were all trying to figure out what to do with our new so-called freedom, and at the same time trying to figure out what freedoms we actually had." Freedom was in flux in the Philippines, then and now.

The Aquino years saw the national Labor Code revised. It became harder to register unions and to legally strike. And Aquino's regional wage boards negotiated worker pay outside Manila that was far lower than in the city. That made it attractive for foreign manufacturers (and local ones) to build plants and plantations, and to invest in export zones outside the city limits.

KMU fought back. The first Philippine rallies for "a living wage" took place in the late 1980s, culminating in a week-long national strike in 1989 involving five hundred thousand workers. This remarkable feat of organizing forced the government to grant the largest onetime wage increase in Philippine history. There was another general strike in 1990. Unions banded together across the political spectrum, demanding a nationwide wage increase. Labor power was at an all-time high in the country. Since 1990, Philippine wages have stagnated, as they have the world over.

Five years after the elation of their peaceful revolution, the country was in a pit of despair. Much of the suffering was a result of "structural adjustments" ordered by the global lenders who had bought up Philippine debt. "There's not a sector in society that has not been kicked around by . . . paying a debt while the country groans under the rubble, taxing the poor . . . raising oil prices and freezing wages," wrote newspaper columnist Conrado de Quiro in 1991.

"The peasants are eating their seeds. The workers have nothing to eat and are shot like dogs by murderous guards while on strike. . . . Public school teachers are . . . selling their bras to earn enough to eat. . . . It is an order dedicated to the International Monetary Fund, the foreign banks, the oil companies . . . thug-hiring employers, and land-reform-busting landlords."[7]

Deep frustration drove thousands into armed insurgencies. Still, the idea of "protracted people's warfare" did not appeal to everyone, says Josua Mata. The idea of picking up a gun, he still feels, "was attractive only to the young and stupid," because any attempt at armed struggle would bring terrible retribution and "guns never bring anything positive."

As a democratic socialist, Mata says he rejected violence and a rigid class analysis that saw only peasants and factory workers as potential revolutionaries. He sought to build a different kind of movement, one that included jeepney drivers, street vendors, hotel cleaners and fast-food workers, students and teachers, street kids and squatters.

In 1996, Mata, Binos, and others founded the Alliance of Progressive Labor. They believed that the changing economy required "a broader sense of what a union is. That's when we started developing our ideals of social movement unionism," he says. They set out to organize workers in the formal as well as the informal sectors, in the dwindling manufacturing sector and the growing service sector.

In 2013, they created SENTRO—a federation that links public and private sector unions, garment, automobile, metal, and service workers. SENTRO is global in its vision, committed to building ties with unions around the world. One hundred years after the Industrial Workers of the World called for "one big union," SENTRO has revived the notion.

Sion Binos's faith in the potential of global organizing grew ever more intense as more and more garment industry jobs were moved to export-processing zones. After 2005, she says, almost "all the garment shops in Metro Manila were transferred to Cavite, where the big export-processing zone had opened. My only choice was to organize inside the zone," a labor environment ruled not by Philippine law but by global trade policies—and brutal force.

It's nearly impossible to make a decent living sewing clothes in Cavite, says Binos. "The prices for food are the same as Manila, but the rents are higher and the wages are almost nothing." Philippine garment factories are more likely than those of any other country to pay subminimum wage. "And jobs in the zone pay less than my old job in Manila," says Binos, "but workers go there because there are no longer jobs in the city."[8]

When I visited in 2015, there were twenty-seven garment factories in Cavite; others produced shoes and electronics. Of the workers, 85 to 90 percent were young women. Many had high school degrees; some even had a little college. "In today's market, that doesn't help them make a living," Binos says. Many saw no future in the zone. They planned to join the millions who each year leave the Philippines to become domestic workers in Hong Kong, New York, London, or the Gulf states. "Workers are our country's biggest export," Binos says ruefully.

Usually they leave the country because they want better food and housing for their children. Binos has seen Cavite garment workers feed their babies Nestlé Milo ActivGo, a malted wheat and barley drink with 402 calories a cup and as much sugar as a glass of Coca-Cola. The Philippines is Nestlé's second-largest Asia market. "You're supposed to mix Milo with milk or water," Binos says. Since workers in the zone often have neither, they "feed their children the powder with a spoon." Families of five live on one package a day, she says, especially when they are waiting for their paychecks.

Hygiene is a challenge. "Each family shares one foil packet of shampoo," says Binos, if they have water. A tiny rented room in the zone costs half of their monthly salary—before taxes. Most workers take home between $41 and $51 a month. The cost of living in the zone is lower than in the US but not by that much. Workers take loans from employers to make it till the next paycheck.

"So they fall deeper and deeper into debt every month because the companies charge high interest on the payday loans. It keeps them almost enslaved. They work till they have no more energy," Binos says, sad and angry in a soft-spoken way.

In 2016, hourly compensation costs for Filipino garment workers were among the lowest in the world. And yet, Philippine government officials and factory owners warn Binos that factories will shut down and move to Bangladesh "if our workers earn too much money." She lays her hands palms-up on the table. "I don't believe it's true. How can they earn less?"

Workers at a Cavite factory sewing for Ann Taylor and Ralph Lauren were earning $7 a day in 2015. That included a cost-of-living allowance and these were women who had been working there for a decade. The women all work overtime, says Binos, because the company offers them "an incentive. What is the incentive? If they finish their quota in two hours they will be paid for four. But if they do not finish in four hours, they must work for free until they are done."

Binos exhales. "I tell the workers, 'You exert all your energy to finish the quota. Then you have no energy for your families, no energy to talk to other workers.' It is a six-day week. They work Saturday too. Workers leave the factory and all they can do is rest."

She does not blame Cavite workers when they tell her they have neither time nor energy to come to union meetings. "The one day they have free," Binos says, "they put into washing, ironing, family bonding. So when you ask, 'Can we have a meeting?' they say, 'There's just no time.'" Some have children who live with grandmothers in the city. On Sundays, they travel for six hours on open-air buses through gridlocked smoggy streets to see their children for a few hours.

After lunch on Sunday is the only time Binos can convene union meetings. "Women have to do laundry and errands in the morning. Those who can, arrive at two o'clock. They talk fast, then rush home because the following morning is another workday. Their husbands live in the city and drive tricycles [pedicabs]. That pays very little and offers no security, so the women feel like they have to stay in the garment shops even if they hate it—for their husbands, parents, kids."

The threat of violence looms as large today as in Marcos's time, Binos says. Under Duterte, maybe worse. She recalls a recent organizing drive. Enough women at one factory had signed union cards that the Labor Department ordered a recognition vote. The morning of the election, five uniformed men carrying automatic weapons stood at the factory gate. "In export zones they have their own special military," Binos says, "but I hadn't seen these men before. We were just two female organizers and two Department of Labor officials monitoring the election. 'Why do you need five armed men?' I asked them."

Shortly before the vote, the guards aimed their guns at the president of the union, ordering her to stop handing out leaflets. They escorted her out. Binos followed and saw the guards lock her up in the guardhouse. "The workers saw and came to protest. So the guards let her go. But it was typical. They try to scare people. Every organizer who is giving out leaflets, they harass them. When I was young, anything that happened the workers would say, 'Let's go on strike.' Now people are scared. It's very difficult to organize now. Very different."

Binos was amazed when the women voted to join the union. "They had to summon up nerve to raise their hands while a few feet from them there were men with machine guns. It takes a lot of courage to vote for a union under those circumstances." I ask where her courage comes from. She answers: "That's easy. My courage comes from workers organizing themselves, not giving all of their energy to the factory owners." After five centuries of colonialism and seventy years of venal, brutal presidents, the Filipino people have no one they can trust but themselves.

Like every garment organizer I met across Asia, Binos spends a lot of time searching for labels. "I look for labels so I can figure out who the buyer is for each factory," she says. "When we find a buyer who has workers in other countries, we make links between the workers." Binos and other ITUC organizers strive to create standards for garment workers across Asia. She has traveled to Singapore, Malaysia, South Korea, and Hong Kong to forge regional bonds.

Like Kalpona Akter, Binos is determined to hold transnational companies accountable for the deaths she believes they have caused. When she started in garment work, it was safer, it paid all right, and you knew who your employer was. By the twenty-first century, Filipino workers seemed to be sliding backward fast.

On May 14, 2015, the Kentex flip-flop and sneaker factory exploded into flames, killing seventy-two and wounding hundreds. Factory doors were locked; fire extinguishers did not work. Windows were barred, preventing workers from escaping. Binos was among those called in to investigate. She found that two different fire inspections had concluded that the factory was unsafe. Still, city officials let it stay open. Investigators began to look for evidence of bribes.

The Department of Labor report, outpourings of grief by victims' families, and angry workers' protests convinced the Philippine government to indict Kentex executives and the officials who had ignored safety warnings. Kentex offered the same argument that owners of the Triangle factory had made a century earlier. There is no proof the doors were locked, they said. Workers had panicked. It was kind of their fault. When those arguments were debunked, Kentex took the tack that Walmart had after Tazreen. The dead were not Kentex employees, executives said. They worked for a subcontractor.

Fifty-seven victims' families sued Kentex and the Philippine Department of Labor. Kentex offered to settle. Without resources to sustain a lengthy legal battle, the grieving families settled for less than $3,500 per victim. It was, said one grieving parent, an insult, salt in the wounds.[9]

Such outrages are possible because of contractualization, says Binos. Few Filipino garment workers are covered by national labor laws anymore. In one factory where she was organizing, Binos found that just two hundred of two thousand workers were official "employees." Only they had a legal right to unionize. The other eighteen hundred were considered "temps." On February 2, 2017, another fire ripped through a Cavite factory, this one injuring 120. They were protected neither by law nor by unions. Sion Binos is tired and angry.[10]

Still, she takes hope in the young organizers she has recruited, women in their twenties and thirties who are savvy and smart and full of new ideas. They communicate and organize via smartphones and social media. "They are inventing something new," she says with hope. Even in the newest "cheapest" place to produce, Ethiopia, where there is not yet a minimum wage law, trade union organizers have won collective bargaining and 25 percent wage increases since 2014. The movement is truly global. Binos continues to believe.[11]

"But we still need the basics," she says. Many workers she organizes are children of farmers who have lost their lands. She points to a poster on the walls of the SENTRO building. A woman with her mouth taped shut holds an empty bowl in outstretched hands: "No Rice Without Freedom. No Freedom Without Rice," the poster says. "The right to organize, bargain collectively, and strike guarantees rice and freedom to all." In the end, it all comes down to land, water, and food.

PART IV

NO RICE WITHOUT FREEDOM, NO FREEDOM WITHOUT RICE

The Global Uprising of Peasants and Farmworkers

CHAPTER 30

"NO LAND NO LIFE"

Uprisings of the "Landless," 2017

CHRISTMAS 2016, MINDANAO, PHILIPPINES. Armed men lounged at the entrance to a banana plantation. Nearby, a sign read "Intruders Will Be Shot. Survivors Will Be Shot Again." Inside the gates, displaced farmers were seven months into an occupation demanding the return of lands that had once been theirs. Philippine land reform officials had ruled for the farmers. But Lapanday Foods, which ships twenty million crates of bananas annually, refused to comply. On Mindanao, home to the largest rubber, banana, and pineapple plantations in the Philippines, disputes are often solved with bullets. Lapanday guards had already shot and wounded ten occupiers. Now, as the farmers ate breakfast with their children, toxic pesticides rained down on them from crop-duster planes.[1]

On New Year's Day, the occupiers were finally driven out. The year 2017 began with bloodshed. By February, five Mindanao activists were dead. Each had fought expansion of banana and palm oil plantations, some on ancestral indigenous lands. One of the murdered men was sitting with his four-year-old niece when gunmen attacked. She was shot, but not fatally.[2]

A thousand miles north, on Hacienda Luisita, the Philippines' largest sugarcane plantation, migratory sugar workers met secretly over the Christmas holidays with UMA Pilipinas, a militant farmworkers' union. The plantation, owned by the family of former Philippine presidents Corazon Aquino and Benigno Aquino III, has been infamous since 2004, when police and troops approved by then-president Gloria Arroyo shot into a picket line of strikers, killing seven, wounding many more. Hundreds were arrested.[3]

Twelve years later, sugar workers charged Luisita, Lapanday, and Dole Philippines with human trafficking and labor slavery. Over the holidays, UMA mounted daring rescues of migrant workers who wanted to go home but said they were being held against their will. The response was swift. Armed men descended under cover of night and burned worker huts, gardens, and their few possessions.[4]

Many of the workers at Luisita had come from Mindanao to find work and to escape an onslaught by federal troops. Indigenous Lumad communities had been under attack since 2015. Under the pretext of fighting terrorism, Benigno Aquino's government had sent in armed soldiers. They occupied elementary schools, warning teachers to leave or be killed. Philippine Special Forces assassinated five people, including two teenagers they claimed were armed "rebels." A fourteen-year-old girl was raped. A teacher was found with his throat slit. Two indigenous leaders were sprayed with bullets in front of their neighbors. Homes and corn granaries were burned. Three thousand Lumad were forcibly displaced. Aquino was making war on his own people.

Eight hundred Lumad, led by women elders in traditional clothing, caravanned to Manila that November. They set up camp in a churchyard, met with reporters and sympathizers, students and legislators, and demanded an end to assaults on their communities. They also announced a civil disobedience campaign called REAP—Resist Expansion of Agricultural Plantations. Despite the government's insistence that it was fighting terrorists, Lumad leaders said the military on Mindanao was attacking land rights activists, farmers, and teachers of Lumad culture.

Not far from the Lumad camp, President Barack Obama met with nineteen Asian heads of state for the 2015 ASEAN (Association of Southeast Asian Nations) trade negotiations. The Lumad and their allies marched in protest. Police blasted them with "sound cannons," playing bad pop music at earsplitting volume. No bullets were used as the ASEAN leaders sang the praises of free trade and global agribusiness. Out of sight, violence continued on Mindanao.

The 2017 murders of Mindanao activists were but skirmishes in a longer war between farmers and the Philippine elite. In April, protesters marched across the Philippines demanding that Duterte and local government officials "Stop Killing Farmers." They carried signs with photographs of the 1987 Mendiola massacre, in which Corazon Aquino's troops had shot into a farmers' demonstration, killing thirteen.

These killings and the protests they sparked were not limited to the Philippines. In the spring and summer of 2017, farmers and farmworkers rose around the world. Infuriated by land expropriations, forced migration, and slave-like conditions for the people who plant and harvest food, self-proclaimed peasants, smallholders, and the landless were on the march everywhere.[5]

In São Paulo, Brazil, on March 7, fifteen hundred women farmworkers carrying machetes and wearing red and black bandannas shut down the Vale Fertilizer plant. They had come to protest the Brazilian government's plans to freeze or cut public services for twenty years. The women vigorously rejected President Michel Temer's assertion that Brazil was hurting financially because its social insurance programs were too generous.[6]

The real problem, they insisted, was government concessions to foreign corporations.

Vale owed Brazil's social security fund $88 million. Together, public and private corporations owed Brazil $150 billion in social security taxes. "The main victims in the social security reform are women of the field." Why, they asked, must the poor always pay for the rich?[7]

International Women's Day has been energetically observed in Brazil since 2006. Each year, Women Without Land, members of the Movement of Landless Workers (MST), has occupied and shut down plantations, factories, and ports. Hundreds have been arrested asking the same question: Why do our taxes go to subsidize foreign corporations while millions of Brazilians live without land or permanent homes? The solution was obvious, protesters said: Brazil should invest in small farms, not industrial plantations that destroy habitat and cause desertification.

Brazil's struggles over land are not new. MST was founded in the 1980s. In a series of occupations, they have moved four hundred thousand landless families onto thirty-five million acres in twenty-four of the country's twenty-six states, establishing subsistence farming communities. When evicted by soldiers and police, they find other vacant lands to farm. The targets of their actions have shifted since the 1980s, says activist Ana Hanauer. Originally, MST battled large Brazilian landlords. In the twenty-first century, she says, they are fighting "multinational agribusiness corporations which are taking over land that should be used for agrarian reform."[8]

Meanwhile in India, battles raged over free trade, farmer debt, and GMO seeds. In March 2017, 170 farmers trekked thousands of miles from Tamil Nadu to Delhi. They asked to meet with Prime Minister Narendra

Modi to demand blanket forgiveness of small farmers' debts. Some activists carried human skulls, remains of a few of the four hundred farmers from their region who, deeply in debt and facing eviction, had committed suicide over the past six months. A few protesters posed with dead rats in their mouths to dramatize hunger and desperation among farm families. They were not seeking handouts, they insisted, but policy change.[9]

Small farmers must have a voice in Indian trade pacts, they insisted. In 2009, an ASEAN–India trade deal had removed tariffs on coffee, tea, pepper, rubber, coconuts, cashews, and coconut oil. Farmers from the state of Kerala fought the pact vigorously. Hundreds of thousands participated in the largest human-chain protest ever. Manmohan Singh, then prime minister, promised he would consider small farmers in the final agreement. He didn't, and commodity prices plummeted across India, ruining many small farmers. Now, the country's leaders were negotiating more trade agreements and protests escalated anew. In June 2017, police shot and killed five farmers at a protest for price supports and debt forgiveness.[10]

Some Indian farmer-activists blame bioengineered seeds for their troubles. Before hybrid seeds were widely adopted in India, they claim, Indian crops were free of the pests that farmers now must fight with chemical pesticides. Vandana Shiva, India's foremost advocate for small organic farms, provocatively refers to "suicide seeds." Because they require expensive pesticides and fertilizers, she argues, bioengineered seeds deepen farmer debt—and increase desperation.

Scientists and government officials insist that GMO and hybrid seeds are good for India because they produce higher yields on large irrigated farms. Whether they do or don't—and that is debatable—most Indian farmers are "smallholders," reliant on rain to water their crops. As large, irrigated farms drain the country's groundwater, droughts are becoming more frequent.[11]

So are protests against industrial farming, extractive industries, and land expropriations. On March 30, 2017, "Day of the Landless" actions took place in India, the Philippines, Bangladesh, Cambodia, Indonesia, Mongolia, Nepal, Sri Lanka, Pakistan, and Thailand. Led by the Asian Peasants' Coalition and Pesticide Action Network–Asia Pacific (PAN AP), transnational farm and fishing networks mobilized to retain or regain land and water rights. "Smallholders," unwilling to wait any longer for their governments to fulfill promises of "agrarian reform," called for "land reform by the people." Sarawak in Malaysia held rituals cleansing their farmlands of "foreign money power." Sri Lankan fishermen rallied on boats to demand their rights to ancestral waters.

Many of the protesters were women because women grow 80 percent of the food in Asia and Africa. Any attempt to fight world hunger must begin with women, they say. In India and Thailand, women's farm groups argued that dispossession of small farmers is a women's issue because governments fail to honor women's customary title to the lands they farm. In Mali, Antoinette Dembélé's garden was destroyed by a Libyan company that built vast rice paddies, then abandoned them. "My garden was very important. It produced a good yield. I depended on no one to eat and pay my taxes," she said. Multiply her story by hundreds of thousands.

In Ghana, angry women farmers confronted owners of a jatropha cooking oil plantation that had uprooted hundreds of shea nut trees and displaced traditional landholders. "The nuts I collect . . . give me cloth for the year," one woman said, "and, also, a little capital." Her shea nut income paid for farm animals. "In a good year, I can buy a cow. Now you have destroyed the trees and you are promising me something you do not want to commit to. Where do you want me to go?" In Mozambique, a single Chinese-owned rice plantation displaced eighty thousand farmers. Without formal land titles, small farmers find little relief from courts.[12]

No place in Asia has been harder hit than Cambodia, where hundreds of thousands of farmers were evicted after 2003 to make way for rubber and sugar plantations. Foreign and local elites, supported by government troops, barred rural Cambodians from traditional hunting and fishing grounds. Farmers say these lands once enabled them to live decently. Modern land enclosures have reduced them to hunger and migrancy.

In the spring of 2017, women battled with police in Phnom Penh, protesting the destruction of entire neighborhoods to make way for "tourist infrastructure" and lodging for employees of foreign corporations. In "cursing rituals," they dragged effigies of plantation bosses and government officials through the streets, sprinkling them with chilies, salt, and dust. In February 2017, a Cambodian court sentenced protest leader Tep Vanny to two and a half years in prison. As protests increased in frequency and intensity, so have government crackdowns.[13]

Farmers marched in the Americas as well. In Mexico and Paraguay, farmers and farmworkers marched for land reform and decent working conditions. From March to May 2017, "Peasant Marches" took place in Texas, California, Oregon, and Washington State. Protesters demanded an end to immigration raids that splintered families. They called for bans on toxic pesticides and for overtime pay and minimum wage protections for field-workers. And in North Carolina, where the Farm Labor Organizing Committee had won pioneering agreements between labor, growers, and food processors, protests erupted after a new Democratic governor signed a bill curtailing their rights to unionize.[14]

There are many places where these battles over land and farmworkers' rights have turned violent. PAN AP recorded 231 murders and 4,685 human rights violations related to land conflicts globally in 2015–16. "The cases include displacements, killings and frustrated killings, arbitrary arrest and detention, filing of trumped-up charges, threats and harassment, and enforced disappearances. . . . Despite this," PAN AP argues in a film about the subject, "peasant resistance . . . is growing."[15]

In March 2017, Via Campesina, the global farmers and farmworkers' federation, hosted a Global Peasants' Rights Congress in Swäbisch Hall, Germany. They gathered on the site of a sixteenth-century Great Peasants' War, during which farmers fought enclosures and drafted the first declaration of peasant rights. Five hundred years later, farmers' groups from around the world issued their own manifesto. "Who we are fighting for," Elizabeth Mpofu of Zimbabwe said, "is every single peasant farmer . . . on the planet. People are eager to join hands in building a global voice."[16]

Corporate land grabs and mass dispossessions of farmers are endangering global food supplies, congress participants argued, sparking mass migrations and generating "new forms of slavery." Attendees at the summit vowed to protect "rights to land, water and natural resources, to seeds, biodiversity, decent income and means of production. . . . Our collective future," they wrote, "and the very future of humanity, is bound up with the rights of peasants."

They called for global unity. "Although we come from countless different backgrounds, we suffer intersecting forms of oppression and must stay in solidarity with each other. South and North, women and men, elders and youth, rural and urban, peasants, migrant and seasonal workers, indigenous people, fishers, pastoralists and beekeepers . . . If one of us loses, we all will lose." For that reason, peasant-activists insist, they cannot lose. "Like a river, our forces will flow together in a mighty stream of life!"[17]

On April 17, the International Day of Peasant Struggle, there were protests by farmers and fishing people in Asia, Africa, Europe, and the Americas. In May, Via Campesina, the IUF, and other global unions and women's and peasant groups came to Geneva to hammer out a UN "Declaration of the Rights of Peasants and Other People Working in Rural Areas." As the meetings came to an end, they released this statement: "The relationship with Mother Earth, her territories and waters is the physical, cultural, and spiritual basis for our existence. We are obliged to maintain this relationship with Mother Earth for the survival of our future generations. We gladly assume our role as her guardians."[18]

CHAPTER 31

"AGRARIAN REFORM IN REVERSE"

Food Crises, Land Grabs, and Migrant Labor

THE 2010s HAVE SEEN A GLOBAL REFUGEE CRISIS on a scale larger than any since World War II. Millions are fleeing war and famine. Millions more have become economic refugees. Between those who move abroad for work and those who migrate internally, something close to half a billion people are on the move, one in fourteen people on earth. Mostly, when people think about labor migration, we imagine rural people choosing to move to cities or other places where workers are needed. But in the twenty-first century, much labor migration has been involuntary. To make sense of the waves of peasant protest, we need to understand that.

In 2007–2008, a global spike in food prices fueled protests in Haiti, Cameroon, Ivory Coast, Egypt, Uzbekistan, Bolivia, Yemen, Indonesia, and other places in a hungry world. UN officials warned that unrest would likely increase as hunger spread. Emissaries from many of the world's nations met in pursuit of "food security." The solution proposed by agribusiness, the World Bank, and some scientists was to modernize farming, to wage a new "Green Revolution."

We will soon be unable to feed the world's people, proponents of this crisis narrative argued, if we do not grow food more efficiently. We can no longer depend on small farmers who have fed the world for millennia. Indigenous seeds do not produce high enough yields. Scientists have invented "better" seeds. Chemical companies have patented and mass-produced them. Global lenders stand ready to help governments buy and distribute them to farmers, and to enable farmers to purchase the fertilizers and pesticides that will make the new seeds produce.[1]

The 2008 global economic meltdown heightened the sense of urgency. As investors scrambled to find lucrative, stable places to invest, corporate consulting firm McKinsey & Company and other analysts argued that investing in agriculture promised higher returns than information technology or heavy manufacturing. A global land rush followed.[2]

Across Asia, Africa, and the Americas, governments eased the way for foreign agribusiness. Plantations spread rapidly. Millions of farmers lost land and income. To get loans, small farmers switched from subsistence to cash crops. Others became contract farmers for foreign buyers. Debt deepened, foreclosure loomed.[3]

How much land changed hands after 2007? The Spanish organization GRAIN recorded land deals in seventy-eight countries for 75 million acres (30 million hectares), an area the size of Italy. The farmers' group No Land No Life counted a thousand land deals over fifteen years in which 67.5 million acres (27 million hectares) of land were transferred from small farmers to corporations. That's an area the size of New Zealand. And these were only the deals for food production. There were also land deals for biofuel plantations, timber, mining, fishing, and resort development.[4]

Across Asia, the twenty-first century has seen what activists call "agrarian reform in reverse." South Korean farmers lost 30 million acres (12 million hectares), Filipino farmers the same amount. In China, 70 million acres (28 million hectares) passed from small farmers to "land trusts" after 2010. Meanwhile, Chinese agribusinesses bought or leased land for mega-farms in thirty-one countries, including the US, Brazil, Mozambique, and Australia. In Indonesia and Papua New Guinea, tens of millions of hectares of rain forests fell as palm oil, rubber, and sugar plantations spread like weeds.

In Cambodia, 70 percent of arable land was leased to rubber and sugar plantations after 2003, and 770,000 farm families were evicted. In 2014, these farmers organized, asking the International Criminal Court in The Hague to charge Cambodia's leaders and private corporations with crimes against humanity. In October 2016, the court broadened its criteria for accepting cases to include land grabs and environmental destruction. Perhaps a new era is beginning.[5]

Sub-Saharan Africa was hit hard by these land grabs: especially Mozambique, Tanzania, Ghana, Mali, Ethiopia, South Sudan, and Sudan. Nine percent of Africa's arable land changed hands. International investors bought the equivalent of the combined farmlands of Britain, France, Germany, and Italy. Vast rice and palm oil plantations displaced small farmers. In Liberia, one official sold rights to one-quarter of the country's forests in 2012, including the last primary rain forest in West Africa. The deal earned forest-dwelling communities $2 a cubic acre for wood that brought $200 an acre on the world market. Mozambican leaders marketed their country as a "biofuel hub," considering leases for millions of hectares every year.[6]

Meanwhile, palm oil plantations swallowed Global South rain forests. Driven by rising demand for biofuels and edible oils, palm oil production grew tenfold in the twenty-first century. Soon, it could be found in half of all supermarket products. Wilmar, which controls nearly half of the global palm oil market, was ranked by *Newsweek* in 2016 the most environmentally damaging company on earth, using up scarce water, spraying banned toxic pesticides, felling rain forests with breathtaking speed. The company was also cited for using child and slave labor. Most palm oil plantations are in Indonesia and Papua New Guinea. But they are spreading across Asia, Africa, and the Americas. The Philippine government announced plans to expand palm oil production from 73,000 hectares in 2016 to 1.3 million hectares by 2020. Mindanao and its people are for sale.[7]

Industrial farming also transformed Latin America and Europe during the twenty-first century. Almost a million hectares of land in Brazil, 750,000 in Uruguay, and 500,000 in Argentina passed from small farmers to corporations after 2007. Small farms in Germany, Italy, France, and Austria were bought by Chinese, European, and Middle Eastern agribusiness companies. Ukraine became home to some of the largest farms in the world—flush with cash courtesy of Cargill, DuPont, and SigmaBleyzer, a global private equity firm based in Houston. In southern Spain, a sea of plastic greenhouses—"*el mar de plastico*"—is filled with tomatoes, citrus, and berries grown for export. Driscoll's, "the world's berry company," bought up smaller Spanish growers to expand their empire.

Small European dairy farms began going under, unable to compete with mega-dairies. Mudanjiang, a twenty-two-million-acre dairy farm in China is the world's largest farm, more than fifty times the size of any European dairy and as large in acreage as the nation of Portugal. The world's second-largest farm is also a Chinese dairy, with acreage equivalent to that of Israel.[8]

European farm consolidation has been intensified by EU subsidies. Many Eastern European farmers went bankrupt when local markets were flooded with subsidized industrial farm produce. By 2013, 3 percent of

European farms controlled more than half of the region's farmland. In February 2017, dairy farmers from across Europe dumped a ton of dried milk on the grounds of the European Parliament in protest. Sardinian farmers occupied land where giant greenhouses were planned. Dairy farmers formed continental cooperatives to market their brands collectively. It is an uphill battle, say small farmers.[9]

Through it all, prices for the world's staples—maize, rice, and wheat—continued to rise. One reason is that many hastily commenced large projects failed. Investors pulled out, leaving abandoned fields and ruined landscapes. In 2014, the UN Food and Agriculture Organization declared the new Green Revolution a failure, announcing that 70 percent of the world's food was still being grown by small farmers. UN food scientists concluded that small-scale organic farming (or agroecology) is the only system that can generate true food security.[10]

By this time, hundreds of millions had been pushed off their lands, though, entering vast migrant streams, hoping to find work far from home. Many have become farmworkers. Global agriculture employs a third of the world's workers. Many are dispossessed farmers.

In every high-income country, commercial farms depend on migrant labor. In the US, 80 percent of farmworkers are immigrants. The industry would collapse without them. Some farms are mechanizing, but that is exorbitantly expensive and only the wealthiest can afford it. Migrant workers feed the world. Without them, food prices everywhere would rise.

Most farmworkers are men under thirty-five, but there are millions of women and children in the fields too. They are common in berry fields where they harvest for the fastest-growing and most profitable sector of the global produce market. In the 2010s, strawberry growers in Spain explicitly recruited Moroccan mothers as guest workers, arguing that they would be compliant, hardworking, and—forced to leave their children behind—unlikely to overstay their work visas. But without homes to which they can return, many farmworkers bring children with them.

Child labor is declining worldwide but agriculture employs more children than any other sector. Of 168 million child laborers in 2016, two-thirds worked on farms: in Uzbekistan, local children were forced out of school and into cotton fields; children from Mali and Burkina Faso labored on cocoa plantations in Côte d'Ivoire; Kyrgyz children picked tobacco in Kazakhstan.[11]

Three hundred thousand migrant children labor in US fields, the majority Mexican and Central American. US law permits growers to hire children between the ages of twelve and eighteen with no special permit. Those under twelve may work with parents' permission. In North Carolina tobacco fields, where child labor is common, nicotine leaches into children's blood through the plants they pick, causing headaches, nausea, and other symptoms of poisoning.[12]

As migrants flood the globe, labor traffickers profit from their desperation. Dispossessed workers go into debt to finance their travel. They pay exorbitantly for food, transportation, and housing. After migrants' arduous journeys, traffickers sell their labor to farmers who have contracted for workers. Women and children, though promised good jobs, are always at risk of being sold as sex slaves.

Labor slavery is widespread in farmwork. When debts for travel, food, housing, and farm gear are not paid off by season's end, migrants may be sold to another farmer and forced to work for free. In Russia, brokers have sold workers to farmers who destroyed their passports and then held them captive. In Malaysia, where a million migrants from Indonesia, Bangladesh, and Vietnam work, an employer may legally confiscate passports and physically "discipline" workers. In Greece, in 2013, a field boss shot twenty-nine Bangladeshi strawberry pickers when they dared to demand long-overdue pay.[13]

Wage theft is endemic. Some employers pay "gang-masters" rather than workers, husbands instead of wives. Or they pay in scrip, food, or alcohol rather than cash. Employers create fake social security numbers and, so they won't be arrested or fined, pay into social insurance programs from which their undocumented workers will never draw benefits.

Dramatically substandard housing is common. Farmworkers are housed in pig stalls, tin sheds, cardboard boxes, greenhouses. And if workers want protection from sun, rain, or pesticides, they usually must buy or devise something themselves. Few farmers supply free protective gear.

As if all this were not hard enough, migrant farmworkers' lives and labor are increasingly being criminalized worldwide. Rising right-wing populism, xenophobic violence, and deportation raids have made life in the twenty-first century difficult and dangerous. And farmworker-activists have become prime targets for arrest and detention by immigration authorities—for the simple reason that they refuse to hide.

CHAPTER 32

MILK WITH DIGNITY

ON A WINDY March afternoon in 2017, protesters circled the steps of the Vermont state capitol. Rain streaked its golden dome as demonstrators sang civil rights songs. It was a classic Vermont rally. There were white-haired activists; Protestant, Jewish, Buddhist, and Muslim clergy; young adults in beards and dreads; children carrying signs that said "We All Belong Here. We Will Defend Each Other." At the center of the circle were a small group of dairy workers from remote mountain villages in southern Mexico.

The protesters sang in Spanish and English: "*Como un árbol firme junto al río, No Nos Moverán*. Just like a tree that's standing by the water, We Shall Not Be Moved." The song rose and fell, followed by a chant: "*¡Ni una más!* Not one more deportation!"

This was the third demonstration in four days to protest the arrest of three Vermont farmworker-activists—Enrique "Kike" Balcazar, Victoria "Zully" Palacios, and Alex Carrillo-Sanchez. Detained by Immigration and Customs Enforcement (ICE), they faced deportation. The three were swept up in a nationwide crackdown ordered by President Donald Trump. During the 2016 campaign, Trump had promised to rid the country of, in his words, "dangerous criminals" and "bad hombres." But farmworker organizers had been targeted and deported for years before Trump's election. "We are Mexicans and immigration is always chasing us," said Vermont dairy activist Maribel Lopes. She was arrested by ICE when she left her workplace to buy diapers for a new baby.[1]

Alex Carrillo-Sanchez's father-in-law, Lyle Deida, addressed the rally. "If it weren't for migrant workers, our dairy products and everything else would go up higher to the point where we couldn't afford it. So I say, let them do what they came here to do, which is to support their families," he said, his voice hoarse and distressed.

Carrillo-Sanchez, Balcazar, and Palacios are all activists in Migrant Justice, an organization that promotes "worker-led social responsibility" on Vermont dairy farms. The National Education Association, the country's largest union, awarded them the Cesar Chavez Civil and Human Rights Award. They also won the John Brown Freedom Award. Senator Bernie Sanders hailed them as "human rights defenders." Twenty-four-year-old Balcazar has been described as "the face of undocumented labor in Vermont." And that's the problem. Migrant Justice activists are intentionally visible.

Balcazar moved to Vermont at sixteen to find work. He considers it home. Asked by local news media if he feared deportation, he replied: "I'm not scared at all. We've been here as a community fighting for our rights to live free and dignified lives and we aren't going back in the shadows." When Vermont ICE let it be known that they planned to arrest and deport Balcazar, allies offered him sanctuary in their homes. He graciously refused.[2]

Balcazar was tired of hiding. Just nineteen when he became active in Migrant Justice, he felt trapped on the farm where he worked seventy-to-eighty-hour weeks. The brutal schedule exhausted him. So did the stress of dodging immigration police.

Until 2013, undocumented Vermonters could not get driver's licenses. Farmers would drive their workers to shop. In rural Vermont, one of the country's whitest regions, vans of Mexicans were easy pickings for ICE. Migrant Justice led successful campaigns to ban racial profiling by state police and to enable undocumented Vermonters to get driver's licenses. That victory came back to bite them.

A few Department of Motor Vehicles employees decided to send ICE copies of license applications "with south-of-the-border names." Though against state law, the practice continued unrestrained. "We're going to have to make you an honorary ICE officer," an immigration agent wrote to a particularly cooperative DMV employee. The ACLU won a $40,000 settlement and DMV employees were warned by the state to stop the practice. But the case highlighted the impossible situation so many farmworkers find themselves in. ICE has continued targeting Migrant Justice activists. In the summer of 2017, two were arrested after a thirteen-mile march from the Vermont State House to Ben & Jerry's headquarters.[3]

The protest was part of Migrant Justice's most ambitious campaign, Milk with Dignity, through which they have tried to bring to Vermont's dairy farms a system of worker-run labor inspections pioneered in 2011 by Florida tomato pickers. The approach has been incredibly effective. In three years, worker-run inspections dramatically improved conditions on Florida tomato farms that had been described by one federal judge as "ground zero for modern slavery." Balcazar says: "I heard about the campaign and I was anxious to bring it here."

Florida's tomato and cane fields, featured in a 1960 documentary called *Harvest of Shame*, had long been infamous for inhumane labor practices. Conditions were little better in 2011. That's when a group of indigenous workers from Mexico and Central America, members of an alternative labor union called the Coalition of Immokalee Workers (CIW), developed a new strategy. They knew that farmers' profit margins were thin in an era of falling food prices. So CIW decided to apply pressure at the top of the supply chain, on the fast-food and retail grocery chains who bought tomatoes in bulk.

To do that, they had to win the support of consumers. The key was making the invisible visible. CIW believed that was best accomplished when workers told their own stories. For fifteen years, from 2002 to 2017, tomato pickers have been doing that on cross-country "Truth Tours." Field-workers have called on consumers, students, and clergy nationwide to pressure big tomato buyers to sign onto a Fair Food agreement. The strategy worked, and fast.

In three years, fourteen major companies—including McDonald's, Taco Bell, Burger King, Whole Foods, Trader Joe's, and Walmart—agreed to pay tomato growers a penny more per pound to increase worker salaries and fund inspections by an independent Fair Food Standards Council. When Walmart agreed in 2014, it was a milestone for international labor. Alexandra Guáqueta, chair of the UN Working Group on Business and Human Rights, attended the contract signing.

CIW's Fair Food Program turned the Florida tomato fields from the most hellish of American agricultural workplaces to among the best. Activists ran peer education programs for twenty thousand tomato workers. They resolved hundreds of wage theft, sexual harassment, and verbal-abuse cases. And by 2015, they had collected $14 million in "Fair Food premiums" from buyers that brought thousands of field-workers above the poverty line.

Fair Food also pioneered effective resistance to slave labor. Inspectors trained workers to identify and report slave labor situations. CIW was credited with helping to free twelve hundred workers being held unwillingly on Florida farms. Unscrupulous labor contractors and farmers were indicted. The UN Commission on Labor and Human Trafficking called CIW's program a model that could raise labor standards on farms worldwide.[4]

The strategy spread through the low-wage workers' movement. Fast-food workers and garment workers also began applying pressure at the top of the supply chain. CIW consulted in framing the Bangladesh Fire and Building Safety Accord and worked with Moroccan migrant tomato and berry pickers. Oxfam pressured UK supermarkets to demand decent conditions in their produce supply chains. And Oxfam US appealed to consumers to improve conditions in chicken processing. (In April 2017, that campaign won major concessions from Tyson, Perdue, and other large chicken processors.)[5]

Enrique Balcazar thought the idea was perfect for Vermont dairy farms. He knew that workers could not squeeze much out of hard-pressed dairy farmers struggling to survive in a time of corporate farming and falling milk prices. Still, migrant workers had leverage because dairy farming is a cold and dirty job that even unemployed Americans are loath to do. Vermont's cows must be milked every twelve hours, 365 days a year, or they will die. And unlike other kinds of farms, dairy farmers are prohibited from using legal guest workers. So undocumented dairy workers and the Vermont dairy industry are inextricably bound together.

In 2014, Balcazar began pressing Vermont's largest dairy buyers to demand improved labor conditions in their supply chains. "Ben & Jerry's is one of the biggest purchasers of milk in Vermont," Balcazar announced. "They've made a powerful brand by advertising that their products are fair trade. Milk with Dignity will make sure that this trade is truly fair." Despite its hippie origins, the famous ice cream company had been sold in 2000 to multinational food conglomerate Unilever. Executives insisted that the company's corporate responsibility code protected workers well enough. Balcazar disagreed.[6]

So Migrant Justice activists protested outside Ben & Jerry's stores in sixteen cities. On International Workers' Day 2015, speakers at a rally outside Ben & Jerry's Vermont headquarters described working conditions in the company's supply chain. Victor Diaz told of injuries he'd received when glass milk bottles exploded and chlorine (used to disinfect milking rooms) sprayed his eyes. Others spoke of sleep deprivation, because Vermont dairy workers do midnight milking. Twelve-to-fourteen-hour shifts, without a day off, are common. And workers have been housed in barns and unheated trailers through long, frigid Vermont winters.[7]

The Vermont dairy workers' movement was born of tragedy: the 2009 death of a twenty-year-old Mayan dairy worker. José Obeth Santiz-Cruz was strangled when his clothing caught in an unsafe farm machine. This kind of injury was not unusual.

Dairy work is dangerous. In New York State alone, sixty-one dairy workers died in workplace accidents between 2006 and 2014. Vermont dairy workers were not strangers to protest and they were angry at having to risk life and limb. Many come from small towns in Chiapas, the southern Mexico region that gave birth to, and has long sustained, the Zapatista rebellion. By 2014, they were ready to rise.

Milk with Dignity was Vermont dairy workers' bid for a brighter future, and Balcazar thought that Ben & Jerry's should be more than willing to give it to them. "Ben & Jerry's has stood up for cows (no RGBH), for chickens (cage-free agreement with Humane Society), and for international farmers (fair trade)," Balcazar argued. "They've pledged support for climate justice, for Occupy Wall Street. . . . So, after four years of us educating them about farmworker human rights abuses in its supply chain, it's time Ben & Jerry's stands up for the rights of the same farmworkers who put the cream in ice cream." In July 2015, Ben & Jerry's agreed.[8]

Then the foot-dragging began. CIW workers came to Vermont to strategize. Migrant Justice activists went on tour again, partnering with student groups to protest at ice cream shops and college campuses. When CEO Jostein Solheim spoke at Stanford, students chanted: "Hey, Ben & Jerry's, can I get some Milk with Dignity in my Cherry Garcia?" Solheim was conciliatory. He agreed that worker-led safety codes were the best way to improve labor conditions. He patted his pocket and swore that he had a Milk with Dignity contract that "I hope I'm going to sign next week." More than two years later, he had not signed.[9]

Thelma Gomez explained why dairy workers were protesting: "In Mexico, where I come from, we don't have an economy where we can make a living, where we can live good lives. So we come here. And yet, when we come here we find ourselves alone, far away from our culture, from our land, from our communities, isolated and living as prisoners on our farms. Especially now, with the president we have, we feel trapped, without the freedom to leave our workplaces, to play with our kids in a park, to spend time with our families."

On June 17, 2017, activists marched thirteen miles from the Vermont State House to Ben & Jerry's headquarters, where Solheim announced that he was "ready to go." Ten days later, Presbyterian congregations across the US sent a joint letter urging him to "not delay any longer . . . and sign in fact what you have already agreed to in principle." Methodists sent one too, urged him to "continue Ben & Jerry's legacy of justice-seeking . . . and fulfill your promise to workers, farmers, and consumers." And Will Allen, Vermont organic pioneer, led organic farmers in challenging Ben & Jerry's, along with Cabot Creamery, owned by Agri-Mark, to stop running "sweatshop dairies" that abuse farmworkers, exhaust cows, and bankrupt small farmers.[10]

Because dairy farms are excluded from the H-2A guest worker visa program, there is bipartisan opposition to deportations in dairy country. A bill forbidding state police from helping ICE easily passed the Vermont legislature and was signed into law by a Republican governor. Meanwhile, nervous dairy farmers organized emergency milking brigades to care for cows who would die if suddenly Vermont's dairy workers were to disappear.

Peruvian immigrant Zully Palacios, who organizes discussion groups to break the isolation of migrant women and their kids, insists: "To fight for our rights is nothing bad. It's a right we all have." From ICE detention, she wrote: "I am sending my energy to you to win our rights and keep on fighting. Together we are more." But days after her release, when she appeared on the news show *Democracy Now!*, she described how scared she was, locked in a tiny, dark cell, allowed no human contact for days.

On March 27, 2017, hundreds circled in a chill rain near the JFK Federal Building in Boston where deportation hearings were under way for Balcazar, Palacios, and Carrillo-Sanchez. The crowd included activists from Cosecha (Harvest)—a nationwide movement led by and for undocumented workers. Migrant Justice came with signs, a marching band, and ten thousand signatures calling on the judge to free "the Vermont Three." Fifty activists went into the courtroom to let the detainees know that "they are not alone. *Estamos en la lucha*. We are fighting."

Outside, protesters sang a 1930s union song, revived in the 1990s by activists seeking to build an international economic human rights movement. In the twenty-first century it has become an anthem of undocumented workers. "I went down to the courthouse and I took back what they stole from me. I took back my humanity. I took back my dignity. Now it's under my feet. Ain't gonna let nobody walk all over me."

That evening, citing letters from Vermont's senators, an immigration judge freed Balcazar and Palacios on bail, though the threat of deportation still loomed. But "the judge looked straight at my daughter and me and denied bail," said Alex Carrillo-Sanchez's wife, Lymarie Deida. "It's OK. We are going to keep fighting." Carrillo-Sanchez was deported on May 7, 2017, leaving behind a wife and daughter who are US citizens. "I'm angry," he said. "But there's no other way." He applied for a marriage visa and began an indefinite wait.

More than five million US children live with undocumented parents, who work and pay taxes. ICE deported five hundred thousand parents of US citizen minors between 2009 and 2015. (That was before Trump took office.) Lymarie Deida wants voters to understand how scared these children are when parents are deported.

On June 30, 2017, Migrant Justice won release of activists arrested at the Ben & Jerry's protest. "You Can't Jail Hope!" they exulted. That was the title of a video they made during an earlier campaign to free detained leaders. In the Trump era, they struggle to hold on to that optimism. Meanwhile, in San Isidro, a town in Chiapas, a new crop of high school graduates with no way to support themselves, began preparing to head north to Vermont.

Then, on October 3, 2017, came a sweet, hard-won victory. Ben & Jerry's finally signed the Milk with Dignity Agreement, giving dairy workers in their supply chain a full day off each week, Vermont minimum wage ($10 per hour), at least eight hours between shifts, and a guarantee that housing will include a real bed (not straw piles), electricity, and clean running water. These amenities for workers hardly seem revolutionary in the twenty-first century, and yet they are. Jostein Solheim, Ben & Jerry's CEO, lauded the company's leadership. "We love to be part of innovation. We believe in worker-led movements." "Kike" Balcazar told a jubilant crowd in Burlington: "This is a historic moment for dairy workers. We have worked tirelessly to get here and now we move forward towards a new day in the industry."[11]

CHAPTER 33

"LIKE THE TIME OF CESAR CHAVEZ"

Strawberry Fields, Exploitation Forever

IN 1970, THE AVERAGE LIFE EXPECTANCY of a California farmworker was forty-nine. The average life expectancy for all US men was seventy-three. In 2015, the average life expectancy of a California migrant farmworker was forty-nine. For US men, it had lengthened to seventy-six.[1]

"It is a very ugly history of injustice, and discrimination," says California berry picker, union organizer, and undocumented immigrant Bernardino Martinez. "Sometimes I feel like we are living in the time of Cesar Chavez. They intimidate us. They beat us. I imagine we feel like they did back then. Scared. But we are still fighting."[2]

Martinez, a Mixteco migrant from Oaxaca, says he knew that his employer would be angry when he convinced his fellow strawberry pickers to strike in March 2012. But "for such a long time, the indigenous community endured discrimination and bad working conditions, not just physically but emotionally. It was bad for us. So I joined the United Farm Workers."

It took a lot of organizing to get a few hundred workers to the UFW office in Oxnard, where Cesar Chavez had lived as a boy and where Driscoll's has its corporate headquarters. When the workers voted to strike, Martinez felt a rush—of elation, and fear.

He believes that God intended him to be an organizer. "I had a hard childhood. I was homeless, almost died in the streets from drugs. God gave me another chance to do something with my life. By organizing, I could do something for my community. We started the *huelga* [the strike] because people had been suffering for years. Nothing ever got better. It was time."

On the day of the strike, he says, "we went up and down the different streets asking people not to go to work. Then we went into the fields and asked people to stop working. We marched with flags [the UFW insignia, a black eagle on a red background]. And we asked God to bless us because we didn't know how it would turn out." It had been years "since there was anything like this in the strawberry fields": fourteen years, to be exact, since a 1998 UFW strawberry strike had brought a union to Coastal Berry (later Dole).

Most of the strikers were Mixteco, indigenous migrants from Oaxacan mountain villages. About twenty-thousand worked in the Oxnard/Ventura area, picking berries, lettuce, kale, and cilantro. "There was a lot of injustice. We were not getting paid what we deserved." State sources show that in 2012, strawberry pickers earned less than other California farmworkers.[3]

And there were hours for which workers were not paid at all, Martinez says. Managers would demand that pickers arrive at 5 a.m., then make them wait, unpaid, until sun dried the dew. Workers wanted a different pay system they called *horas y cajas*—hours and boxes. That would give them a minimum salary for every hour they were at work. On top of that they would be paid per box. Those who picked a lot would be rewarded. The company agreed, he says. "Then, year after year, they wouldn't do it."

The 2012 strike was also sparked by wage theft and racial prejudice, he says. "The indigenous community saw not just low wages but also discrimination." Workers asked Martinez to negotiate with field foremen because he spoke both Spanish and Mixtec. But many indigenous migrants, especially older women who never attended school, speak neither Spanish nor English, he says. Many cannot read or write at all. It burned him when supervisors purposely undercounted the number of boxes these women had picked. He fumed watching young foremen humiliate women old enough to be their mothers.

Indigenous workers were never promoted to "higher-level positions," Martinez says. "*Mayordomo*, supervisor; *ponchador*, the people who run the time clock. Those positions were never available to us." Those jobs were given to nonindigenous immigrants who cheated and derided the workers they oversaw. Some supervisors charged field-workers for rides to work. Without licenses, undocumented immigrants had few other options. But wage theft and contempt rubbed salt in the wounds, says Martinez. It built a fever for change.

Racism toward indigenous undocumented workers is not anomalous, he says. It's how the system works. Mexican American growers hire nonindigenous Mexicans as foremen, then sow division. As labor control tactics go, says Martinez, this one is as old as the hills.

Driscoll's earned public relations points for helping Mexican Americans and Japanese Americans start their own berry farms. But the real profits are made in distribution. Growing is delicate and risky. Driscoll's "partner growers" earn little comparatively. At first, Driscoll's partnered with Japanese Americans returning to California from internment camps after World War II. By the 1970s, they worked increasingly with Mexican American growers. Some did well growing for Driscoll's. But for many, it was glorified sharecropping. Partner growers leased their land from Driscoll's, grew berry varieties it bioengineered, and paid hefty fees for both.[4]

Martinez believes that Driscoll's and Anacapa—California's largest frozen berry distributor—moved increasingly toward small partners because large farms are easier to unionize. When you organize a large farm, you get a large local. On small farms, foremen know workers' names and surveillance is intense. And even if you win, the struggle yields few members.

Early in the 2000s, Martinez and the UFW successfully organized a large Anacapa farm. But right away, he says, the company announced that "they were broke because the UFW made it too expensive for them to operate. That's not true."

The company reorganized, using small farms. "We saw the same trucks, portable restrooms, materials, the same varieties, the same supervisors," he says. "The only difference was that workers did not have union contracts." He slowly clenches his fingers. "The big and powerful companies don't want employees to understand how the system works. They want to be the only ones who know."

When he began organizing the 2012 strike, it was challenging for Martinez to bridge the divides between indigenous and nonindigenous workers. "It was hard to get non-Indian workers from Michoacan, Hidalgo, and other parts of Mexico to join. They didn't want to be linked to us. They didn't want to feel similar to us in any way." After long days in the field, Martinez walked from door to door, explaining how the union would benefit everyone if they stuck together. Still, few non-Mixtecos struck. Later, when wages rose for everyone, he says, some of them pulled him aside later to apologize. "Now they understand: nothing improves without *la huelga*."

Convincing indigenous workers to strike wasn't easy either, he says. "They didn't trust the union." So Martinez started by working on his relatives. "I explained that this was good for the community. I told them that the UFW could help us when we faced powerful companies. If only two or three of us talk about injustices at work, they will find reasons to fire us. But if we unite, I told them, we can make change." Martinez says he did not underplay the power of companies like Anacapa and Driscoll's. "I wanted to be honest with my people."

Still, he was shocked when they sent men to assault him. "I should have known something was coming," he says. "At work, the supervisors looked at me like I was some kind of weird insect. They would make things up to make me look bad. One foreman said I was intimidating my coworkers. People would spit in front of us when we walked by." But he figured he was safe. It was 2012, not 1972. California had an Agricultural Labor Relations Board (ALRB), won through the struggles of the UFW. There were laws on his side.

"Then they beat me up," he says. "I was standing outside the gate. We were trying to get people to join the strike when these guys started to hit me." He was pretty sure he knew who had ordered the beating. "There was this guy, I have a picture of him." He pulls a picture up on his iPad. "His name was Rhett Searcy."

A Republican Party activist with ties to white supremacist militias, Searcy started his career in the mid-1990s as a "one-man ranch patrol" helping California sheriffs catch cattle thieves. By the 2010s he had recast himself as "a strike management and labor relations consultant" hired by growers from California to Canada.[5]

Despite Searcy's scare tactics, says Martinez, they persuaded enough workers to sign union cards that the state ALRB scheduled an election. "The company put people dressed like soldiers at all the entrances," he recalls. The union filed a "notice of intent to take access" and the farm was legally bound to let them in. When they refused, the UFW filed a complaint with the ALRB and sued in Ventura County Superior Court. Martinez was a named complainant. Undocumented status be damned. He was all in.

Court records describe Searcy and his "strike management" consultants as wearing "camouflage pants, gray baseball caps with an image of a black spade under a skull and crossbones, and 'special forces' buttons on a jacket embroidered with 'Heli Assault' and 'US/NAS INM.' . . . Rhett Searcy was armed with a gun and a taser. He kept the gun in a visible holster on his side. Mr. Searcy clicked his taser while approaching employees in their vehicles. . . . Mr. Searcy also approached striking employees, swinging his arms, brandishing the taser and clicking it to emit sparks of electricity."[6]

Searcy did more than click the Taser, says Martinez. "He was walking around with his taser gun and he would taser people to let them know not to join us. And they had these people driving around the fields in tanks." Martinez took pictures. He shows one: an armed guard in uniform drives an ATV past rows of workers bent low, picking. The point was to scare people, he says. The company wanted undocumented workers to think that the US military had been sent to stop the union. "When I came to work wearing a UFW button, the supervisors looked at me with real hatred, like we were in a war."

UFW organizers were eventually allowed onto the farm as federal and state law required. But whenever they approached workers, Searcy and his men would hover. Supervisors would interrogate employees afterward, demanding to know whether they supported the union. Then Martinez was beaten as foremen watched. One supervisor drove his truck up inches behind a UFW organizer's car, honking and screaming. Then he did it again, to make sure workers were watching. It didn't surprise Martinez that the union lost the election. He was amazed that they lost by only eighteen votes. "Workers were so afraid." Martinez didn't blame them.[7]

Margarida still regrets her vote.[*] "I regret that I didn't fully understand why they wanted to strike. I was so afraid. If they were to let me go, I worried I wouldn't be able to find another job, even though they were paying us very little." Many strikers were fired, she says. Martinez was one. Margarida says the firings scared her. But now, "I understand more. You have to strike to make things better. I am not fearful now. The next time, I am ready to go on strike." She feels that those who did not strike benefited from the courage of the strikers. Everyone's wages went up. "Five, ten dollars extra is good money. Nobody will just give that away."

---

* In this chapter, I use first names only for the safety of undocumented workers.

Martinez won his lawsuit too. The judge ordered the company to re-hire him and pay him for the time he missed. The California ALRB was granted a restraining order, preventing the company from intimidating workers. "With that strike, we won a real raise around the county," Martinez says, "because growers saw we would strike."

The day Martinez returned to the fields felt like a movie, he says. "This congresswoman accompanied me to the work site. The cops gathered around me. I walked down this dirt road between the rows and I could see people watching. The company wanted me to leave so they told the *obreros* [the people who run the machines] to make my life difficult. Still, I could feel that the foremen had respect for me now because I led a revolt." He sits up in his chair, satisfied. "And maybe some fear, because they knew I was capable of doing it again."

The workers seemed to stand up straighter as he walked by that day, Martinez says. "I felt good. They opened their eyes. They woke up. They saw that they could make change. The government sided with me. I got my job back. We were not helpless."

The next year, on Cesar Chavez's birthday, Martinez spoke at UFW rallies in Oxnard and Salinas, where he was then organizing. "When the people in Salinas heard what we were doing here, they came and asked us to organize because they had the same problems, especially wage theft." In Salinas, he worked with another Mixteco organizer named Juvenal Solano.

The Salinas growers used the same tactics to intimidate workers, Martinez noticed. "We were collecting signatures for the union and we saw the same security guards, the same lawyers. It was the same devil." This time, though, the anti-union tactics were more sophisticated, Solano says. "Psychologists, counselors they called them, would go into the fields and gather the crews. They would say all these negative things about the union. We would talk back and ask the psychologists questions and tell the truth about the UFW."

The two men convinced enough workers to sign union cards that a vote was scheduled. Still, the workers were afraid. Martinez and Solano stood guard all night outside a camp where workers met and debated. The union lost the vote, but again not by much. The workers showed courage, Solano and Martinez say. They stood up. They were proud.

Martinez is philosophical about his losses. "I wouldn't recommend this life to anyone. My family has suffered. I have been hurt and humiliated.

But we did win a lot of important changes so I have peace. In my mind, in my heart, I know I've done what I can for my people."

He stands in his small rented apartment and paces. "There's still so much to fight for. There is so much racism against us. We are paid so little. We want consumers to know how much we contribute to the economy of this country and the world." For that reason, he says he would do it all again. "If someday the people revolt, if someday the people go on strike again, I will be there," he says, sounding like a character out of a twenty-first-century John Steinbeck novel. "They are the ones who suffer and go through struggle. I will be there for them."

Martinez places callused, scarred field-worker's hands on the heads of his seven-year-old son and four-year-old daughter. "A lot of us who work in the fields are undocumented but those who are born here have a voice. They will have a vote. We may not have a voice, but they will. I am working for them. I do what I do for them." Then he stood. There was packing to do as the family prepared to leave Oxnard for Salinas. The autumn picking season was beginning.

CHAPTER 34

BITTER GRAPES

HENRIETTE ABRAHAMS, a leader in South Africa's Sikhula Sonke farmworkers' union, says that "farmworker communities are the forgotten segment of our society, hidden away and ignored in our rural areas, where exploitation is rife."[1] Legacies of slavery continue, and she believes that "the farmer appears to see the workers as subjects and property." As a result, "the struggle for decent lives and decent work . . . is a long and arduous fight." And it has not generally been taken up by well-funded big unions but by "small, independent, under-resourced trade unions."

Still, in the summer of 2012, women workers in the Western Cape Winelands came out of the shadows and got the world's attention—at least for a while. Over centuries, in a region where white Afrikaner nationalism still rules, the hard labor of black South Africans has profited white winemakers. In the twenty-first century, wine became South Africa's most lucrative agricultural export. And yet starvation wages, abysmal living conditions, brutal mistreatment and exposure to pesticides afflicted workers who pruned the vines, picked the grapes, and made the wine.

Then something snapped. An old vineyard was sold. The new owners slashed workers' wages, and eight hundred pickers walked out. Conflict between workers and bosses in this region was nothing new, nor were brutal crackdowns by growers and police. Both dated back to the era of colonial slavery. But something was different here. This strike spread quickly, sweeping up thousands of workers in sixteen towns. By fall, the strike had engulfed the Western Cape and threatened to spread across South Africa.[2]

At one winery after another, workers decried "hunger wages." Police and private security guards shot into peaceful crowds, wounding and killing strikers. Infuriated, the strikers blocked roads, set fire to vineyards, cars, and farm machinery, and clashed hand-to-hand with police.

Government officials and growers condemned the destruction but the workers were unapologetic. No one pays attention, they said, until the vineyards burn. In November, workers rejoiced when authorities arrested a farmer who had shot live ammunition into a crowd of protesters, killing three. They felt sure that were it not for the strike, he would not have been charged with murder. Still, larger victories were a long way off.[3]

The strike lasted seven months, workers say, because they wanted a lot: improved housing, free water and discounted electricity, an end to evictions and police brutality, and a chance for their children to attend local public schools. (Local authorities often refused to enroll migrants' children because they were born in other towns or countries.) Women strikers demanded equal pay with men, paid maternity leave, yearly paid vacations, hourly rather than daily wages, and the right to negotiate directly with employers instead of labor brokers. By strike's end, they had made progress on all of these goals, raising their salaries by 52 percent. They still did not earn enough to live on, they said, but they had demonstrated the power of organizing. They knew they could rise again.[4]

Media and politicians described the strike as "leaderless" and "organic," words so often attached to workers' actions, especially those led by women. It was true that the strike had not been organized by one of South Africa's large, male-dominated labor unions. But it was hardly a spontaneous, emotional outburst. It was a well-planned action.

Journalists and union leaders have frequently used those words to describe woman-led political actions: the 1909 general strike by women garment workers in New York; the 1955 Montgomery bus boycott in Alabama. It wasn't true of those actions. Nor was it true of the 2012 Cape strike.

The strike had been planned by a self-described "feminist social movement union" called Sikhula Sonke, Xhosa for "We Grow Together." Founded in 2004, the union attracted mostly mothers from 112 Western Cape farms. The women banded together around safety and health issues, children's education, violence against women. And they had been organizing collective actions for years whenever farmers mistreated members or stole their wages.[5]

Sikhula Sonke was a rare creature: a women-led trade union in South Africa. Though men could and did join, the bylaws mandated that the secretary-general, president, and two-thirds of delegates to union congresses must be women. And the union explicitly addressed women's issues: unequal pay; sexual harassment; maternal and infant health; farmers who paid "family wages" to husbands but not wives; migrant children's rights; and government refusal to recognize women's title to land. They also fought "contractualization," because most women grape workers were classified as "temporary" or "seasonal." As such, they were unprotected by South African labor laws and ineligible for social security and disability benefits.

Above all, the union focused on stopping violence against women and children. Sikhula Sonke members (male and female) had to promise to fight violence against women wherever they found it. Whether the perpetrator was a farm owner, a foreman, or a male farmworker, union members promised to intervene, and they did.

The union was interested in women's whole lives—in and outside of work, says founder Wendy Pekeur. And that resonated strongly with workers. A child of farmworkers, Pekeur saw vineyard bosses pay workers in alcohol, a practice she says damaged worker health and family life. Pekeur fought for payment in cash, hoping to reduce fetal alcohol syndrome among winery workers' children. Rates in the Western Cape are some of the highest in the world.

By 2009, Sikhula Sonke had five thousand members on two hundred farms. Three years later, it had over six thousand spread over three hundred farms. There were many reasons the movement grew so quickly.

Human Rights Watch (HRW) likened the lives of Cape wine workers in the 2010s to slavery. South African activists said conditions were worse than under apartheid. They had deteriorated over thirty years of land grabs. From 1984 to 2015, between two and three million South Africans were evicted, creating a vast pool of desperate labor, vulnerable to unscrupulous labor brokers and field bosses.

HRW found grape workers living in pig stalls, wooden shacks, and tin sheds without heat, electricity, or running water. Farmers beat and tasered workers for not picking quickly enough. Some workers were shot for minor offenses, including picking a bit of fruit for their families to eat. Though the practice was banned in 1960, farmers continued to pay workers in alcohol or scrip. Reports of extreme cruelty abounded. In 2015, Henriette Abrahams received a letter describing a horrifying public punishment. A farmer bound two women to ox harnesses and forced them to pull a tree up by the roots while other workers watched.[6]

Sikhula Sonke leaders understood that such cruelty deeply damaged workers. So they developed exercises to build members' self-esteem. Like United Sisterhood Alliance in Phnom Penh and Bangladesh Center for Worker Solidarity, they ran consciousness-raising groups. Two feminist NGOs—Gender at Work and Women on Farms—provided funding and training.

Women workers said the groups were transformative. One recalled: "I was a closed flower. I never spoke and always thought that everything I am about to say is wrong and that people will laugh at me. . . . I began to grow and the flower opened. . . . I have learned to stand up for my rights and to practice my rights. I tell my children: I am leaving my footprint for you."

Another felt a surge of power: "If I can speak to farmers and change things, then . . . I am not afraid of anyone—farmer, man, policeman, president. . . . I can now look at the farmer's eyes without being intimidated. I am able to listen to my fellow workers more. I am now confident and speak English without feeling inferior. I am able to stand up."[7]

The workers have needed such resolve. Though the 2012 strike raised farmworkers' wages, attracted attention from South Africa's large unions, and opened Cape wineries to investigation by global human rights and consumer groups, conditions for many wine workers remained dismal. In 2016, Danish television exposed them in a documentary called *Bitter Grapes*. After it aired, Scandinavian unionists asked to inspect South Africa's wineries. Since Scandinavia is among the largest buyers of South African wines, the move caused a fuss.

Workers at Robertson winery, featured in *Bitter Grapes*, struck for fourteen weeks in the autumn of 2016. Consumers demanded that Danish supermarkets stop carrying their wines and many did. Still, the vintners refused to settle. The workers wanted $615 a month. The winery paid $300. Striker David Everson says his family survived the strike by "borrowing and friends giving us food." The union sent food, but as creditors closed in, Everson told his kids there would be "no Christmas goodies" this year. Through it all, Robertson wines continued to sell well in the US. A global economy has seemingly endless markets.

Since then, workers have continued to organize, and a new Sikhula Sonke continues to educate, running a network of early childhood education centers. They boast of sending their students on to good public schools. Cooperative wineries are popping up on the Cape, black-owned and worker-led. Still, for workers on the worst white-owned wine estates, progress is hard-won. "My dream is like everyone's dream," says one worker. "To have a proper job that can pay you a living salary, so you know that at the end of your life your family will benefit." Sikhula Sonke's optimistic slogan remains aspirational: "We Grow Together."

CHAPTER 35

"WHAT ARE WE RISING FOR?"

BETWEEN 2013 AND 2015, Mixteco and Triqui berry pickers repeatedly struck one of the largest growers in Washington State—Sakuma. Berries and apples had made Washington a force in global produce, especially in Japan. And as the fruit market boomed, farmers drove their field hands harder and harder. Pickers labored without breaks, earned paltry wages, and slept in leaky bunkhouses, wet and cold when the Northwest rains fell.

Washington's migrant berry pickers organized for years before the strikes began. Oaxacan migrants Ramon Torres and Filemon Pineda led the efforts. Sakuma claimed to pay $10 an hour, said Pineda, "but they demanded fifty pounds per hour to get to ten dollars. . . . Only workers who work fast could get that." Workers said the company engaged in systematic wage theft. Sakuma insisted this was a computer glitch. The pickers were unconvinced: "These 'glitches' have been going on for years."

Constant pressure to pick faster was aging them prematurely, they said. "When my body's all used up, they'll dispose of me (fire me or deport me)," one worker said. "I've been coming here to pick berries since I was fourteen. I'm twenty-five now. This company has taken my youth."[1]

The pickers wanted $14 an hour, watertight housing, clean water and bathrooms in the fields. Basic stuff, but Sakuma would not budge. Instead they brought in seventy "guest workers" on temporary H-2A visas. Sakuma fired Torres and hired an anti-labor public relations firm to spread misinformation about the organizers. They asked police to remove Pineda from the fields and brought in TransWorld Security Services to ensure that union organizers stayed out. A global labor control outfit, TransWorld sent Sakuma a familiar figure—Rhett Searcy.

Security posts soon ringed the berry fields. Workers had to enter and leave each day through electrified gates. Armed guards patrolled the fields wearing uniforms emblazoned with the words "Food Defense and Safety

Officer." The "officers" quickly moved beyond the fields, following organizers, spying on families, recording conversations.[2]

The pickers sued Sakuma for interfering with their legal right to organize, entering into evidence a phone conversation in which Searcy had threatened force against strikers. Owner Steven Sakuma testified that he had never told Searcy to use force. The judge ordered Sakuma to cease and desist, to withdraw the security guards, and to let workers organize.

But before the decision, Sakuma applied for and was granted guest workers. When they arrived, the company laid off all pickers involved in organizing. The workers sued again. This time Sakuma was cited for lying on its guest worker application by saying that there were no labor disputes prompting their request. It is illegal to use guest workers to break a strike.

As the situation evolved, the berry pickers organized an independent union—Familias Unidas por la Justicia (Families United for Justice)—and demanded that Sakuma recognize it. They also reached out to friends, family, and comrades working in the San Quintín Valley in Baja California, where most guest workers for US farms are recruited. Pickers are connected all along the Pacific Coast, says Juvenal Solano, because "we have relatives in the fields everywhere." Having followed the crops from Baja to British Columbia, migrants know the conditions on many different farms.

Solano's story is typical. He migrated with his parents from Oaxaca after NAFTA made it impossible for them to remain on their own farm. Baja's San Quintín Valley was their goal. The site of massive irrigation and desalinization projects, it had become the center of strawberry production in Mexico.

"I began work in the fields when I was seven. We started every day at four or five every morning," he recalls. "They would drive workers in an open truck and you had to jump on while it was moving." He remembers "running, and my father would reach down and lift me into the truck. Only people who made it to the truck would have work that day. You had to be fast."

Living conditions were primitive. "There was no water in workers' houses. We would take water from the irrigation tanks. My mom boiled the water as a remedy for bacteria. There was a lot of mistreatment and injustice, and very low wages." Alfreda (not her real name), a Zapoteca migrant, says she had to "carry water like I was a camel. We had to buy gallons and gallons to drink, to bathe in, to wash our clothes." Sadly, both say, conditions did not improve much over the years.[3]

By the twenty-first century, Baja's industrial farms were growing more berries than US farms, earning fortunes for Mexican and transnational companies. Many Mexican state legislators were Baja strawberry growers, and so they got away with paying subminimum wage and not contributing to social security. Driscoll's affiliate BerryMex obeyed state laws, investigators reported. But workers said picking quotas were brutal and the hours inhuman.[4]

Lack of clean water was what finally moved them to organize. "They say what they offer is safe," said Alexandra, "but it tastes like pond water and it has green slime on it." People get "a tremendous sore stomach" from drinking it. Decades of industrial agriculture had drained the aquifer till salt seeped into San Quintín's groundwater. Workers' children got sick when they drank it and developed rashes when they used it to bathe. In the spring of 2015, San Quintín pickers formed the Alliance for Social Justice. Their first demand was clean water.[5]

But they soon moved beyond that. The $6 daily wage that was standard in Baja berry fields in 2015 had not increased since 1994. The amount they received per box had last been raised in 2001. Still, a gallon of milk cost the same in Baja as it did in San Diego. Baja workers wanted a $13 daily wage, drinkable water in their homes and fields, and an end to sexual harassment and violence. And they wanted employers to start paying into social security, so workers could eventually retire and draw pensions.[6]

This was the first independent union Mexican farmworkers had organized in generations. Very different from the corrupt, government-dominated "yellow" unions that had long controlled Baja farmwork, it was strongly influenced by farmworkers' activism in the US. Leader Bonifacio Martinez consulted with Sakuma organizer Filemon Pineda to create a "union that will defend our rights. We're the same workers, and we're talking about the same kind of union."[7]

Other San Quintín organizers had worked for the UFW or for Florida's Coalition of Immokalee Workers. In the 1990s, San Quintín leader Fidel Sanchez worked in Florida, where he joined CIW. That helped him see how profitable a commodity berries were. He believed that big supermarket chains would press growers to improve conditions and pay more if they struck. (Indeed, Walmart would soon do that.) Sanchez also organized for the UFW in Washington's apple orchards. "Cesar Chavez was an example I learned from," he said, "that we shouldn't live submissively."

San Quintín activist Justino Herrera knew how dangerous organizing in Baja could be. His brother was assassinated in the 1990s building a union. Herrera was radicalized. He led a "work stoppage against an abusive labor contractor" in Oregon. Later he helped build the movement in Baja. Finally, there was Eloy Fernandez, sixty-five. He too had organized for the UFW, back in the 1970s.

These men urged Baja berry pickers to form an independent union, different from the corrupt unions that had long held power in northern Mexico. Indigenous identity was central to their organizing. "We're not the Indian lying against a nopal cactus sleeping with the hat over his head," Fernandez said. "We want to be heard."[8]

On March 17, 2015, after farmworkers and government officials failed to reach an agreement, Baja berry pickers walked out of the fields. There had been food and labor protests in San Quintín before, but the 2015 uprising was like nothing Mexico had seen for decades. Over fifty thousand farmworkers struck, immobilizing berry production for two months.

Thousands of strikers soon shut down the Transpeninsular Highway on which Mexican produce is shipped to US markets. They staged sit-ins over 120 kilometers (about 75 miles). They piled roads high with burning tires. They drove a farm truck onto the highway, set it aflame, and left it there.

The twelve largest farms in Baja were paralyzed. Walmart, Costco, Safeway, and other large chains reported shortages of strawberries, tomatoes, and other Mexican produce. The strike cost BerryMex $20 million. Driscoll's CEO, J. Miles Reiter, stepped down two weeks into the strike.

Baja's governor came. The Mexican federal government sent police and soldiers who shot rubber bullets, teargassed workers, and made two hundred arrests to open the highway. The growers offered a raise but it was insulting, workers said, just one dollar a day more. Growers insisted the state's produce industry would collapse if they paid $13 a day, as workers wanted. Thousands marched to state offices in anger. Their banners said: "We Are Workers, Not Slaves."

To make sure that US companies got the message—especially Driscoll's and Walmart—strikers rode buses to Tijuana and marched to the US border with fists raised. "We deserve a just wage," they shouted. A few weeks later, some growers came back with a more respectful offer. Hungry, many returned to work. But thousands stayed out, insisting that the proposed increase was not enough. Strikers continued to block farms and roads, slowing the flow of produce north toward the border.

On May 9, Mexican police in armored trucks called *tiburónes* (sharks) roared down the dusty streets of Baja's farmworker barrios. They stormed into houses and beat parents in front of their children. They shot into the backs of fleeing strikers.

Worker rage exploded. Strikers burned a local police station and occupied government buildings, calling for Baja's governor to step down for sending police to attack workers. Again, they blocked a major highway. They set fire to fields. Like South Africa's grape workers, they were unrepentant. Baja's government only cared about them when fields were burning. Workers could smell the profits going up in smoke.

Sakuma workers joined their friends and family in San Quintín to organize an international boycott of Driscoll's. "Why target Driscoll's?" they were asked. Precisely because it was, as it self-identified, "the world's berry company." Distributing around the globe, Driscoll's had the power to influence wages, hours, pesticide use, and pretty much everything to do with the industry.[9]

In June the strike was settled, and Baja workers got a 50 percent raise. The *Los Angeles Times* called the deal historic. While not the 100 percent raise strikers had asked for, it was far more than the 15 percent that growers initially offered. It brought Baja pickers' wages to between $9 and $11.50 a day. Growers committed to pay into social security and provide some benefits. Baja's government promised to enforce the agreement. Walmart offered to monitor.[10]

Since consumer pressure on Walmart, Costco, and Safeway had encouraged growers to settle, pickers along the Pacific Coast continued to boycott Driscoll's, Sakuma, and Häagen-Dazs ice cream, the largest buyer of Sakuma berries. Like Florida tomato pickers and Vermont dairy workers, Sakuma field hands went on tour to tell consumers about the people who harvested their breakfast berries. Farmworkers and students picketed supermarkets. Seattle's Puget Consumers Co-op, the country's largest cooperative grocery, took Sakuma and Driscoll's off their shelves.

In the fall of 2016, Sakuma gave in. They allowed a union election. Workers voted overwhelmingly to unionize. As part of the settlement, Sakuma paid $900,000 in back wages.[11]

Conditions also improved in Baja, but union activist Gloria Gracida Martinez said in the fall of 2016 that pickers there had not yet achieved justice. The long-term goal is for Driscoll's to sign an agreement for workers on all "partner" farms from Baja to British Columbia. It's a long shot but indigenous people think long-term, says Oxnard activist Irene Gomez. "We try to educate our community that you must speak loudly about your rights, many times—or nothing will change."[12]

CHAPTER 36

"THESE BORDERS ARE NOT OUR BORDERS"

ARCENIO LOPEZ'S GRANDFATHERS came to California from Oaxaca as guest workers in the 1950s. Like all braceros, they were given short-term contracts, worked longer, and were paid less than US-born workers. When the season was over, they were sent home.[1]

Arcenio's father, Abelardo Lopez, came during the 1970s. California strawberry growers had sent recruiters to his town to lure indigenous workers they hoped would undercut the wages that newly unionized Mexican American field hands had fought for.

"Men from my community were the first Mixteco pickers in Oxnard," Lopez says. "They made holes underground. They lit candles for light; sometimes they had no light at all so no one would know they were there. There were snakes in the dark holes with them. Those are the stories I heard growing up." Every November, Abelardo Lopez returned home for a few weeks, to till and plant the family fields.

Anastacia Lopez tended those fields, harvested, traveled to pick strawberries in California, then took her earnings back to Oaxaca, where she used them to buy cows. Selling milk enabled her to keep her kids in school. "I did my best, working my fields, growing my corn, saying to my sons: 'Keep working hard in school.'"

Selling milk, corn, and beans at the indigenous market at Custlahuaca, Anastacia earned just enough to live. "If we broke a pencil or lost a notebook," Arcenio says, "Mom got very mad. We were just making it." Anastacia says she loved those cows. "It was very hard to sell them." But she did so her family would have money to emigrate.[2]

The Lopez family decided to leave Oaxaca after Mexico, Canada, and the US signed the North American Free Trade Agreement (NAFTA) in 1994. Over the next few years, Mexico was flooded with cheap, genetically modified American corn that drove down corn prices and contaminated Oaxaca's diverse corn crops. Two million Mexicans lost their farms.

Millions more lost farm jobs. Half a million Mexicans a year were soon fleeing to the US. This was double the number who had left each year before NAFTA.[3]

Fortunately for the Lopez family, Abelardo was one of 2.7 million undocumented workers granted amnesty and a green card under Ronald Reagan's 1986 Immigration Reform and Control Act (IRCA). That enabled him to bring his family to the US. One by one he brought his sons. Arcenio waited for word from US authorities that it was his turn. It took ten years.

A long backlog makes legal entry into the US painfully slow. A decade-long wait is not unusual. But Arcenio Lopez turned twenty-one while he was waiting. And US officials told him he was no longer eligible to join his family legally. He grimaces, remembering. "I told my brother, 'I have no other option. I'm going to walk over the border.'"

The family hired a *coyote* (human smuggler), and "with people from all over Mexico," Arcenio Lopez set off on what he was told would be a three-hour walk. "Then this guy showed up with a rifle," he recalls. "He told us to lie facedown. It was night in the middle of the desert. I thought: 'This is it. My life is over.'" Lopez had hidden twenty dollars in the cuff of his pants. "This guy started touching our bodies and going in our pockets. He said, 'If I find any money, I will kill you right now.' Thank God he didn't."

The *coyote* had brought three chickens and two gallons of water to feed the migrants on their three-hour walk. The bandit left one chicken and one gallon of water for twelve people who walked for four days. "There was an old guy carrying a suitcase who started crying, 'I can't make it,'" Lopez recalls. "The *coyote* said, 'Just leave him. Just let him die.' I said, 'How are we going to just let him die? No.'"

After four days, they were caught by the US border patrol and sent back to Tijuana. There they were sold to another *coyote* who held them in a brothel. "My mother thought I was going to die. She told me to stop trying." It took four attempts before Lopez made it to Oxnard. There, with his parents and his brothers, he started picking *fresas*—strawberries, "red gold."

Strawberries had become immensely valuable during the years that the Lopez family had been coming to the US. Between 1974 and 1994, California's strawberry output tripled and American demand doubled.

Driscoll's, its largest distributor, went global. By 2011, berries had become the largest and fastest-growing sector of the global retail produce market.[4]

The berry boom produced incredible profits both for distributors and grocers. Driscoll's, which began on two small California farms, grew to enjoy near monopolies in the US and giant market share around the world. Berries also fueled Walmart's growth. In 2002, one in fifteen American grocery dollars were spent in Walmart. By 2011, one in four were. Walmart sells more groceries than anything else and berries drive produce sales.

Not so long ago, berries were a summer treat in northern lands. Then the berry revolution began. Affluent Americans and Europeans began to crave berries at breakfast daily. The history of the Lopez family and of so many other Oaxacan migrant pickers in California, Moroccan migrants in Spain, Bangladeshis in Greece, Thais in Finland, lies behind the shelves of beautiful berries now sold year-round across the US and Europe.

Arcenio Lopez's family, like many Mixtecos, had farmed for generations. But by the late 1950s, their *milpa* (cornfields), beans, squash, and sisal no longer brought high enough prices to carry farm families through the winter. So Arcenio Lopez's grandfathers became Braceros. His paternal grandfather, Nicanor Lopez, was easily able to cross into California, he says. He was light-skinned and spoke Spanish. His mom's father, Delfino Lopez, looked indigenous, and his Spanish was limited. His road was much harder.

"Every time, at the border, they would make him take all his clothes off. They would ask him to bend, so they could search his genitals. And they put some gas on them because they thought he had bugs. My grandmother Alfonza would cry telling me these things." As a child, Arcenio felt embarrassed for his grandfather. "After all that, sometimes they sent him back. They wouldn't even let him cross."

His grandparents started following the crops in Mexico. They picked cotton in Chiapas, tomatoes in Sinaloa, and cut sugarcane in Veracruz. "They would leave us for three, four, five months and then come back to our little town to plant and harvest our fields." His grandfathers did learn some Spanish, Arcenio says. Indigenous children were punished for speaking their native tongue in Mexican schools. But his grandmother Alfonza, like so many indigenous women of her generation, never had time or money for school, he says. She spoke only Mixtec.

Arcenio says that her stories of those years radicalized him. "My grandmother couldn't speak Spanish well, so she felt impotent when people made fun of her. I remember thinking, 'How is this possible even in Mexico? Are we not all citizens of the same country? What makes us different?'" From his earliest years, Arcenio vowed to fight back.

In 2015, when he was thirty-five, Lopez became director of the Mixteco/Indígena Community Organizing Project (MICOP), in Oxnard, California, a nonprofit that offers healthcare for field-workers and runs empowerment groups for teens and women. It helps survivors of domestic violence, and trains field hands to promote healthcare in their communities and translate for indigenous speakers in California schools, courts, and hospitals.

Lopez tries to promote a strong positive indigenous identity among Mixtecos living and working in California. MICOP hosts "Indigenous Knowledge" conferences that bring together activists, public school teachers, scholars, and community organizers. Radio Indígena broadcasts talk and music in Mixtec. The "Indigenous Voices" speaker series sends young activists to schools and community groups. And MICOP's Mixteco food, music, and dance festivals fund-raise for scholarships to send indigenous migrant students to college.[5]

He is keen to link indigenous Oaxacan migrants to Native American organizations because he feels they have more in common than not. "We did not cross the border," Lopez says. "The border crossed us." He sees this argument, popular among Mexican immigrant rights activists, in specifically indigenous terms. "It's not just that the border between Mexico and the US is meaningless," he says. "These borders are not *our* borders. Any indigenous person should have a right to automatic citizenship because all of this land was ours."

It makes him angry that many of the people he meets in MICOP's crowded Oxnard offices had to pay *coyotes* to smuggle them across the border. On a hot September day, MICOP activists shared with me stories of that journey. Most never finished high school, becoming field-workers at eight, nine, or ten. In their thirties and forties, some began taking GED classes. Others wished aloud that they had the time.

Alfreda, a Zapoteca packinghouse worker in Port Hueneme, first left Oaxaca for Sinaloa to pick tomatoes on the giant export farms there. In the late 1990s, she picked berries in San Quintín before walking across the border. Working in the US, Alfreda believed "I could help my family more." Her daughter was born in California in 1997. No one wants their children to have to work in the fields, she says. "So even though I had to walk in the mountains and the desert it was OK. We got caught and sent back. That was OK too. I walked again."

Alfreda attends a women's empowerment group at MICOP called Avanzando: "We Are Advancing." She is training to be an interpreter for Zapotec speakers in schools, courts, and hospitals. Her proudest accomplishment is a daughter who graduated high school and was admitted to UC Davis. "She wants to be a doctor for our community," Alfreda says. "And she wants to work in Oaxaca, too, to help our people." Alfreda holds up a photograph of her daughter's college ID. "The only part that is hard," she says, is that she has not seen her parents since she left Mexico. She is afraid that if she visits them she will not be allowed back into the US. And her parents do not have the money to come north.

Irene Gomez was a migrant worker for years. She followed crops up the Pacific Coast from fourteen to twenty. In her thirties, through MICOP, she became a women's healthcare activist. She worked in the fields during the day. At night, she would do "our work." Being a "*promotora*" changed her, she says. "We were acquiring new skills and knowledge to help our community. That was so gratifying."

She says her life changed when she met Sandy Young, the nurse from Los Angeles who founded MICOP in 2001. "She was the one who identified a whole community that was unable to communicate with health providers because they didn't speak Spanish or English. We started doing monthly meetings and we began to realize how big our community was."

Young sent Gomez and other *promotoras* to find and survey indigenous migrants in Ventura County. Gomez says they asked every Mixteco they met if they knew other Oaxacans in the area. "It was not easy. People were afraid to talk to us."

In 2007, MICOP won a grant to help indigenous migrants access healthcare. Soon after, Young hired Gomez to teach parenting classes. These were, she says, as much immersion in a new culture as how to care for kids. She taught the importance of car seats. "We told them it was important to read to their children, even while they were still in the womb." She laughs. "They thought we were crazy."

Every night, the *promotoras* walked and drove through Oxnard and Port Hueneme to find migrant families and sign them up for MediCal, California's health insurance for the poor. "At first people were afraid they might be deported if they signed up. But eventually they heard about a relative or a friend who went to a clinic and nothing happened to them, so they began to feel it was OK."

The *promotoras* helped women get mammograms, gave them contraceptives, and taught them about reproductive health. They encouraged young people to think of becoming medical professionals through a program for *promotoritos*, young healthcare promoters. Perhaps that was how Alfreda's daughter found her path. Activism enabled Gomez to "leave the fields behind," and she feels proud to help others do the same.

"This is my road," she says. One of the "programs that I am proudest of is being able to work with women that go through domestic violence. I provide them with information about options, not something they had in our town when I was growing up. I witnessed violence in my family as a child, so I feel a special connection. I want the women to understand that they can leave, even if they have kids. This is something very emotional."

Battered women's shelter staff need help communicating with indigenous families, Gomez says. "So we translate from Mixtec or Zapotec." Cultural translation is needed too. "We are from very different cultures. Sometimes it's little things—serving rice and beans instead of white bread so the women feel at home."

Gomez believes that indigenous women are more candid with their own. "I am not a therapist," she says, "but indigenous women confide in us. Mental health issues are not spoken about in our communities. We provide survivors with a space to talk about abuse, to talk about self-esteem, to realize they have the capacity to change their lives."

When women are ready to tell their stories, some join La Voz Indígena (the Indigenous Woman's Voice). They speak at women's and youth groups, to social workers and healthcare professionals. To do that they have to smash cultural taboos, Gomez says. Some speak on Radio Indígena, reaching a far bigger population than MICOP can touch in person. "The speakers give women the information they need," she says quietly, "so they know they are not alone."

Some activists see this kind of work as service delivery, not political organizing, Gomez knows. She disagrees. Like women workers' consciousness-raising groups around the world, she believes that MICOP's discussion groups are empowering. "Women say to us that these programs make a difference in their lives. We help them come out from dark places and begin to see themselves as people capable of making change."

Juvenal Solano, MICOP's labor and community organizer, says that the work he does is not so different from that of the *promotoras*, except that he works more with men. He visits field-workers in their homes, shows them how to organize meetings, teaches them their legal rights. They learn that they can get better benefits, salaries, health insurance for their families. "But they have to work together," Solano says. The former UFW organizer calls what he does for MICOP "secret union-organizing. Mixtecos don't like the word 'union,'" he says. "So I talk to them about community service."

There are indigenous farmworkers who are more union-friendly than the Mixtecos, he says. "The Triqui spoke up for their rights in Mexico and they do here too. Growers try to frighten workers. But the Triqui are very powerful people. They are not easily threatened."

With the Mixtecos and Zapotecos, Solano uses a social movement–organizing approach. "I help them see that they have power to change many dimensions of their lives, their homes, streets, schools, and work. I train community leaders to speak out for their communities, for labor justice. They learn what rights they have when the landlord doesn't provide heat, when the company steals their wages. It's mostly men who come but there are women too."

He tries to build on the indigenous tradition of *tequio*, communal service. That's what MICOP members feel they are doing when they march for immigration reform and for amnesty for undocumented workers. In that spirit, MICOP clients traveled to lobby for a 2016 law granting California farmworkers overtime pay.

They learned that farmworkers are treated differently from other kinds of workers, under federal, state, and even county law. Minimum wage and maximum hour standards are lower and weaker. Seventy-eight years after other US workers earned overtime through the Fair Labor Standards Act, agricultural employers were still permitted to demand ten-hour days from field-workers—with no extra compensation.

"That is a long day when you are doing field work," Irene says. "Bent all day." Especially when you are working on your knees, Anastacia Lopez says. Margarida is happy they won. "I work too hard for too little. I want that to change that for me and for my children."

Dynamic activist Maricela Vargas, founding director of Central Coast Alliance United for a Sustainable Economy (CAUSE), has worked hard to pass a "Farmworker Bill of Rights" in Ventura and Santa Barbara Counties. (Eventually they hope to pass one statewide.) The bill seeks to protect field-workers from wage theft, sexual violence, and other forms of employer abuse. Designed to strengthen enforcement of existing laws, it also cuts new legislative ground.

If the bill passes, pregnant workers will have the right to refuse to handle dangerous pesticides. The bill would create county programs to fight sexual violence and harassment. Finally, says Vargas, it would "push local government to support farmers who want to do the right thing, who have an enlightened vision." Toward that end, the proposed Bill of Rights offers financial incentives for farmers who treat workers well and who avoid dangerous pesticides.[6]

Rising militancy among indigenous workers has sparked a backlash, some of it shockingly petty. MICOP gives diapers to farmworkers' families and, each autumn, hands out backpacks stuffed with school supplies. For a long time, the Reiter family of Driscoll's paid for these. Driscoll's is headquartered in Oxnard and it was good publicity. But in 2015, after MICOP activists demonstrated in support of the San Quintín strike, the Reiters stopped paying for these programs.

That's OK, says Arcenio Lopez. "I have a vision of labor justice for my people. And whatever we can do here at MICOP to make that happen, we will." He remembers working in the strawberry fields, how ashamed and angry he became listening to foremen mock Mixteco workers. "That was life-changing for me because I realized I need to teach my people how to read and write Spanish and English so they can defend themselves. I need to teach them how to stand and not be ashamed. How to be strong."

He says that Sandy Young—MICOP's founder—started him on a different path. "Now I have bigger ideas." He laughs. Around him, the MICOP offices buzz with meetings, discussion groups, a radio show in progress. The rooms echo with a lively mix of Mixtec, Spanish, and English.

"The system works by putting fear into people," he says, "using electric shocks, both the Taser kind and shocks to the mind." Donald Trump's campaign sent shock waves through his community, he says, more frightening than those from Rhett Searcy's gun. People are afraid. "To organize indigenous people, we have to educate. We must build trust and provide space for them to talk and grow. That's what MICOP is trying to do. And I think we're doing it pretty well."

CHAPTER 37

AFTER THE COLONIZERS, RICE

VICKY CARLOS GARCIA strolls into the vast, dark wood lobby of the Manila Hotel, a slight drag on one leg. The white hotel on Manila's harbor was General Douglas MacArthur's headquarters in the 1930s. His rooms are now a museum.

Garcia smiles as she passes a gingerbread house and a stand of fake pine trees rising from wads of cotton snow. It's late November and steamy hot outside. Inside the air-conditioned lobby, a pianist jazz-riffs languidly. American Christmas songs echo off twenty-foot ceilings. Garcia gestures up at the beams. "The high ceilings are from the Spanish," she says. "Almost everything else here is from the Americans."[1]

A survivor of childhood polio, Garcia is raising funds for a hip replacement. "I grew up in a poor family, one of ten children. There was no money for polio care." She's been in pain since then. But she has never let that stop her. Garcia has long been a woman on a mission.

Since 2006, Vicky Carlos Garcia has made the same journey again and again, riding fourteen hours on buses, "jeepneys" (open-air mass transit), and jeeps to remote mountain communities in northern Luzon—the largest Philippine island. Sparsely populated by indigenous farming communities, the area is known as the Cordillera. After the last jeep stop, it is a long hike to villages of brightly colored multistory buildings set amid two-thousand-year-old rice terraces. "It's difficult to understand how isolated these communities are," she says, gesturing. "On a mountain called Sleeping Beauty, there is a stairway to heaven."

Hand-carved into steep, lush mountains by ancestors of the people who now live and farm there, the Philippine terraces produce some of the most delicious rice in the world. "These terraces were built a long time ago," one indigenous activist says, "before the time of Jesus." They have been designated a UNESCO World Heritage Site. Built of mud and stone, they capture water ingeniously, in a series of ponds laced together with elaborate irrigation canals that tap mountain rivers. Some have called the terraces "the Eighth Wonder of the World."

Since 2006, Garcia and Montanan Mary Hensley, who first came to the Cordillera as a Peace Corps volunteer in the 1970s, have been trying to help farmers revitalize their communities and preserve their way of life by marketing their heirloom rice to gourmet groceries and restaurants from Manila to Manhattan. They know it is ironic. They are tapping transnational slow-food networks to preserve ancient Cordillera farming traditions nearly destroyed by the rise of a global food economy.

Hensley believes that the "Green Revolution" that promised to modernize agriculture in poor countries instead caused the "extinction of hundreds of thousands of rice varieties. That's not an exaggeration," she says. "It's just true." The Philippines was ground zero for rice engineering, she says, home to the International Rice Research Institute (IRRI), founded in 1960 with grants from the Rockefeller and Ford Foundations. IRRI spearheaded the Green Revolution in Asia, bringing industrial agriculture to a region that had been fed by small farmers for millennia.[2]

The results were dramatic, but not in the way Green Revolution advocates promised. The global seed and pesticide industry pushed governments in poor nations to reject small farmers' customary seed preservation and exchange techniques. Global lenders offered agricultural loans to poor countries if they would pass "plant variety protection" laws that gave companies like Monsanto and Syngenta intellectual property rights to bioengineered seeds. Some countries even criminalized seed banking and farmers' seed exchanges. By 2015, five companies controlled half of the world's seed market, giving them, activists say, "a stranglehold on the world's pantry."

Few small farmers could afford the costs associated with bioengineered seeds, Hensley says. Nor could they compete in price or volume with cheap, subsidized imports from the US, Thailand, and India, where rice is grown on vast industrial farms. As in Oaxaca after NAFTA, as in so many parts of Africa after the land grabs and flooding of markets with cheap, subsidized grains and produce, millions of small Asian producers were ruined.[3]

Farmers' groups began to resist. "It's a choice between abundance and scarcity," says Indian activist Vandana Shiva, who has called for civil disobedience through continued seed exchange. Via Campesina's Elizabeth

Mpofu also has urged farmers to continue exchanging seeds, even where it is illegal. Both women argue that pursuing "food security" via industrial farming and patented seeds has increased hunger in Asia and Africa.

"The periods of starvation . . . in Africa result primarily from the restrictive trade rules that favor big corporations and prohibit the seeding of traditional, indigenous foodstuff by the small-scale farmers," Mpofu says. In the 1960s, Africa exported food. In the twenty-first century, the continent has to import 25 percent of what its people need. Mpofu believes it could be different. So do Garcia and Hensley. In the twenty-first century, the Philippines became the world's largest rice importer, this in a country where climate-resilient high-protein rice was pioneered millennia before IRRI.[4]

Rice is the most important food in the world, a staple for more than half the world's people. It accounts for 40 percent of calories consumed in Asia, for poor people more than 50 percent. It is the fastest-growing food in Africa, where rice consumption has doubled since 1970. The same is true in the Middle East.[5]

Supporters of industrial rice production argue that growing global demand necessitates high-yield rice seeds and large-scale farming, and that falling rice prices help the poor and hungry. And genetically modified rice strains can address nutritional deficiencies caused by poverty, advocates insist. Since the 1990s, IRRI scientists have been working to perfect "golden rice," a strain infused with beta-carotene. Meanwhile community activists reduced Philippine vitamin A deficiencies by helping the urban poor plant community gardens.

Because the Philippines plants more GMO crops than any other country, it is also a center of resistance. Some feel that laboratory-made seeds are endangering biodiversity. In 2013, four hundred Filipino farmers and Greenpeace activists destroyed a golden rice test plot. Scientists and journalists painted them as provincial and naive. Protesters insisted that there are serious downsides to industrial farming and GMO crops, among them the disappearance of small farms planted with diverse, unique seeds.

In the 1990s, President Bill Clinton pressured Haiti to drop tariffs on US rice in exchange for aid. Cheap American rice imports destroyed indigenous Haitian rice farms, turning a desperately poor country into a staple food importer. After the devastating 2010 earthquake, Monsanto donated GMO seeds. Haitian farmers worried they would contaminate indigenous crops. They knew they could not afford to buy new seeds each year or pay for pesticides and fertilizer. As hunger raged throughout Haiti, former President Clinton apologized for his "mistake." In Thailand, India, and China, too, small rice growers struggle to compete with agribusiness. Even China, since 2010, has become a rice importer.[6]

Across Asia, heirloom rice strains disappeared, deemed too expensive to grow and not sufficiently high-yield. In the Cordillera, by the 1990s, numerous rice varieties faced extinction. Chong-ak rice, from Kalinga province, was one. A cold-tolerant rice suited to high mountains, it was a staple of the Taguibong people, served at holidays, funerals, and other ritual gatherings.

Hensley recalls other varieties from her Peace Crops days that were in danger. Tinawon and Unoy, each with an intense taste and smell, were different from any commercial rice sold in the US. Cultivating these was a sacred act. Their growth cycles defined the year for the Ifugao people, who celebrated twelve rice rituals annually to keep balance between people and the environment, water and soil, air and earth.[7]

Indigenous farmers practice agroecology of the most sophisticated kind, says Garcia. She believes we must look to them instead of industrial farms and agricultural engineers to strengthen global food security. She was not surprised when the 2014 UN report said the same. Instead of chemical pesticides, Cordillera farmers have always used soil conservation and herbal pest control. They were "organic before there was organic." Garcia says she and Hensley "want to help these farmers in a cooperative way, to create an enterprise they work by themselves, so that they can make a living, sustain their lands, be able to meet their needs, and improve their quality of life."

Cordillera rice-growing techniques were passed down through generations in ritual chants sung by old women as seeds were sown. These rice-growing experts were called "seed keepers." Every year, they scoured the terraces to find the healthiest, hardiest, tastiest seedlings and cultivate seeds for future harvests. Over generations, the seeds they chose yielded three hundred heirloom rice varieties unique to the Cordillera.[8]

Rice-growing communities helped preserve Luzon's biodiversity, says Garcia. They maintained small forests at the top of each terrace comprising hundreds of species of native plants. These filtered rainwater, replenished the soil, and supported fish, berries, mushrooms, and waterfowl.

Their unique growing system allowed Cordillera communities to cultivate rice at very high altitudes, some more than three thousand feet above sea level. UNESCO designated the Cordillera a "Globally Important Agricultural Heritage Site" and the rice rituals, "Treasures of the Intangible Cultural Heritage of Humanity." But it was all teetering on the brink of extinction by the 2010s, and UNESCO named the Cordillera a "World Heritage Site in Danger."

When Garcia and Hensley began working to revitalize indigenous rice growing, Cordillera farming communities were in decline. Farmers' children were migrating to the city. Rapid urbanization was endangering the delicate ecosystem. Between 1987 and 2007, the Philippines lost half its arable land to urbanization, extractive industries, and resorts. That doesn't count the losses for palm oil, sugar, rubber, and banana plantations.[9]

The country began to plant more GMO crops than any other. The Philippine government, like many in the Global South, distributed the seeds to small farmers. Proponents argued that they would help reduce hunger. Opponents say now there was little or no increase in yield.

Either way, there were losses, activists say. Heirloom rice was high in protein. More "modern" rices were not. One indigenous journalist who returned to the Cordillera after time away found high rates of diabetes in communities where modern commercial rice had become a staple. The disease was striking people as young as thirty-five.[10]

Many indigenous Cordillera communities tried hard to sustain traditional ways of living. Kankanaey activist Joan Carling fought three successful battles to block World Bank-funded dams there. She also helped farmers formalize land titles. When she was bedridden with malaria, farmers trekked hours on foot to visit her. But by 2006, she had become fearful. Three activists she knew were murdered that year. Then a friend in the military told her that he had seen her name listed among "enemies of the state." In 2008, "suspicious men on motorbikes" began following her everywhere. With regret, Carling left her home, but continued her work from Thailand.

There, Carling created the Asian Indigenous Peoples Pact, linking farm and environmental activists from the Philippines, Nepal, Taiwan, Japan, Indonesia, and other countries. The battle to help small farmers, feed the hungry, preserve dwindling forests, rivers, and the sea is global, she says. And indigenous people are the shepherds. "It's part of our being to protect and conserve."[11]

Indigenous farmers have long been caught in the crosswinds of violence that is not of their making, says Mary Hensley. As far back as the 1970s, Hensley remembers that "fighting between the military and Communist guerrillas left mountain villages cut off. People were suffering from iodine deficiency and severe hunger."

While in the Peace Corps, Hensley traveled from village to village delivering iodized salt to promote healthy hormone production and fight birth defects. For years afterward, she says she was haunted by what she saw, and wondered what could be done to help these communities. In the early twenty-first century, she met Garcia, a former social worker and Philippine Labor Department official, at the School for International Training in Brattleboro, Vermont. The women became friends and spent long hours talking about Hensley's memories of the Cordillera. In 2005, they began work on a plan to market heirloom rice worldwide.

By this time, most young people were fleeing—or had fled—the Cordillera, says Garcia, hoping for an easier life in the city. The average age of Filipino farmers had risen to fifty-seven. "Young people no longer wanted to till the land and work on a farm. They abandoned their lands, settled in Manila. They wanted to have a cell phone instead of only a little shovel. They traded farm equipment for cash because they wanted nice things like anyone else."

To aid their families, she says, many rural women went "overseas to become domestic helpers. The Philippines is the world's number one exporter of people. Mostly women. Three Filipino families out of ten have a family member overseas. They became the lifesavers for poor people, especially in the countryside. Someone from the family sacrifices herself by going abroad. They became our heroes but at what cost?"

Like many activists in an era of involuntary migration, Garcia believes that dispersion was damaging families, that everyone should have "a right to stay home," to make a decent living off their own lands. She and Hensley "wanted to see young farmers embrace their culture, their environment, their traditions," Garcia says. "What would keep me here? What would make me want to stay? That's what we asked. We thought selling heirloom rice might earn them enough that people could stay if they wanted to."

Garcia says she also hoped to promote healthier agriculture and food systems in the Philippines. "There was no organic movement here at that time," she says. "Our government was only into hybrid seeds. Because of our RICE [Revitalize Indigenous Cordilleran Entrepreneurs] project, all that has been turned upside down."

There are 11.5 million Filipino families earning a living growing rice. Increasingly, they are returning to agroecology. Via Campesina, Philippines, says that pesticides have depleted the country's rich soil. PAKISAMA, a Philippine smallholders' confederation with a hundred thousand members in twenty-eight provinces, argues that a return to organic is the only path toward a higher yield. They are retraining farmers in eight provinces and helped pass an Organic Law in 2010 channeling government resources toward small organic farms. Agroecology is booming in the Philippines, and RICE was one of the catalysts. Garcia feels great about that.[12]

Organic heirloom rice brings farmers higher prices, Garcia says, and those extra few dollars "have made a difference in the lives of Cordillera farmers, improving the future for their children and their communities. This means a life that is more than mere survival. They can have more to drink than coffee with no sugar. When they cook, they can have soy sauce. They can grow greens to eat with their rice. They can afford salt, sugar, vinegar, and oil. You need all of that to be healthy." (On the other side of the world, in Vermont, promoters of organics are making the same argument: that it will help keep struggling farmers in business.)

The heirloom rice business has helped Cordillerans educate and care for their kids too, Garcia says. "They can keep their children in school, because they have cash to pay school fees. They can buy medicine for those who are sick. And once their children are educated, they can become part of the rice marketing. They have a business of their own."

Through the heirloom rice business, indigenous Cordillera women have become political advocates for their communities, says Hensley. They travel through Asia and Europe, connecting with other farmers and slow-food activists. They have become part of the global fight for "food sovereignty." Each country's citizens should control local food supplies, policies, and growing practices, they argue, not global seed and chemical companies.

Garcia's remarkable energy helped spark a little revolution in the Cordillera, says Hensley. "I can still see her in my mind, visiting a hundred

little communities, finding ways to speak to farmers in their own languages (which are different in every town). She helped them to see the
benefits to developing global markets for their rice." Each setting was
different; each community reached decisions through unique processes
of discussion and debate. "Vicky is an amazing facilitator," says Hensley.
"Completely dedicated to empowering local people."

Garcia has spent her life serving Filipino workers, poor people, and
children. Her personal story encapsulates the history of her country. A child
of farmers and teachers, she was raised in Cavite, home of Emilio Aguinaldo, the guerrilla leader who fought for independence against the Spanish
and then the Americans. "I know what it's like to till the land and grow your
own food," she says. In a region famous for intricate embroidery, she and
her sisters sold their handiwork to supplement the family harvest.

Her oldest brother worked at one of Cavite's early garment factories, making jeans. "He was killed by the henchmen of the Marcos regime
because he was organizing a union," she says. His life and work shaped
her. "Every day he came home and told me how Levi's and Wrangler
mistreated the workers," she says. "I listened, sucked these images up. I
became an activist."

Marcos declared martial law in September 1972, Garcia recalls. "They
killed my brother in February, five months later. I had to testify in court
about his death. It was the scariest thing I ever did. I told nothing but the
truth, so help me God. My brother was shot twenty-one times. Then he
walked home so he could see my mother one more time. His will was so
strong. His heart was so strong, he made it home, walking the crooked
streets. Before he died he told me about the shooting. I was with him,
holding him." She was twelve.

A few weeks later, Garcia found out that her brother had made her
the beneficiary of his insurance. "He thought I could make a difference,
young as I was. He wanted me to finish school." And she did. "I studied
labor relations so that I could figure out what rights workers had under
the law, and what rights they should have." She felt indulgent spending
days in school when her country was racked by famine and her family was
living on hamburger buns and dried milk donated by the US military. But
she continued, earning a master's degree.

When Marcos fell, Garcia was a twenty-four-year-old social worker,
helping street children in Manila. The commute from Cavite took hours

on hot, crowded buses. She listened to "people talk about Marcos, his secret ties to the CIA, to Jimmy Carter and Ronald Reagan. I realized our government was the puppet of the Americans. In college, you study history, but here it was before my eyes. I felt I had to do something."

The People Power revolution that brought Marcos down in 1986 sucked Garcia in. "This was my chance to be there in the streets. My friends came with me because of my physical disability. They worried I'd be in danger." Even the memory is electric. "There were more than a million people on EDSA, Manila's main street. From all sides, all walks of life. We closed down the streets. Neighbors came because they knew the story of my brother and because everyone was affected by Marcos. We felt maybe we can end it and we'll have a beautiful tomorrow. Everyone was looking for a better day."

Garcia draws in breath. "But it didn't come." People trusted Corazon Aquino in ways they shouldn't have, she believes. "Everyone thought Cory was the mother of our country. So when she said we have to tighten up security, we didn't talk back, because you don't talk back to your mother. So the Philippines remains in turmoil to this day. We have been favored by the Americans. They use us for militarization in Asia. Their little brown brothers." She laughs a little bitterly at the phrase used often by American colonial officials to refer to the Philippine people during the period of the American occupation, from 1901 to 1946. "And now globalization. History has changed us. We are all caught up in it."

Garcia says her desire to help farmers stay on their land was fueled by years of working with "urban settlers" in the tin, wood, and cardboard shantytowns of Manila. "Ask them why they are there," she commands. "Agricultural lands were converted during the Green Revolution. That was just the beginning. They're not all there because they want to be."

Every day Garcia walked the sprawling shack cities along the Pasig River where millions live off what they can scavenge—fast-food waste, engine parts, discarded clothing—detritus of the global economy. Everyone there is always working, she says, harder than affluent people can ever imagine. Girls and women peel garlic all day and pile it high. Women sell clothing they've sewn from discarded fabrics. A hundred families sleep in a stinking, hot warehouse full of fast-fashion waste. Living at the center of a steaming garbage dump, they pick through refuse all day, carefully piling and gathering usable items for resale.

That world so shocked her that she says it reset her mind. "By any other standards, I would be considered a marginal, oppressed minority. But not here. That work made me understand what it really means to have rights and privilege."

A piece of her heart remains with the street kids. "The Philippines is number one in Asia for street children," she says. Garcia worked "undercover" to gather evidence on sales of Filipino children. "It was my first understanding of globalization," she says. "I thought I was taking on a few pedophiles. They were drugging children and kidnapping them. I was even drugged one time." She came to believe that human trafficking is systemic, an integral part of the global economy. She says she expected to have to fight thugs but instead found herself fighting "the pillars of society: the police, the justice system, the schools, even the Church."

What she saw in the streets of Manila drove her commitment to create opportunities for farmers to flourish economically and stay on their lands. "In the slums, once you're thirty, if you don't have a job, you probably never will. I started to think people should be able to stay on the land if they want to. That is better for many people."

The heirloom rice project educated hundreds of Cordillera farmers and put them in control, she says. It helped to kick-start the organic movement in the Philippines. Then came the backlash. Things were going well. By 2016, Mary Hensley had found investors willing to build infrastructure that would enable RICE to expand deeper into the Cordillera, to ship new kinds of heirloom rice—especially the region's trademark purple rice. But it was not to be.

The Philippine government began its own heirloom rice project. "They realized how lucrative it could be," says Hensley, "and they wanted to run it." Since the scope of the government program is large, Hensley admits, it will reach many more farmers than she and Garcia could. But since the death of a key RICE ally in government, those developing the project have shown little commitment to empowering Cordillera communities. A new generation of Cordillera activists are starting to work on that, through heirloom rice production and marketing plans of their own. It's dangerous but potentially lucrative, and danger, they say, is part of life.

Vicky Garcia was warned in no uncertain terms to back off. She has had to take the threat seriously. She is not downhearted about it, she says.

Donations from friends around the world enabled her to have her hip replaced. She lives with her adult son and the two care for each other. She feels good about what she has accomplished. And ready for the next phase of her story.

"Our history is a mix of everything you are talking about in this book. Frustrations, tragedies, and triumphs." She looks forward to figuring out what comes next, she says, for her, and for her people. "My work is in the Philippines. But, you know, what I am experiencing is true for people all over the world. Our fight will never end." She stands, a little shaky but firm. "And that's OK. I have always been a fighter. I will just keep on fighting."

PART V

"THEY SAID IT WAS IMPOSSIBLE"

Local Victories and Transformative Visions

CHAPTER 38

"WE CAN TURN AROUND THE LABOR MOVEMENT. WE CAN REBUILD POWER AND WE CAN WIN!"

AFTER DECADES OF NEOLIBERALISM and in an era of rising right-wing nationalism, it is tempting to give in to despair. And yet, as the young Filipina labor activist Em Atienza says, there is no time. There is too much work to be done. This book has highlighted the successes of many different low-wage workers' movements but also noted the costs of struggle. In the end, they leave us with this: Change is possible on small and large scales, even against overwhelming odds. But progress is neither linear nor easy.

Los Angeles Alliance for a New Economy cofounder Madeline Janis feels there is little to be gained by mourning what's been lost. To win progressive change, she argues, we must look forward. LAANE has achieved significant victories, in Los Angeles and nationally. They've built broad coalitions linking labor, community, academic, and environmental groups; registered new voters and marshaled them to push through groundbreaking policies; tapped urban development projects and cutting-edge manufacturing technologies and turned them to aid poor and working people. Janis and other LAANE leaders argue that we *can* harness the future for women and people of color, immigrants and veterans, and for the greater health of our planet. If we resist grief and fear and keep facing forward.[1]

In that spirit, I devote these last pages to a few more stories of success. These are, I believe, more than local or momentary victories. They are pieces of potentially transformative activist projects. We can use these and other flashes of light to strike sparks, to build models, to cast seeds of change to nourish a new world.

Maria Elena Durazo has described the 2010s as a time of activist convergences. From the confluences of many movements— for labor, gender, race, immigrant, and environmental justice—visions and practical plans are taking shape. The "new economy" movement is working to create more humane local, national, and global economies driven by renewable energy. Roots of Change, Food Policy Councils, Via Campesina, Food First, and others are laying the groundwork for healthier, more inclusive farm, food, and water systems. The Worker Rights Consortium, International Labor Rights Forum, and global unions including the ITUC, IUF, UNI Global Union, and IndustriALL are constructing new global values chains—built on fair trade and worker justice.

To build these ambitious new systems, activists are organizing broad coalitions, rejecting internecine battles and tests of ideological purity. Workers, labor and community organizers, consumers, faith, civil rights, and youth groups, politicians, government officials, environmental and philanthropic networks are entering alliances built on flexibility, mutual respect, creativity, and courage. Navigating their differences is not easy. This is not naive Pollyanna politics. It is a fusion of idealism and pragmatism. Using what Janis calls "a comprehensive kitchen-sink approach to organizing," many people are trying to do "big things." And in some very real ways they are succeeding. We just have to pay attention.

CHAPTER 39

FLASHES OF HOPE

ON JULY 17, 2017, BYD, the world's largest electric-vehicle manufacturer, signed an agreement to recruit and hire 40 percent of its Los Angeles workers from communities long underrepresented in manufacturing. The possibility of good new jobs shimmered for women and people of color, veterans and the formerly incarcerated living in poor, depleted towns around Los Angeles. BYD committed to fund expansive apprenticeship and training programs and even to provide transportation for workers and trainees who do not own cars. This was not ordinary corporate behavior.[1]

The agreement was negotiated by Jobs to Move America (JMA), a coalition of labor, community, environmental, and philanthropic groups directed by Madeline Janis and working to bring manufacturing back to US cities. And these would be union jobs. SMART (the sheet metal workers' union) would represent workers and help BYD design apprenticeship training. Two days later, the Ports of Los Angeles and Long Beach committed to invest $14 billion to replace their fleets of diesel trucks with electric vehicles. This marked a huge next step toward cleaning the air around the busiest ports in the country, a project LAANE had launched more than a decade earlier. And it created a need for electric vehicles produced by companies like BYD.[2]

Meanwhile, on the South Side of Chicago a new factory was rising. After a fifty-year hiatus, trains would again be built in the Windy City. Linda Nguyen was there at the groundbreaking, representing JMA. Nguyen led negotiations between Chicago's Transit Authority, unions, and Chinese railcar manufacturer Sifang. The company agreed to invest $100 million in a state-of-the-art factory, hire from the surrounding community, and establish training and apprenticeship programs. These, too, would be union jobs. The International Brotherhood of Electrical Workers would design training programs and represent many newly hired workers. The Transport Workers Union would represent the rest.

After decades of offshoring, union manufacturing jobs were returning to the Midwest. And it was not Donald Trump (or his allies) who brought them.[3]

When New York announced a $3 billion purchase of 1,025 subway cars, one of the largest mass transit purchases ever, city and state officials said they were not just buying "trains that will improve New York's transit system" but working to "create good jobs and revive manufacturing in our communities that need it the most." After months of negotiation by Janis and Nguyen, President Obama's transportation secretary, Anthony Foxx, sent letters to city transport agencies nationwide lauding new public purchasing criteria written by JMA. They called it the "U.S. Employment Plan." (The Trump administration Department of Transportation rescinded that support in August 2017.)[4]

Still, JMA's plan remains a blueprint for mass transit purchases by city and county governments in New York, Illinois and California. The plan, as adopted by these local governments, required every company bidding to build city buses, trucks, and trains to indicate how many local jobs they would create, how they would ensure that women, veterans, and people of color were trained and hired, and how they would use clean, renewable energy. It also outlined mechanisms to ensure transparency and compliance. Researchers estimated that New York City's transit purchase could create thirty-three thousand well-paying local jobs.[5]

What became the US Employment Plan was first rolled out in Los Angeles. After years of lobbying by LAANE and labor unions, Los Angeles Metro announced in 2015 that, in awarding contracts worth $1 billion for the purchase of 247 new railcars, it would score proposals based on how much production would be done in Los Angeles, how many jobs the project would create for communities suffering chronic underemployment, and how clean the trains would be. City experts said the project could create as many as ten thousand local jobs.

"For too long, American transit agencies have purchased buses and passenger trains for our cities without considering the ability to use these dollars to create quality jobs and generate opportunities for struggling communities," said JMA activist Rudy Gonzalves. That is beginning to change. Unlike others who have promised to bring manufacturing jobs back to the US, JMA is doing it. They are, as they say: "Making Our Transportation Dollars Go the Distance."[6]

. . .

Across the world, outside Cape Town, South Africa, another jobs creation movement is fast growing. In Philippi, a township known for violence and hopelessness, a farmer cooperative has taken root. In 2011, a group of mostly older women with exceptional gardening skills began growing wine grapes in their yards—the first wine grapes planted on the Cape Flats since before World War II. Virgin Wines in the UK funded their dream of turning those grapes into exportable wine. A little revolution had begun.[7]

Philippi arose from the wholesale resettlement of black families under the Apartheid Group Areas Act of 1950, says Nomhle Zondani, a township girl turned wine marketer. "Before the resettlement of people in the 1960s, the Cape Flats had vineyards. All of them are gone now but the soil is still fertile. We want to bring this part of Cape Town back to its former glory." The goal is to create as many new jobs as possible. In addition to farms, they are opening a wine-making school, restaurant, and bottling plant.

Western Cape vintner Graham Knox says that the limestone-rich soil in the Gugulethu section of Philippi township is a vinicultural treasure, as good as the land on which white-owned wineries have stood for centuries. South Africa is a top-ten global wine producer because of that soil. The women of Philippi have only little plots between tin shacks and abandoned factories, dirt roads and railroad tracks, but they are using them to bring change. Almost all field-workers in the Cape's multibillion-dollar wine industry are black. Until recently, fewer than 3 percent of owners were.

Since the late 1990s, black-owned and collectively owned wine estates are taking hold. Many hope that producer cooperatives will bring economic opportunity and improved labor conditions to the region. None of these success stories is more unlikely than that of Township Winery. Its wines—Little White Lies, Outlaw, and Storm—evoke the turbulent history of race-gender labor relations in South Africa's fields. Zondani directs marketing for Township wines. Like many poor students, she had to drop out of college, unable to pay tuition. Broke and jobless but interested in making a career in wine, she found Knox and real estate developer Kate Jambela. They were willing to invest in Philippi.[8]

The growers are excited, sixty-four-year-old Judith Xabanisa says. "I always enjoyed farming but I never thought I'd be growing grapes." Arlene van Wyk says: "I have been poor all my life. Now today, even the farmworkers' kids . . . can become farmers. . . . Black people will have opportunity to have our own vineyards."

Zondani says she "had to explain to the community that this is not going to bring easy money, that the success would come once we harvest." But Xabanisa hopes her work will lay the foundation for a family business. "I am hoping to pass on the skills I have learned to my four children and grandchildren so they don't end up in the streets or as criminals."[9]

So far, the results are promising. "People can't believe that something of this great quality came from a group of women with nothing," says Nkosi Madotyeni, who manages a Cape Town liquor store. Philippi Little White Lies Sauvignon Blanc sells well there. "Things are changing slowly but surely," he says. "It's inspiring to watch." By 2017, Township wines were being sold to five-star restaurants in South Africa, as well as the UK, Italy, Germany, Switzerland, and China. And sales continue to grow.

An hour away, in the Western Cape with its centuries-old estates and deeply rooted Afrikaner nationalism, a black producer's cooperative is now bottling wine at Koopmanskloof—a venerable white estate. It has been majority worker-owned since 2007, when owner Stewie Smit transferred 51 percent ownership to two hundred workers. The winery is now managed by Rydal Jeftha, a former field-worker who lives on the land.

Thandi winery (Xhosa for "nurturing love") is another producer collective, majority owned by 147 worker-families. Thandi was South Africa's first BEE (Black Economic Empowerment) project, funded through 2003 legislation to redistribute some of the country's vast resources to citizens of color. Thandi was the first winery in the world to win Fair Trade accreditation. By 2009 it was self-sustaining. Worker-owners run every phase of production from planting and picking, to marketing across Africa, Europe, and Asia.[10]

To compete with the region's older, larger white-owned wineries, these collectives have had to build economies of scale. Fourteen black- and woman-owned wineries have banded together into the Treasure Chest Collective. In recent years, these new collectives have sponsored township wine festivals that draw tourist dollars to Gugulethu, Soweto, and other townships in South Africa, supporting local businesspeople, creating decent jobs and income. They promote "Women in Wine," "Cape Dreams, "African Roots."

There are also several hundred employee-owned, democratically run companies in the US. As of 2017, 160 had organized into the national Federation of Worker Cooperatives, and aligned with European co-op federations in a "movement for workplace democracy and economic justice." Allied with and often funded by labor unions, worker cooperatives have become particularly popular among Latinx immigrants in the US who have formed trucking, housecleaning, and home-care cooperatives.[11]

Outside Santa Cruz, California, a different fair farm model has been offering hope for more than thirty years, improving workers' lives, along with the health of consumers and our planet. Swanton Berry Farm founder Jim Cochran traces his roots to farmworker cooperatives. Swanton is not a producer's cooperative but it boasts the first stock ownership plan in US agriculture. Of the eleven thousand employee stock ownership plans in the US only some are majority owned and operated democratically. Swanton is one of those.

The people who founded Swanton were an interesting mix, disciples both of environmentalist Rachel Carson and union leader Cesar Chavez. In the mid-1980s, they started the nation's first organic strawberry farm. Most berry farmers then and long afterward were wedded to methyl bromide, says Cochran, a chemical used to kill house termites. It enabled farmers to get a 50 percent higher yield than organic farmers could, but it was "deadly stuff," Cochran believed. Swanton's founders decided to try something different.

They were ultimately proven right. By the twenty-first century, methyl bromide had been banned in the US and many other countries because of its toxicity and the damage it did to the ozone layer. But California strawberry farmers, arguing they couldn't grow their crop without it, were exempted from the ban. Activists fought to change that. The UFW, MICOP, and other farmworker groups documented the pesticide poisoning of farmworkers and their children. Cochran offered proof that you could grow strawberries organically. Finally, in 2016, methyl bromide was banned completely.[12]

Swanton's founders always wanted the farm to be more than an environmental beacon. When he became self-sufficient economically, Jim Cochran began trying to find "a way for farmworkers to get a better deal in the system." Organic farms were already being certified so that consumers would know they could trust farmers' growing practices, Cochran said. Why shouldn't farms be certified for their labor practices? "If we can do that with fertilizers and plants and soil," he asked, "why can't we do that with people?" Cochran worked hard to convince other farmers, but it was an uphill battle at first. "There wasn't much interest in the organic community in . . . certifying labor standards," he says.

So Cochran reached out to the United Farm Workers. In 1998, Swanton became the first unionized organic farm in the country. Contract negotiations were "an excellent learning process," Cochran says. There is a myth that labor relations will remain harmonious on organic farms if we just don't talk about the issues. Labor "was not being addressed in any formal way by other farms," he says, "and I felt it was really important to do that." Swanton workers have a union contract, health and dental plan, vacation pay, paid sick leave, and a stock ownership plan. The farm gained one of the most stable workforces in agriculture, with workers who stay for ten and twenty years. And when Swanton workers retire, the company buys back their stock, so they have savings to live on. As Swanton's workers purchase ever greater shares of the company, says Cochran, the farm is returning to his roots in producer cooperatives.[13]

Swanton's environmental and labor practices have won numerous awards. In 2002, it won the EPA's Stratospheric Ozone Protection Award for pioneering techniques for growing berries without methyl bromide. In 2003, Swanton became the first US farm chosen by Social Accountability in Sustainable Agriculture (SASA) for a pilot audit to establish international standards for agricultural labor. Cochran and his partner Sandy Brown were invited by the United Nations Food and Agriculture Organization to testify about fair farm labor standards. Swanton is globally acknowledged as a pioneer and a model.

Swanton's worker-owners believe consumers will pay for labor justice as they do for chemical-free produce. One of the few US farms that is Food Justice-certified and bears the UFW label, Swanton advertises that on all its products: "Organically Grown by Union Labor."[14]

Since 2005, Jim Cochran has been working to expand his model into broader policy. Together with other food, farm, and antipoverty activists he created the Vivid Picture Project, to envision and lay the groundwork for a food, farm, and water system that feeds farmers, urbanites, and farmworkers alike. In 2013, they created the California Food Policy Council. It is now one of two hundred food policy councils across the US that are playing an increasingly large role in driving state and local food policy in fairer, healthier, more inclusive directions.

Among their victories is the Market Match program to make locally grown fresh fruits and vegetables available to food-insecure families and people who qualify for SNAP (Supplemental Nutrition Assistance Program). This initiative was introduced into the US Farm Bill in 2014. Now between $16 million and $32 million annually are granted to schools and farmers' markets to enable low-income Americans to enjoy fresh local produce at affordable prices.[15]

GrowNYC has a similar initiative, providing freshly grown local produce free or affordably through greenmarkets, youth markets, community gardens, and fresh-food box drop-offs. These programs benefit underserved communities that were food deserts not long ago. The projects employ two thousand local residents, and support small farmers around the city.[16]

On a larger scale, Food Policy Councils and the Roots of Change foundation are crafting and sponsoring legislation to build healthy food policy across the country. In California, the world's sixth-largest economy, proposed legislation that stands a good chance of passage includes laws improving access to clean drinking water for all, farm-to-school free meal programs, incentives for organic farming, and eased access to land and cutting-edge farm machinery for underserved farmers: young farmers, women, veterans, and farmers of color. Perhaps most important is their Food Chain Workers' Bill of Rights. The food-chain bill is potentially transformative, they say. One in six US workers labor in food-chain jobs. So do millions more worldwide.

Food First director Eric Holt-Giménez and Berkeley professor Miguel Altieri see similar kinds of coalitions being formed worldwide as "agroecologists build strategic alliances with food sovereignty and agrarian movements." These alliances, they believe, are creating "considerable political will for the transformation of our food systems." As Via

Campesina argues, the future of our world and its creatures may depend on their success.[17]

Cotton farming is being transformed as well. And, once again, global worker protest and consumer pressure have catalyzed change. In May 2017, thirteen of the world's largest clothing, retail, and textile companies, which together use 300,000-plus tons of cotton annually, signed a Sustainable Cotton Communiqué. Signatories included IKEA, H&M, Nike, Inditex, Gap, Marks & Spencer, Tesco, and other mega-companies. Negotiations were led by Prince Charles of England and driven by Marks & Spencer, the company that in 2017 earned the highest rating of any apparel retailer for protecting human rights in its supply chain.

Coalitions of workers, students, consumers, and farmers brought important changes in cotton farming between 2012 and 2017. They proved that cotton could be grown without destroying soil, polluting watersheds, or using child labor. Still, only one-fifth of cotton used by the major brands came from responsible growers. The Sustainable Cotton pact was an important step toward reducing "the negative environmental and social impacts" associated with cotton production. And it proved again that the big transnational buyers are key to improving conditions for workers on the ground.[18]

Small experiments in clothing manufacturing are also modeling broader possibilities for change. The Dominican town of Villa Alta Gracia is a free trade zone where export garment factories provide most of the jobs. From the 1980s on, workers at a Korean-owned headwear factory tried unsuccessfully to unionize. Activists toured US college campuses to describe their struggle. Student support helped them win the right to unionize in 2003, and with that came large wage increases. But in 2007, the company decamped for countries where it was cheaper to produce clothing, as manufacturers were doing across the Dominican Republic. Everyone in Alta Gracia felt the impact of the plant closures. The town withered.

Then, in 2010, Knights Apparel, the largest provider of collegiate-licensed sportswear in the US and a clothing provider for the National Hockey League, opened a new factory with a radical vision. Knights owner Joe Bozich wanted to show that you can profit by supporting worker justice. The Alta Gracia Project hired workers who had lost their jobs when the old factories closed. It recognized the workers' union and negotiated and signed a historic contract, agreeing to supply workers' health insurance, allow independent safety inspections, and pay what is called in Latin America *una salario digno*, a dignified wage. Alta Gracia workers earn three times the zone minimum and well above the national wage.

United Students Against Sweatshops activists pushed US colleges to have their logo-wear made at Alta Gracia. A sympathetic executive at Barnes & Noble, operator of college bookstores across the country, carried and promoted the product. By 2016, Alta Gracia was providing logo-wear for eight hundred US colleges and universities and moving into the black financially. For the first time, its workers had indoor plumbing, electricity, healthcare, and the chance to finish high school and attend college. Said one worker, "This has allowed us to dream."

Opening a unionized garment shop with a livable wage and decent conditions was unprecedented in the modern global apparel trade, says Scott Nova, founder and director of the Worker Rights Consortium. WRC, which investigates and certifies labor conditions worldwide, said that despite "a vast proliferation of 'corporate social responsibility programs' . . . no major apparel brand is doing what Knights Apparel is doing at the Alta Gracia factory."[19]

Knights CEO Joe Bozich says personal tragedy moved him to create a new model for garment manufacturing. In one short period, he lost family members in their twenties and thirties, two of his children faced death, and he was diagnosed with multiple sclerosis. His grief and longing for hope fueled in him a "NEED to KNOW that what I'm doing for work every day is making a real difference in the lives of people our business touches."[20]

Knights subsidized Alta Gracia for the first few years. By 2015, when Knights was bought by Hanes, Alta Gracia had become self-sufficient. Bozich says he hopes to open more garment factories like it. His slogan: "Changing Lives One Shirt at a Time."[21]

Tonlé, the largest ethical apparel manufacturer in Cambodia, represents another compelling model in fashion, offering living wages and safe working conditions while alleviating some of the massive environmental problems generated by garment production. Pioneering zero-waste manufacturing techniques, Tonlé began in 2013 to make clothes from fabric scraps. In its first year, it prevented 22,000 pounds of fabric from ending up in landfills and waterways.

Tonlé provides good jobs for rural women, partnering with village-based women's weaving collectives to turn scraps into new fabric. Environmentally friendly production techniques save water, and prevent pesticides, toxic dyes, and other chemicals associated with clothing production from entering landfills, air, and water. And, like Alta Gracia, it offers shop-floor democracy to women who would otherwise be working under sweatshop conditions.[22]

Branding and marketing labor justice is key to the success of small to midsize models like Swanton, Alta Gracia, and Tonlé. Whether it's Food Justice certification or a union or labor justice label, consciousness is growing worldwide. How fast it grows will depend on the willingness of entrepreneurs to commit to farming and manufacturing fairly, and on consumers' willingness to research and pay for those products.

Are these small models reproducible on a larger scale? Georgetown professor John Kline calls Alta Gracia "the anti-sweatshop." He argues that it is reproducible, indeed that it must be. "If this small factory can start from nothing, pay a 'Living Wage' and gain market share against well-established, heavily advertised brands," he says, "there are no excuses why large brands with an existing customer base cannot much more easily afford to pay workers a decent wage."[23]

Until that happens, consumers, NGOs, students, and government officials must continue demanding that global clothing brands and retailers be held legally accountable for the safety of their supply chain. The Bangladesh Fire and Safety Accord has done so with dramatic success, says Kalpona Akter, making factories safer for 2.5 million garment workers. Before the accord, an average of two hundred workers were dying every year in Bangladesh garment factories. In 2013, the death toll was much higher. In 2016–17, there were "zero deaths." Akter credits the accord, with its mandatory inspections and mechanisms for sanctioning companies that do not cooperate.

Still, the original accord is set to expire in 2018. As this book goes to press, global unions, thirteen major clothing brands, and NGOs including Clean Clothes Campaign, United Students Against Sweatshops, and International Labor Rights Forum have signed a second accord that will go into effect as soon as the first expires. "An agreement that holds signatory companies legally responsible for the commitments they made to worker safety is unprecedented in the modern global apparel industry,"

Clean Clothes Campaign argued in 2017. There are moves afoot to expand it to other industries and other countries.

In four years, 1,600 factories were inspected, 100,000 safety improvements were made, and there were 7,000 follow-ups to monitor improvements. Accord inspectors were often the first qualified building inspectors to see the inside of Bangladesh garment factories. Eighty percent of safety code violations identified by accord inspectors were remediated. There is much more work to do, but experts call the accord "a massive advance in worker safety." The challenge is to expand and reproduce it widely.[24]

CHAPTER 40

BIG IDEAS, NEW MODELS, SMALL COURTESIES BUILD A NEW WORLD

NEW IDEAS ARE TRANSFORMING our global economy a bit at a time. Worker-written social responsibility codes, like the Bangladesh Fire and Safety Accord, have improved conditions, raised wages, and educated workers from Florida's tomato fields to Bangladeshi garment shops, Texas construction sites, and electronics sweatshops worldwide. The global uprisings chronicled in this book, and the broad coalitions they have generated, have chipped and cracked the gospel of free trade. Increasingly, global companies have been forced to at least pay lip service to the idea of corporate social responsibility, if only because the public is now paying attention to worker deaths, child labor, and wage theft. And that damages global brands.

The proliferation of corporate social responsibility codes since 2010 may be seen as mostly an attempt to repair companies' public image, but that doesn't mean they have done no good. Nike, Gap, H&M, and other global companies who have been targeted by protesters and boycotts have made real improvements in their supply chains in response to pressure. But they only go so far.

Worker-led social responsibility codes are driven by a very different motivation: to end human rights violations in the workplace. And they have been very successful very quickly. Coalition of Immokalee Workers cofounder Greg Asbed argues that this is because no one understands as workers do the labor and safety issues in each industry. When workers conduct investigations, they get more accurate accountings of workplace conditions because employees are willing to speak candidly to them. ILO and UN investigations have affirmed this, showing worker-written social responsibility codes to be the single most effective tool available for raising wages and labor standards, educating workers, and fighting labor slavery. Even some corporate CEOs have admitted as much. The effort now is to push more companies to sign on to worker-led codes of conduct, and workers are building coalitions with consumers to press the electronics, dairy, and many other industries on this.

Community Benefits Agreements have arisen as an equally important and potentially transformative tool in the movement for worker and poor people's justice. Like so many important progressive strategies, the idea of harnessing the twenty-first-century urban real estate development boom to benefit poor and working-class communities was incubated in a small ground-floor office in downtown Los Angeles—home to progressive think-tank and organizing dynamo—the Los Angeles Alliance for a New Economy.

LAANE was founded in the early 1990s as a brainchild of Maria Elena Durazo, Miguel Contreras and attorney Madeline Janis, then an activist in the sanctuary movement for refugees from Central America. Janis says that the massive civil unrest after the 1992 police beating of Rodney King shook her. "It was a bread riot, significantly about low-wage poverty," she knew. And yet, "there weren't enough organizations representing regular people, organizing regular people."[1] Local 11 of UNITE HERE, then headed by Durazo, hired Janis to do just that.

In 1995, Janis began "traveling around and talking to a lot of people" to figure out how to bring together labor, environmental groups, religious leaders, academics, and politicians. At that time, says LAANE director Roxana Tynan, Los Angeles was the epicenter of wage theft and low-wage poverty in the US. Over the next twenty-five years, LAANE, its labor allies, and the unusually broad coalitions they helped build and sustain, made Los Angeles a national leader in creating policies that promote fair wages, strong unions, equitable and environmentally friendly urban development, and enlightened mass transit.

Janis and LAANE used an organizing style Janis calls "the kitchen-sink approach. Comprehensive campaigning, the idea that you need a lot of different types of tactics to accomplish something big. You need real people affected by policy. You need research, communications, policy development, and a legal strategy. And, of course, you need money."

Together with allies in UNITE HERE and the Los Angeles Federation of Labor, which Contreras and Durazo led sequentially (except for one year) from 1998 to 2014, LAANE began to "really look at the relationship between government and the private sector," Janis says. "What were all the ways you could impact corporate behavior? What were the ways we could impact regional, state, and national economies by using the power of government?"

Contreras argued that unions needed to stop writing checks blindly (mostly for Democratic candidates) and figure out how to elect "warriors for workers." Under Contreras and Durazo, the LA Federation of Labor trained workers—documented and undocumented—to identify and register immigrant working-class pro-union voters. "Then we started to elect real warriors," says Janis.

Once they had allies in government, she says, the next step was to frame policies that would benefit labor, immigrants, women, people of color, and the environment. LAANE researchers under Janis's guidance began to look at ports and logistics, retail, construction, waste, and recycling. Its organizers knocked on doors, garnering broad community support for environmentally friendly, labor-friendly policies. They pulled in everyone they could think of, says Tynan, to pressure city and county officials.

Clean ports were a priority, since diesel trucks from the ports generated a sizeable part of LA's air pollution. "When we were trying to win cleaner trucks at the Port, we reached out to mothers of asthmatic children," Tynan recalls. "They saw how it benefited their kids." Working in that way, Janis says, LAANE began winning victories.[2]

Their first big victory was a retention ordinance that LAANE framed and championed, motivated by threats of mass layoffs at the airport. The ordinance directly addressed what Janis calls "the willy-nilly practice of outsourcing to get a cheaper labor force." It was simple, Janis recalls: If you change contractors, you must give workers ninety days' notice, move them to a new job, recognize their union if at least 50 percent are unionized. That model for fighting the worst effects of subcontracting is as replicable as any anti-labor law generated by the American Legislative Exchange Council (ALEC), Janis believes. But in the age of state preemption laws, activists will have to work on the state level as well as the local. In California, they have been able to do that.

Los Angeles also passed the first broad living-wage ordinance in the country, in 1997, expanding a narrower one that had passed in Baltimore in 1994. The LA law, which became the model for living-wage ordinances later passed by a hundred cities, paved the way for the global living-wage movement. "It was the first time in a hundred years that anyone had heard the phrase 'living wage,'" Janis says. "It was very, very contentious."

Since that time, demands for a living wage have spread around the world. And support is growing steadily across partisan lines. The legislative struggle is far from over. Quite the contrary in the age of Trump, the Koch brothers, and authoritarianism ascendant from Poland to the Philippines. But Durazo, Janis, and Tynan are unfazed. The struggle is ongoing.

That is why, says Janis, it is so crucial to fight on many fronts at once and to leverage the economic power of local government to bring private sector developers to the bargaining table. That was the root of community benefits agreements (CBAs). "Corporations were talking out of both sides of their mouth," Janis says. "Keep the government out of business except when we need money: subsidies, tax breaks, bailouts." As urban real estate development boomed in the 1990s, LAANE and other community coalitions fought to ensure that poor communities would benefit.

The greatest achievement of the community benefits movement has been to ensure that private developments—the Staples Center, the Los Angeles airport expansion, the Hollywood and Highland development where the Academy Awards are held—generate well-paid jobs, affordable housing, gender equity in hiring, union recognition. Janis and attorneys for Partnership for Working Families helped write "project-specific contracts between developers and community organizations . . . safeguards to ensure that community residents share in the benefits . . . [and] have a voice in shaping the project," and legally binding contracts so that community organizations can make developers keep their promises.[3]

Leveraging the power of their newly expanded voter bloc, LAANE and the LA Federation won Janis a seat on the LA Redevelopment Agency Board, the largest of its kind in the country, with a billion-dollar annual budget. Janis says she used her ten-year term to push multiple Community Benefit Agreements. She saw them as "experiments writ large." Though Los Angeles has the most CBAs in operation, the strategy has now been used in dozens of cities. Using that tool, activists have been successful at redistributing some of the massive profits generated by galloping urban redevelopment to poor people, women, children, the elderly.

There have been some failed CBAs. In some cases, says Tynan, the community organizing was not energetic enough, contracts were not planned carefully, so city agencies did not fully involve and empower community residents. The new Yankee Stadium in the Bronx and Atlantic Yards in Brooklyn were instances of that. But CBA proponents consider these cautionary tales as teachable moments, demonstrating the need to organize broad alliances of stakeholders early. Community organizing is how you win support from government agencies, says Tynan. And it is how you pressure private developers.

To build durable community networks, she says, you have to organize around issues with broad appeal. The living-wage campaign, Tynan says, has energized constituencies who were not politically engaged previously. LAANE, SEIU, and UNITE HERE saw the living-wage struggle as "a way of getting people engaged and organized and excited and motivated, whether or not they could vote." It has helped make undocumented workers full participants in political battles, around a whole range of issues, she says. That's a good thing.

LAANE has identified community leaders and organized them to fight wage theft, sexual harassment, and environmental degradation while campaigning for a living wage. The group provides trainings to "build capacity" and expand skills for poor people, immigrants, environmental activists, mothers' groups, and many others. "Many different kinds of people saw that the capacity to win something real comes in partnership with the labor movement," says Tynan. Those allegiances have proven to be lasting.

During the Long Beach, California, living-wage campaign, she says, LAANE found allies in places that surprised even the organizers. Cambodian and Filipina immigrant girls' groups proved tireless and ebullient. They dove in enthusiastically, she says, making videos for the community: "If my mom made a living wage we could . . ." Community-based activists convinced 150 small businesses to hang signs and send letters to the city council explaining why a living wage would be good for business—because more people would have money in their pockets to spend. "It really shifted the politics in Long Beach," she says. "And we now have a city council that is majority progressive."

Tynan, Janis, and others believe that LAANE offers a model that can be (and has been) used elsewhere. In 2012, they published a comic book called *They Said It Was Impossible!: How to Win Progressive Change When the Odds Are Against Us*. A series of case studies and guidelines for campaigns, the book suggests strategies for "reclaiming our country the smart way."

Don't focus on losses, says Janis: decline in unions, outsourced jobs, gentrification. Look to the future and figure out how to build unions, create jobs, construct or rehab affordable housing. The Community Benefits Agreement they negotiated when LA's airport expanded brought half a billion dollars in benefits back to the community. Community Organizing for Responsible Development (CORD) did the same with a CBA around construction of the Yale-New Haven Medical Center in 2006. It brought jobs, job training, union recognition, housing, and environmental protections to ever-struggling New Haven.[4]

Janis believes that progressives must consistently channel procurement funds to benefit poor communities and labor. Government agencies spend $1.3 trillion a year on "buying things," she says. "That's a lot of shit we the taxpayers buy. That means we have leverage." Janis grins. "I'm an old Communist. I love the idea of getting back to manufacturing, making things, seeing union workers on production floors." A full-time activist since the 1970s, she acknowledges: "I know this will take the rest of my life." Like Vicky Carlos Garcia, she's fine with that.

Tynan believes that the successes of Los Angeles's progressive coalition have been built, too, on "multiracial organizing, labor community partnership, and not talking trash about each other, working with respect and solidarity." Los Angeles has benefited from the perspective of immigrants from Central and Latin America, she says, whose experiences of violent conflict at home made them keenly aware of how essential broad solidarities are. Alongside them, she says, were activists from the UFW, from the African American freedom struggle, from the Justice for Janitors campaign in the 1990s, many of whom remembered "the internecine craziness of the 1960s and wanted no part of it."

"We believe in mass organizing," says Tynan, a former hotel union organizer in Las Vegas. "That means reaching regular people, not sounding insane and not being blinded by ideology." And at the end of the day, Tynan argues, it still means organizing people into strong unions. Like UNITE HERE, she says, we must remain "committed not just to worker organizing but to building worker leadership." There is no real, lasting change without that.

On a blisteringly hot June day in 2017, OUR Walmart activist Denise Barlage and I sat drinking margaritas in plastic cups on the shores of Lake Champlain, in Burlington, Vermont. She had flown across the country for a meeting of the Food Chain Workers Alliance, where she strategized with Familias Unidas por la Justicia, Sakuma's newly unionized indigenous berry pickers, Enrique Balcazar and the leaders of Migrant Justice, and many others. She met with fast-food and grocery workers from across the US, Canada, and Mexico. Barlage was feeling buzzed by all the ideas, all the connections, all the visions, all the hope.

She had recently been hired by LAANE to organize workers fighting for paid time off: sick leave; family leave to care for ailing parents and children; vacation days. It was her first paid job since Walmart and she was excited. LAANE wanted her to reach out to retail workers across Southern California. "Paid time off," she said with energy. "It's the next thing."

As the sun set over the high peaks of the Adirondacks, Barlage looked out over rose-streaked water and flashed the OUR Walmart OK hand sign. For a moment she grew somber, remembering her final visit to Evelin Cruz in the hospital a year earlier. Barlage had never escaped Evelin Cruz's last words to her: "Keep with the program." Denise raised her glass, toasting Cruz, the movement, the falling night. "Keep with the program." She nodded. "Yes, we will."

ACKNOWLEDGMENTS

FIRST AND LAST, I thank the activists, organizers, farmworkers, fast-food, garment, retail, and hotel workers whose story this book tells. You opened your hearts, homes, union halls, and workplaces. You let me interview and Liz photograph. You shared your lives, struggles, dreams, and challenges. Your candor and courage changed me, and I know that the pieces of your stories that are published here will remain in the hearts and minds of those who read this book. Special thanks to Kalpona Akter, Denise Barlage, Bleu Rainer, Nice Coronacion, and Arcenio Lopez, who put up with numerous interviews and follow-up questions.

Thanks to Wim Conklin of the Cambodia Solidarity Center for introducing me to Vathanak Serry Sim, and thanks beyond measure to Vathanak for all he did to set up and transport me to interviews throughout Phnom Penh. I am grateful to the women of United Sisterhood Alliance, not only for in-depth interviews but for enabling me to visit one of their worker drop-in centers on the outskirts of the city. Gratitude goes as well to the organizers who helped me set up interviews with workers: Heather Nichols in Providence; Glen Arnodo and Tg Albert in Los Angeles and Pico Rivera; Joanna Coronacion and Em Atienza in Manila; Donna Foster and Sandy Young in Oxnard; Kelly Benjamin and Idallis Marrero in Tampa; Virgilio Aran and Liz Schalet in New York. Much appreciation to Nafisa Tanjeem for introductions to Bangladeshi activists.

I am grateful to Gayatri Patnaik, my editor at Beacon. Thanks for believing in this project from the first day I told you about it and for your wisdom and support throughout. Thanks as well to the entire Beacon team for your energy, enthusiasm, and skill.

Thank you to Kimberley Phillips and Marcus Boehm for a grant to subsidize publication of the photographs in this book. And thanks, Kim, for many years of friendship and conversation.

Dartmouth College provided a Scholarly Innovation and Advancement Grant that funded travel and research and gave me time off from teaching. I could not have written this book without that support.

Caroline Hansen, Julia Marino, and Mercedes Mariola did important background research and transcribed crucial interviews. You are fine scholars in your own right. Thank you.

To my dear friend Elizabeth Cooke, whose amazing photographs lend urgency, immediacy, and aesthetic depth to this book, I owe you more than I can say for decades of creative collaborations. Together we've made books and articles that are immeasurably richer for your contribution. Thank you for working with me, challenging me, laughing and crying with me and for an ongoing grand conversation that is far from over.

To my brilliant, edgy, funny, dramatic, wise family—my life partner Alexis Jetter, and our children Evann and Raphael—thank you for keeping me afloat, inspiring me, making me laugh, loving me. I love you back and will have more time to spend with you now.

And, last—to those whose struggle this book chronicles, thanks for a world-changing gift: giving us hope in dark times.

NOTES

PROLOGUE—BRANDS OF WAGE SLAVERY, MARKS OF LABOR SOLIDARITY

1. Material for this reflection derived from interviews conducted between March 2015 and April 2017—in the US and abroad. All interviews cited in the book were conducted by this author.

CHAPTER 1—INEQUALITY RISING

1. Thomas Piketty, *Capital in the Twenty-First Century* (Cambridge, MA: Harvard University Press, 2014); Joseph Stiglitz, *The Price of Inequality: How Today's Divided Society Endangers Our Future* (New York: W. W. Norton, 2013); David Harvey, *The New Imperialism* (New York: Oxford University Press, 2003).

2. David Harvey, *A Brief History of Neoliberalism* (New York: Oxford University Press, 2005); Friedrich Hayek, *The Road to Serfdom* (London: Routledge, 1944).

3. Milton Friedman, *Capitalism and Freedom* (Chicago: University of Chicago Press, 1962); George Monbiot, *How Did We Get into This Mess? Politics, Equality, Nature* (London: Verso, 2016); Nancy MacLean, *Democracy in Chains: The Deep History of the Radical Right's Stealth Plan for America* (New York: Penguin, 2017); Jane Mayer, *Dark Money: The Hidden History of the Billionaires Behind the Rise of the Radical Right* (New York: Doubleday, 2016).

4. "An Economy for the 1%," 210 Oxfam Briefing Paper, January 18, 2016.

5. "62 People Own Same as Half World," Oxfam, press release, January 18, 2016, http://www.oxfam.org.uk/media-centre/press-releases/2016/01/62-people-own-same-as -half-world-says-oxfam-inequality-report-davos-world-economic-forum; Social Security Administration, "Wage Statistics for 2014," https://www.ssa.gov/cgi-bin/netcomp.cgi ?year=2014.

6. Emmanuel Saez, "Striking It Richer: The Evolution of Top Incomes in the United States," University of California, Berkeley, September 3, 2013, http://eml.berkeley.edu //~saez/saez-UStopincomes-2012.pdf.

CHAPTER 2—ALL WE'RE ASKING FOR IS A LITTLE RESPECT

1. Bruce Douglas, "McDonald's Discrimination Lawsuit Seeks to Stop Chain Expanding in Brazil," *Guardian*, February 25, 2015.

2. Telephone interview with Bleu Rainer and Kelly Benjamin, September 2, 2015; Bruce Douglas, "McDonald's Faces Global Scrutiny at Brazil Senate's Human Rights Hearing," *Guardian*, August 20, 2015.

3. Interview with Benedict Murillo, Manila, November 22, 2015.

4. Telephone interview with Denise Barlage, April 20, 2016.

CHAPTER 3—"WE ARE WORKERS, NOT SLAVES"

1. Interview with Vicky Carlos Garcia, Manila, November 20, 2015; Harvey, *A Brief History of Neoliberalism*, 146.

2. "We Are Organized and We Know What We Want: An Interview with Elizabeth Mpofu," February 8, 2016, Thousand Currents, https://thousandcurrents.org/we-are-organized-and-we-know-what-we-want.

3. Katherine Zavala, "Farmworkers' Strikes: From Washington State to South Africa," September 6, 2013, International Development Exchange (now Thousand Currents).

4. "We Are Workers, Not Slaves! Farmworkers in Baja California Stand Up!," *Revolution*, April 11, 2015, http://www.revcom.us/a/382/farmworkers-in-baja-california-stand-up-en.html.

5. Lauren Carlson, "NAFTA Is Starving Mexico," *Foreign Policy in Focus*, October 20, 2011. http://fpif.org/nafta_is_starving_mexico.

6. Interview with Anastacia Lopez, Oxnard, CA, September 7, 2015; Eric Perramond, "The Rise, Fall, and Reconfiguration of the Mexican *Ejido*," *Geographical Review* 98, no. 3 (July 2008): 356–71.

7. Interview with Arcenio Lopez, Oxnard, CA, September 5, 2015.

8. Interview with Bernardino Martinez, Oxnard, CA, September 6, 2015.

CHAPTER 4—"I CONSIDER THE UNION MY SECOND MOTHER"

1. Interview with Tep Saroeung, Phnom Penh, November 29, 2015.

2. Chhay Channyda and Vincent MacIsaac, "Beer Girl Allies Target Carslberg," *Phnom Penh Post*, August 9, 2011.

3. "CFSWF Response to the Carlsberg Statement Issued on February 9, 2016," March 4, 2016, https://sarmorablog.wordpress.com.

CHAPTER 5—HOTEL HOUSEKEEPERS GO NORMA RAE

1. Skype interview with Massimo Frattini, October 20, 2015.

2. "The Law of Hotel Housekeeper Occupational Health & Safety," Transnational Development Clinic at Yale Law School, February 25, 2014, http://www.iuf.org/w/sites/default/files/TheLawofHotelHousekeepers.pdf.

3. Interview with Chhim Sitthar and Pao Chhumony, Phnom Penh, November 26, 2015.

4. Conversation with Vathanak Serry Sim, Phnom Penh, November 28, 2015.

5. Interview with Sok Kin, Phnom Penh, November 26, 2015.

6. Peter Amsel, "NagaWorld Staff Go Norma Rae," June 29, 2013, http://calvinayre.com/2013/06/29/casino/nagaworld-casino-staff-go-norma-rae-on-nagacorp.

7. Chhay Channyda and Shane Worrell, "NagaWorld Casino Staff Roll Dice on a Strike," *Phnom Penh Post*, February 26, 2013; Kaing Menghun, "Court Order Ends NagaWorld Strike," *Cambodia Daily*, June 27, 2013; Jonathan Cox, "NagaWorld Union Shoots for New Status," *Khmer Times*, January 14, 2016.

8. "Spain: Unions Challenge Fake 'Service Providers' Impoverishing Hotel Workers," IUF, July 10, 2017, http://www.iuf.org/w/?q=node/5630.

9. Frattini interview, October 20, 2015.

10. Interview with Santa Brito, Providence, RI, September 3, 2015.

11. Susan Buchanan et al., "Occupational Injury Disparities in the U.S. Hotel Industry," *American Journal of Industrial Medicine* 53 (2010): 116–25.

12. Interview with Maria Elena Durazo, Los Angeles, September 11, 2015.

13. Interview with Laphonza Butler and Rusty Hicks, Los Angeles, September 8, 2015.

14. David Whitford, "A Mess: Hyatt's Housekeeping Scandal," *Fortune*, October 2, 2009.

15. Bruce Vail, "'Hyatt Hurts' Boycott Inflicts Pain on the Hotel Giant," *In These Times*, March 18, 2013; Laura Clawson, "Hyatt and Union Announce Deal," *Daily Kos Labor*, July 1, 2013, http://www.dailykos.com/story/2013/7/1/1220371/-Hyatt-and-union -announce-deal-just-days-after-Pritzker-s-confirmation.

16. "Hunger Strike! Hilton Mission Valley: We Say ¡No Más!," Facebook post, 2013, https://www.facebook.com/events/121946677997953/?active_tab=highlights; "Hotel Workers Continue Hunger Strike for Jobs," *Fox5*, April 7, 2013, Sandiego.com/2013 /04/07.

17. Frattini interview, October 20, 2015.

CHAPTER 6—UNITED FOR RESPECT

1. Interview with Venanzi Luna, Pico Rivera, CA, September 9, 2015.

2. Steven Greenhouse, "Wal-Mart Labor Protests Grow," *New York Times*, October 9, 2012; Emily Jane Fox, "Why Wal-Mart Workers Are Striking on Black Friday," *CNN Money*, November 20, 2012, money.cnn.com/2012/11/20/pf/walmart-black-friday /index.html; Josh Eidelson, "The Great Wal-Mart Walkout," *Nation*, December 19, 2012; "Wal-Mart Workers in 12 States Stage Historic Strikes," *Democracy Now!*, October 10, 2012, https://www.democracynow.org/2012/10/10/walmart_workers_in_12_states_stage.

3. Telephone interviews with Denise Barlage, September 9, 2015, and January 18, 2017.

4. Interview with Evelin Cruz, Pico Rivera, CA, September 8, 2015.

5. "UNI Walmart Global Union Alliance Is Launched to Support Walmart Workers," National Union of Public and General Employees, Canada, https://www.nupge.ca /content/uni-walmart-global-union-alliance-launched-support-walmart-workers.

6. T. A. Frank, "A Brief History of Walmart," *Washington Monthly*, April 2006; *International Directory of Company Histories*, vol. 63 (Detroit: St. James Press, 2004); Dina Specter, "Walmart," *Business Insider*, November 15, 2012; Ellen Israel Rosen, "The Walmart Effect: The World Trade Organization and the Race to the Bottom," *Chapman Law Review* (Spring 2005).

7. "Kalpona Akter at Walmart's Annual Shareholder Meeting," June 10, 2013, YouTube video, https://www.youtube.com/watch?v=AcC-yCyF4f0; "Bring Bangladesh Voices to Walmart's Headquarters," Indiegogo, 2013, https://www.indiegogo.com/projects/bring-two-bangladeshi-garment-workers-to-the-walmart-shareholder-meeting; Clare O'Connor, "Former Bangladesh Sweatshop Worker to Billionaire Walton Family: Use Your Wal-Mart Fortune to Stop Worker Deaths," *Forbes*, June 7, 2013.

8. Phil Wahba, "Walmart Says Outside Labor Agitators Forced It to Take Action," *Fortune*, November 25, 2015.

CHAPTER 7—SUPERSIZE MY WAGES

1. Telephone interview with Vance Sanders, November 28, 2015; Joseph Piette, "Fight for $15 Links Racism, Low-Wage Economy," *Workers World*, August 22, 2016.

2. Piette, "Fight for $15."

3. Sarah Jaffe, "'We Triggered Something Epic': Naquasia LeGrand and the Fight for $15," *Progressive*, August 8, 2016; Karen Matthews, Associated Press, "Wage Fight Propels KFC Worker to White House," *USA Today*, March 2, 2014.

4. "I'm Sick and Tired of Being Sick and Tired," December 20, 1964, in *The Speeches of Fannie Lou Hamer: To Tell It Like It Is*, ed. Maegan Parker Brooks and Davis W. Houck (Jackson: University Press of Mississippi, 2011), available at http://www.crmvet.org/docs /flh64.htm; Jaffe, "'We Triggered Something Epic.'"

5. "NYC Law Gives Fast Food Workers Scheduling Rights," *US News & World Report*, May 30, 2017.

6. Jaffe, "'We Triggered Something Epic'"; Tony Wilsdon and Brent Gaspaire, "Manifesto of the Fastfood Worker," *Socialist Alternative*, January 2013.

7. Interview with Samuel Homer Williams, Pasadena, CA, September 10, 2015.

CHAPTER 8—1911–2011

1. Annelise Orleck, *Common Sense and a Little Fire: Women and Working-Class Politics in the United States, 1900–1965* (Chapel Hill: University of North Carolina Press, 1995).

2. Interview with Kalpona Akter, Montreal, August 5, 2016.

3. Telephone interview with Kalpona Akter, October 15, 2015.

4. Ibid.

5. Ibid.

CHAPTER 9—PEOPLE POWER MOVEMENTS IN THE TWENTY-FIRST CENTURY

1. Alina Carrillo and Shalmali Guttal, "When Murder and Abuse Become Systemic," *Focus on the Global South* (blog), Summer 2016, http://focusweb.org/content/when-murder -and-abuse-become-systemic; Human Rights Watch, *World Report 2016*, https://www.hrw .org/sites/default/files/world_report_download/wr2016_web.pdf.

2. "Wages and Working Hours in the Textiles, Clothing, Leather and Footwear Industries," International Labour Organization, Geneva, 2014, http://www.ilo.org.

3. National Employment Law Project, "The Growing Movement for $15," November 4, 2015, http://nelp.org/publication/growing-movement-15.

4. Human Rights Watch, *World Report 2016*.

5. Interview with Chhim Sitthar, Phnom Penh, November 27, 2015; e-mail correspondence with Em Atienza, June 22, 2016; Rishi Iyengar, "The Killing Time: Inside Rodrigo Duterte's War on Drugs," *Time*, August 25, 2016.

6. Interview with Maria Elena Durazo, Los Angeles, September 11, 2015; interview with Josua Mata, Manila, November 22, 2015.

7. Skype interview with Moshrefa Mishu, October 10, 2015.

8. Kim Scipes, *KMU: Building Genuine Trade Unionism in the Philippines, 1980–1994* (Quezon City: New Day Books, 1996).

9. Iain Boal, "Up from the Bottom," in *First World, Ha Ha Ha! The Zapatista Challenge*, ed. Elaine Katzenberger (San Francisco: City Lights Books, 1995).

10. Diana Denham and C.A.S.A. Collective, eds., *Teaching Rebellion: Stories from the Grassroots Mobilization in Oaxaca* (Oakland, CA: PM Press, 2008); author's observations and interviews, Oaxaca, Mexico, June 10–13, 2006.

11. Marta Sanchez articles on *Teacher Solidarity*: "Mexican Education Reform Is Stained with Blood," July 21, 2016; "Dissident Teachers Lead Resistance in Mexico," July 28, 2016; "Mexican Teachers Strike Today," August 22, 2016, http://www.teachersolidarity .com/.

CHAPTER 10—"YOU CAN'T DISMANTLE CAPITALISM WITHOUT DISMANTLING PATRIARCHY"

1. Interview with Joanna Bernice Coronacion, Manila, November 22, 2015.

2. Ibid.

3. Michèle Asselin, *Women on the March Until We Are All Free! A Brief History of the World March of Women* (2010), https://www.dssu.qc.ca/wp-content/uploads/a_brief_history _of_world_march_of_women.pdf.

4. Ibid.

5. "Moudawana: A Peaceful Revolution for Moroccan Women," Tavaana, https://tavaana.org/en/content/moudawana-peaceful-revolution-moroccan-women; Katja Zvan, "The Politics of the Reform of the New Family Law (the Moudawana)," Faculty of Oriental Studies, University of Oxford, May 2007; Amancio Vilankulos, "Young Mozambican Activists Call on Leaders to Support Reproductive Health," UN Population Fund, January 16, 2015, available at http://www.aidsfocus.ch/fr/actualites/young-mozambican-activists-call-on-leaders-to-support-reproductive-health-efforts.

6. Morgan Winsor, "Congo's Conflict Minerals," *International Business Times*, September 8, 2015.

7. *The World March of Women 2010: Third International Action*, http://www.world-governance.org/IMG/pdf_WMW_Book_2011_ENGLISH-2.pdf.

8. Ibid.

9. "Congo-Kinshasa: Bukavu—World March of Women," UN Stabilization Mission in the DR Congo, October 18, 2010, http://allafrica.com/stories/201010211042.html; Dunya Kadın Yuruyuşu, "Women on the March," January 27, 2015, http://www.dunya kadinyuruyusu.org/index.php/duyurular/3-women-on-the-march-until-we-are-all-free.

10. "Flashmob Sings 'Bread and Roses' to Demand Respect for Women's Rights and Dignity," Alliance of Progressive Labor, SENTRO, press release, March 8, 2014, http://focusweb.org/content/flashmob-sings-bread-and-roses-demand-respect-womens-rights-and-dignity.

11. Interview with Jamaia Montenegro, Quezon City, November 24, 2015.

12. Interview with Vun Em, Phnom Penh, November 30, 2015.

13. Womyn's Agenda for Change, see http://www.unitedsisterhood.org/; interview with Sok Thareth, United Sisterhood Alliance, Phnom Penh, November 30, 2015.

14. Vun interview, November 30, 2015.

15. "Statement by Global Unions to the 2016 Meetings of the IMF and World Bank," October 7–9, 2016, https://www.ituc-csi.org/IMG/pdf/statement.imfwb.1016.pdf.

16. UNITE HERE Local 1, *Hands Off, Pants On: Sexual Harassment in Chicago's Hospitality Industry*, report by UNITE HERE Local 1(Chicago: July 2016), https://www.handsoffpantson.org.

17. Communications with Asuncion Binos, November 26, 2015.

18. Interview with Kalpona Akter, Montreal, August 8, 2016.

CHAPTER 11—THIS IS WHAT SOLIDARITY FEELS LIKE

1. Telephone interview with Kalpona Akter, October 15, 2015; Frattini interview, October 20, 2015.

2. Interview with Ruby Duncan, Las Vegas, September 2, 1992.

3. George Katsiaficas, *Asia's Unknown Uprisings*, vol. 2, *1947–2009* (Oakland, CA: PM Press, 2013), 33.

4. Laundry Workers Center, http://laundryworkerscenter.org.

5. Interview with Virgilio Aran, New York, April 16, 2015.

CHAPTER 12—RESPECT, LET IT GO, 'CAUSE BABY, YOU'RE A FIREWORK

1. "The Dancers' Union of Bagong Silangan," April 5, 2014, YouTube video, https://www.youtube.com/watch?v=-EIIQrmoBzcs; interview with Lei Catamin, Quezon City, November 24, 2015.

2. "The Dancers' Union of Bagong Silangan."

CHAPTER 13—REALIZING PRECARITY

1. Skype interview with Ann Buckner, April 2, 2015.

2. Interviews with Eric Webb-Fiske, Bleu Rainer, Keegan Shepard, and Cole Bellamy, Tampa, FL, March 25, 2015.

3. "Women at Work: Trends, 2016," International Labour Organization, http://www .ilo.org/wcmsp5/groups/public/---dgreports/---dcomm/---publ/documents/publication /wcms_457317.pdf; *The Employment Situation—April 2014* Bureau of Labor Statistics report (Washington, DC: US Department of Labor, May 2, 2014), https://www.bls.gov /news.release/archives/empsit_05022014.pdf.

CHAPTER 14—DAYS OF DISRUPTION, 2016

1. "Minimum Wage and Living Wage: Recent Developments," Results: The Power to End Poverty, http://www.results.org/issues/minimum_living_wage, accessed October 6, 2017.

2. Elaina Athans and Angelica Alvarez, "Durham Protesters Demanding Wage Increase Arrested," ABC11 *Eyewitness News*, November 29, 2016, http://abc11.com/news /durham-protesters-demanding-wage-increase-arrested/1631168; SEIU Facebook page, "North Carolina Home Care Workers Are Standing Up," https://www.facebook.com /SEIU/posts/10153040583282680?comment_id=10153042499002680.

3. Interviews with Vance Sanders, November 29 and December 20, 2016.

4. Thomas Friedman books: *The Lexus and the Olive Tree: Understanding Globalization* (New York: Farrar, Straus and Giroux, 1999), and *The World Is Flat: A Brief History of the Twenty-First Century* (New York: Farrar, Straus and Giroux, 2005).

5. Jonathan Maze, "Why McDonald's Won't Ever Get Rid of Its Real Estate," *Nation's Restaurant News*, February 26, 2015; Adam Brownlee, "McDonald's Corporation: A Real Estate Empire Financed by French Fries," *The Motley Fool*, March 6, 2016.

6. Randy James, "A Brief History of McDonald's Abroad," *Time*, October 28, 2009; "McDonald's Total Assets Quarterly," *YCharts*, June 30, 2017, https://ycharts.com/companies /MCD/assets.

7. "Trump's Labor Pick, Fast-Food CEO Andrew Puzder, Opposes Minimum Wage Increase & Paid Sick Leave," *Democracy Now!*, December 9, 2016.

8. Diane Thao, "Protesters at Nevada Capitol Demand $15 Minimum Wage," News 4/Fox 11, September 12, 2016, http://mynews4.com/news/local/protestors-at-state -capitol-demands-for-15-minimum-wage.

9. Ock Hyun-Ju, "Workers and Students Up Pressure on Park to Resign," AsiaOne, December 1, 2016, http://news.asiaone.com/news/asia/tens-thousands-workers-and -students-ups-pressure-s-korea-president-park-resign; TeleSUR, "General Strike in South Korea," November 30, 2016, http://www.telesurtv.net/english/news/General-Strike-in -South-Korea-Demands-Impeach-President-20161129-0013.html.

10. "Union of Part-Timers to Launch First Collective Bargaining with McDonald's Korea," Yonhap News Agency, April 26, 2017, http://english.yonhapnews.co.kr/national /2017/04/26/0302000000AEN20170426012100315.html.

11. "Brazil Stoppages Against Government Agenda," *Prensa Latina*, November 11, 2016; Ed Taylor, "Brazil McDonald's Fined $30 Million," *Bloomberg News*, December 7, 2016, https://www.bna.com/brazil-mcdonalds-fined-n73014448238.

12. Ian Hodson, "European and U.S. Workers United in Fair Pay Fight," *Morning Star*, November 29, 2016, https://www.morningstaronline.co.uk/a-4624-European-and -US-workers-united-in-fair-pay-fight.

13. Abi Wilkinson, "Labour's Ban on McDonald's Is No Snobbery, It's Crucial Support for Its Staff," *Guardian*, April 22, 2016; Graham Reddick, "McDonald's Offers Fixed Contracts to 115,000 UK Zero-Hours Workers," *Guardian*, April 25, 2017.

CHAPTER 15—THE NEW CIVIL RIGHTS MOVEMENT

1. "Low-Wage Workers Hold 1st Annual 'Fight for 15' Convention," *Ebony*, August 12, 2016.

2. Interview with Bleu Rainer, New York City, April 15, 2015.

3. Interview with Reika Mack, Tampa, FL, March 25, 2015.

4. Interview with Maia Montcrief, Pasadena, CA, September 10, 2015.

5. Telephone interview with Vance Sanders, November 28, 2016, and subsequent e-mail correspondence.

6. Rainer interview, April 15, 2015; interview with Vance Sanders, February 16, 2017.

CHAPTER 16—COUNTING VICTORIES, GIRDING FOR AN UPHILL STRUGGLE

1. "State Minimum Wages 2017," National Conference of State Legislatures, http:// www.ncsl.org/research/labor-and-employment/state-minimum-wage-chart.aspx.

2. Peter Dreier, "How Fight for $15 Won," *American Prospect*, April 4, 2016.

3. Leah Zitter, "Top 8 Companies Raising the Minimum Wage," *Investopedia*, August 14, 2016; Stephen Miller, "Big Companies Are Raising Wages," Society for Human Resource Management, July 15, 2016, http://www.shrm.org/resourcesandtools/hr-topics /compensation/pages/raising-low-earners-wages.aspx.

4. "Current Sick Days Laws," Support Paid Sick Days, http://www.paidsickdays.org /research-resources/current-sick-days-laws.html, retrieved February 14, 2017.

5. "NY/NJ Airport Workers Bargaining Committee," n.d., filed in New Jersey and New York, 32BJ SEIU, http://www.seiu32bj.org/spotlights/nynj-airport-workers -bargaining-committee; Jeff Amy, "Former Contract Workers Crucial in Canton Nissan Union Vote," *Clarion-Ledger*, July 25, 2017.

6. Interview with Prince Jackson and Canute Drayton, New York City, April 15, 2015.

7. Francisco Mariano, "The Airline Industry Is Global. So Are We," SEIU blog, November 2016, http://www.seiu.org/blog/2016/11/the-airline-industry-is-global-so -are-we.

8. National Employment Law Project, "Fight for $15: Four Years, $62 Billion," data brief, November 2016; Dreier, "How Fight for $15 Won."

9. Interview with Laphonza Butler, Los Angeles, September 9, 2015. All future quotes from Butler are from this interview unless otherwise noted.

10. Quoctrung Bui, "50 Years of Declining Union Membership," *Planet Money*, NPR, February 23, 2015.

11. National Employment Law Project, "Fighting Preemption," policy brief, July 6, 2017, www.nelp.org/publication/fighting-preemption-local-minimum-wage-laws; Bill Kramer, "Localities Challenging State Preemption Laws," *MultiState Insider*, August 22, 2016, https://www.multistate.us/blog/insider/2016/08/localities-challenging-state -preemption-laws; "Living Wage Mandate Preemption Act," American Legislative Exchange Council, reapproved by ALEC Board of Directors on January 28, 2013, https:// www.alec.org/model-policy/living-wage-mandate-preemption-act.

12. "Right-to-Work Resources," National Council of State Legislatures, http://www
.ncsl.org/research/labor-and-employment/right-to-work-laws-and-bills.aspx.

CHAPTER 17—*HUELGA DE HAMBRE*
1. Steve Ahlquist, "2014: The Year RI Jailed Workers in Poverty," *RI Future*, December 31, 2014, http://www.rifuture.org/2014-the-year ri-jailed-workers-in-poverty.html.
2. Interview with Santa Brito, Providence, RI, September 2, 2015.
3. Steve Ahlquist, "Renaissance Employee Suffers Heart Attack While Firing," *RI Future*, December 15, 2014, http://www.rifuture.org/fired-renaissance-employee-suffers
-heart-attack.
4. Interviews with Heather Nichols and Shelby Maldonado, September 3, 2015; Peter Makhlouf, "Laboring for Democracy: The Minimum Wage in Rhode Island," *College Hill Independent*, April 3, 2015.
5. John Hill, "Renaissance Downtown Housekeepers Vote to Unionize," *Providence Journal*, November 12, 2015.
6. *Providence's Pain Problem: Procaccianti Hotels Hurt Workers* (Providence, RI: United Here! Local 217, 2015), https://www.scribd.com/document/278093339/Providence-s
-Pain-Problem.
7. Alisha Pina, "Rally at Providence Business," *Providence Journal*, March 22, 2017.
8. Interview with Mirjaam Parada, Providence, RI, September 3, 2015.
9. Telephone interview with Denise Barlage, January 26, 2016.
10. "L.A. Women Fast for 15," testimony before LA City Council, April 29, 2015, https://www.facebook.com/LA-Women-Fast-for-15-1576428089312871.
11. Interviews with Denise Barlage, December 10, 2015, and January 26, 2016; telephone interview with Tyfani Faulkner, February 17, 2017.
12. Rainer interview, April 15, 2015.
13. Ned Resnikoff, "The Return of American Hunger," *Atlantic*, July 19, 2016.
14. Peter Dreier, Megan Bomba, and Rosa Romero, "Food Insecurity Among University of California Employees," Urban and Environmental Policy Institute, Occidental College, October 2016.
15. Barlage interview, January 26, 2016.
16. Padraig O'Malley, *Biting at the Grave: The Irish Hunger Strikes and the Politics of Despair* (Boston: Beacon Press, 1991); "Gandhi: The Previous Fasts," *Indian Express*, March 4, 1943.
17. Patrick J. McDonnell, "37 Protesters Arrested in Hotel Labor Dispute," *Los Angeles Times*, December 1, 1994; Nancy Cleeland, "26 Activists Arrested During Pro-Union Protest at LAX," *Los Angeles Times*, May 13, 1999; Maria Elena Durazo, "Fasting to Right Worker Injustices," *Los Angeles Times*, May 25, 1999.
18. Gustavo Arellano, "Disney's Hotel-Workers' Union Is Still Trying to Bring Down the Mouse," *OC Weekly*, October 7, 2010.
19. Patrick Cooligan, "Hunger Strikes and Happiness Pickets," *Las Vegas Sun*, April 25, 2012; Associated Press, "A Station Casinos Property to Unionize," *Las Vegas Sun*, September 6, 2016; Bethany Kahn, "Station Casinos Agree to NLRB Settlement," UNITE HERE Local 226 press release, Las Vegas, March 14, 2017, http://www.culinaryunion226
.org/news/press; K. Morrison, "Station Casinos Agree to Settlement," March 16, 2017, World Casino Directory, https://news.worldcasinodirectory.com/station-casinos-agrees
-to-settlement-palace-station-now-unionized-43633.

20. David Yaffe-Bellamy, "Local 33 Presents Yale with Petition," *Yale Daily News*, April 5, 2017.

21. Amy Hungerford, "Why the Yale Hunger Strike Is Misguided," *Chronicle of Higher Education*, May 9, 2017; Jennifer Klein, "Why Yale Graduate Students Are on a Hunger Strike," *New York Times*, May 9, 2017.

22. Author's observation; "The Fast Against Slow," www.local33.org.

CHAPTER 18—SOCIAL MOVEMENT UNIONISM AND THE SOULS OF WORKERS

1. Interview with Maria Elena Durazo, Los Angeles, September 11, 2015.

2. Interview with Josua Mata, Quezon City, November 22–23, 2015; interview with Rusty Hicks, Los Angeles, September 7, 2015; Kim Scipes, "Understanding the New Labor Movements in the 'Third World': The Emergence of Social Movement Unionism," LabourNet Germany, June 5, 2003, http://archiv.labournet.de/diskussion/gewerkschaft /smu/The_New_Unions_Crit_Soc.htm.

3. Interview with Bleu Rainer, Tampa, FL, March 25, 2015; Durazo interview, September 11, 2015.

4. John Nichols, *Uprising: How Wisconsin Renewed the Politics of Protest* (New York: Nation Books, 2012); Sarah Jaffe, *Necessary Trouble: Americans in Revolt* (New York: Nation Books, 2016).

5. Josh Eidelson, "How a $15 Minimum Wage Went from Fringe to Mainstream," *Bloomberg News*, March 29, 2016.

6. Ibid.

7. Interviews with Joanna Bernice Coronacion and Josua Mata, Quezon City, November 22–23, 2015.

CHAPTER 19—"CONTRACTUALIZATION"

1. Interview with Joshua Noguit, Quezon City, November 22, 2015.

2. Steven Greenhouse, "Fight for $15: Meet the Enfant Terrible Who Turned Minimum Wage into a National Battle," *Guardian*, April 9, 2016; Michael Greenberg, "Tenants Under Siege," *New York Review of Books*, August 17, 2017.

3. David Cooper and Teresa Kroeger, "Employers Steal Billions from Workers' Paychecks Each Year," Economic Policy Institute, May 10, 2017.

4. Fight for $15, "Day of Disruption November 29," video, fightfor15.org.

5. Ibid.

CHAPTER 20—"STAND UP, LIVE BETTER"

1. Interview with Girshriela Green, Pico Rivera, CA, September 9, 2015.

2. Interview with Venanzi Luna, Los Angeles, September 10, 2015.

3. Nelson Lichtenstein, *The Retail Revolution: How Wal-Mart Created a Brave New World of Business* (New York: Metropolitan Books, 2009).

4. Cantare Davunt, "I Cannot Continue to Live and Work Like This," *Salon*, October 21, 2014; "Walmart: Our Locations," http://corporate.walmart.com/our-story /our-locations; C. Ehrbacher and Becca Aaronson, "Walmart Private Plan Stirs Concern Over Workers' Compensation System," *Texas Tribune*, April 9, 2012; "Accident in Walmart Claims," Legally Firm, http://www.legallyfirm.com/accident-in-walmart-claims, accessed October 6, 2017.

5. Ellen Bravo, "Respect the Bump Gets Results as Well as Respect," *Huffington Post*, September 29, 2014.

6. Interview with Girshriela Green, June 9, 2016.

7. Katie Johnston, "Pregnant Workers' Bill," *Boston Globe*, July 20, 2017.

8. Interview with Elizabeth Gedmark, June 9, 2016.

9. Barlage interview, September 10, 2015; Amien Essif, "Wal-Mart's Inhumane Policies for Pregnant Workers," *In These Times*, November 6, 2014.

10. Nicole Flatow, "U.S. Supreme Court Sides with Pregnant Workers in Major Discrimination Case," *ThinkProgress*, March 25, 2015; Jeffrey Toobin, "Betty Dukes vs. Wal-Mart," *New Yorker*, June 20, 2011; "1.5 Million Female Wal-Mart Employees Lose Historic Sex Discrimination Case," *Democracy Now!*, June 21, 2011; Liza Featherstone, *Selling Women Short: The Landmark Battle for Workers' Rights at Wal-Mart* (New York: Basic Books, 2004).

11. Green interview, September 9, 2015; Ari Bloomekatz, "Thousands Rally Against Wal-Mart in Chinatown," *Los Angeles Times*, July 1, 2012.

12. Interview with Evelin Cruz, Pico Rivera, CA, September 9, 2015.

13. Interview with Jenny Mills, Pico Rivera, CA, September 9, 2015.

14. Interview with Barbara Collins, Pico Rivera, CA, September 9, 2015; Ashlee Kieler, "Labor Board Orders Walmart to Rehire 16 Employees Fired for Striking," *Consumerist*, January 22, 2016.

15. Interview with Denise Barlage, Burlington, VT, June 12, 2017.

16. Telephone interview with Tyfani Faulkner, February 17, 2017.

CHAPTER 21—"IF PEOPLE WOULD THINK ABOUT US WE WOULDN'T DIE"

1. The official name is the Accord on Fire and Building Safety in Bangladesh, http://bangladeshaccord.org.

2. "Powerful Brands, Powerful Platforms: One VF," http://www.vfc.com.

3. "Tangled Thread," video produced by Sara Ziff, 2014, https://vimeo.com/92582309.

4. "Prospects for Democratic Reconciliation and Workers' Rights in Bangladesh," US Senate Committee on Foreign Relations, press release, February 11, 2014, https://www.foreign.senate.gov/press/chair/release/chairman-menendez-opening-remarks-at-the-hearing-prospects-for-democratic-reconciliation-and-workers-rights-in-bangladesh.

5. "GSP Review of Bangladesh Recognizes Progress, Urges That More Be Done on Worker Safety and Rights," Office of US Trade Representative, press release, January 2015, https://ustr.gov/about-us/policy-offices/press-office/press-releases/2015/january/gsp-review-bangladesh-recognizes;www.foreign.senate.gov/imo/mediadoc/Akter_Testimony.pdf.

6. Dave Jamieson, "Rana Plaza Survivor Left with Debilitating Trauma," *Huffington Post*, March 19, 2014.

7. "Rep. George Miller Speaks Out About Garment Factory Conditions in Bangladesh," February 12, 2014, *Feminist Daily Newswire* (blog), https://feminist.org/blog/index.php/2014/02/12/rep-george-miller-speaks-out-against-garment-factory-conditions-in-bangladesh.

8. Interview with Sok Thareth, Phnom Penh, November 29, 2015.

9. Interview with Roth Minea, Phnom Penh, November 28, 2015.

10. Sok Thareth interview, November 30, 2015.

11. Mech Dara and Alex Willemyns, "Workers Turn Models on Political Catwalk," *Cambodia Daily*, May 26, 2014.

12. Marc Bain and Jenni Avins, "The Thing That Makes Bangladesh's Garment Industry Such a Huge Success Also Makes It Deadly," *Quartz*, April 24, 2015, http://qz.com/389741/the-thing-that-makes-bangladeshs-garment-industry-such-a-huge-success-also-makes-it-deadly.

13. Skype interview with Nazma Akhter, October 9, 2015.

14. Michelle Chen, "Congress Has Only Now Banned Slave Labor in U.S. Imports," *Nation*, February 23, 2016; Matea Gold et al., "Ivanka Inc.," *Washington Post*, July 14, 2017.

CHAPTER 22—HOW THE RAG TRADE WENT GLOBAL

1. Messenger Band, "Suffer from Privatization" (2009).

2. Ibid.

3. Glynis Sweeny, "Fast Fashion Is the Second Dirtiest Industry on Earth," EcoWatch, August 17, 2015, http://www.ecowatch.com/fast-fashion-is-the-second-dirtiest-industry -in-the-world-next-to-big--1882083445.html.

4. Lina Stoz and Gillian Kane, "Facts on the Global Garment Industry," February 2015, https://cleanclothes.org/resources/publications/factsheets/general-factsheet-garment -industry-february-2015.pdf.

5. Gordon Laird, *The Price of a Bargain: The Quest for Cheap and the Death of Globalization* (New York: Palgrave Macmillan, 2008).

6. Cecile Fruman and Douglas Zeng, "How to Make Zones Work Better in Africa," *Private Sector Development* (blog), World Bank, July 27, 2015; Douglas Zeng, "Why Are More Countries Embracing Industrial Zones?," May 5, 2015, *Special Economic Zones* (blog), World Bank, http://blogs.worldbank.org/category/tags/special-economic-zones; Matt Kennard and Claire Provost, "Inside the Corporate Utopias Where Capitalism Rules and Labor Laws Don't Apply," *In These Times*, July 25, 2016.

7. "Export Processing Zones Growing Steadily," International Labour Organization, September 28, 1998; Bangladesh Export Processing Zones Authority, "About BEPZA," http://www.epzbangladesh.org.bd; Aycil Yucer and Jean-Marc Siroen, "Trade Performance of Export Processing Zones," *World Economy* 39, no. 7 (April 2016).

8. *H&M Annual Report*, 2016, https://about.hm.com/content/dam/hmgroup/groupsite /documents/masterlanguage/Annual%20Report/Annual%20Report%202016.pdf.

9. "Global Garment and Textile Industries: Workers, Rights and Working Conditions," Solidarity Center, November 2015, http://www.solidaritycenter.org/wp-content /uploads/2015/11/Global.Garment-Workers-Fact-Sheet.11.15.pdf.

10. Ibid.

11. Hsiao Hung Pai, "Factory of the World: Scenes from Guangdong," *Places*, October 2012.

12. Elizabeth Cline, "Where Does Discarded Clothing Go?," *Atlantic*, July 28, 2014; Anthony Roberts, "Walmart's Limited Growth in Urban Retail Markets: The Cost of Low Labor Investment," UCLA Institute for Research on Labor and Employment, July 2015; Steve Hargreaves, "Your Clothes Are Killing Us," *CNN Money*, May 22, 2015.

CHAPTER 23—"THE GIRL EFFECT"

1. "Our Purpose," mission statement, Girl Effect, http://www.girleffect.org/our -purpose.

2. Jill Ker Conway speech, Dartmouth College, April 1998.

3. Maria Hengeveld, "Nike Boasts of Empowering Women Around the World," *Slate*, August 26, 2016.

4. Messenger Band, "Workers' Tears" (2006).

5. Interview with Sok Thareth, Phnom Penh, November 29, 2015.

6. Messenger Band, "Fate of Garment Workers."

7. Messenger Band, "Land and Life."

8. Interview with Kalpona Akter, Montreal, August 14, 2016; interview with Roth Minea, Phnom Penh, November 28, 2015.

9. Hengeveld, "Nike Boasts."

10. Hyun Soo Lee, "Former Nike Factory Worker Shares Story," *Daily Collegian*, March 21, 2016, http://www.collegian.psu.edu/news/campus/article_4fcbbb98-efe1-11e5 -9e95-6fc988b86843.html.

11. Tanya Talaga, "Garment Workers Making Less Money Than 10 Years Ago," *Star* (Toronto), July 19, 2013.

12. Anu Muhammad, "Wealth and Deprivation: Ready-Made Garments Industry in Bangladesh," *Economic and Political Weekly* 46, no. 34 (August 20, 2011).

CHAPTER 24—"MADE WITH LOVE IN BANGLADESH"

1. "Bangladesh: Out of War a Nation Is Born," *Time*, December 20, 1971.

2. Bangladesh Export Processing Zones Authority, "About BEPZA," http://www .epzbangladesh.org.bd; Akter interview, August 14, 2016.

3. Interview with Ath Thorn and members of CCAWDU, Cambodian Coalition of Apparel Workers Demoncratic Union, Phnom Penh, November 29, 2015.

4. *Wages and Working Hours in the Textiles, Clothing, Leather and Footwear Industries*, International Labour Organization, report for the Global Dialogue on Wages Forum, Geneva, September 23–25, 2014.

5. John Barker, "A Stitch in Time: The 'Orchestrated Networks' of Bloody Taylorism," *Mute Magazine*, July 10, 2013, http://libcom.org/tags/bangladeshi-garment-workers.

6. Akter interview, August 14, 2016.

7. Red Marriott, "Death Traps: Work, Home, Fire and the Poor in Bangladesh," March 10, 2010, libcom.org.

8. Ibid.

9. Red Marriott, "Tailoring to Needs: Garment Workers Struggles in Bangladesh," *Insurgent Notes*, October 28, 2010.

10. Accord on Fire and Building Safety in Bangladesh, update on progress, April 2016, http://bangladeshaccord.org; telephone interview with Kalpona Akter, October 15, 2015; Akter interview, October 9, 2015.

CHAPTER 25—"WE ARE NOT A POCKET REVOLUTION"

1. Reuters, "Bangladesh Garment Workers Hold Largest Protest Yet," September 21, 2013.

2. Global Nonviolent Action Database, Swarthmore College, http://nvdatabase .swarthmore.edu.

3. All quotes from telephone interview with Moshrefa Mishu, October 12, 2015.

4. Global Nonviolent Action Database, Swarthmore College, http://www.human rightskorea.org/wp-content/uploads/2011/01/khis-press-statement-bangladesh-hrd -26-jan-2011.pdf.

CHAPTER 26—"A KHMER WOULD RATHER WORK FOR FREE THAN WORK WITHOUT DIGNITY"

1. Interview with Khloek Outrok, Phnom Penh, November 27, 2015.

2. "Clothes Retailers Accused of Labor Abuses in Cambodia," BBC News, March 12, 2015, http://www.bbc.com/news/business-31842046.

CHAPTER 27—"AFTER POL POT, WE NEED A GOOD LIFE"

1. All quotes from Chea Mony in this section are from interview, Phnom Penh, November 27, 2015.

2. Interview with Wim Conklin, Phnom Penh, December 4, 2015.

3. Interview with Ath Thorn, Phnom Penh, November 28, 2015.

4. Interview with Yang Sophorn, Phnom Penh, November 28, 2015.

CHAPTER 28—CONSCIOUSNESS-RAISING, CAMBODIA STYLE

1. Interviews with Vathanak Serry Sim, Phnom Penh, November 25–28, 2015, and with Vun Em, Phnom Penh, November 30, 2015.

2. Interview with members of the Women's Information Center discussion group, Phnom Penh, November 29, 2015.

3. Interview with Dany, Danu, and Sreypon, Phnom Penh, November 29, 2015.

CHAPTER 29—FILIPINA GARMENT WORKERS

1. Interview with Josua Mata, Quezon City, November 23, 2015.

2. Interview with Asuncion Binos, Quezon City, November 24, 2015.

3. Scipes, *KMU*.

4. Ibid.

5. Ibid.

6. Raisa Serafica, "Four Things to Know About the Mendiola Massacre," *Rappler*, January 21, 2017, http://www.rappler.com/move-ph/159028-mendiola-massacre-anniversary.

7. Conrado de Quiros, *Dance of the Dunces* (Manila: Anvil Publishing, 1991), 51–52.

8. Matt Cowgill and Phu Huynh, "Weak Minimum Wage Compliance in Asia's Garment Industry," International Labour Organization, August 2016, http://www.ilo.org/wcmsp5/groups/public/---asia/---ro-bangkok/documents/publication/wcms_509532.pdf.

9. Nathaniel R. Melican, "57 Kentex Victims' Kin Settle with Firm," *Philippine Daily Inquirer*, June 23, 2015.

10. Associated Press, "More Than 120 Injured in Fire at Philippines Factory Complex," *Star Tribune*, February 2, 2017.

11. Andrea Dijkstra, "Low Wages Draw International Textile Companies to Ethiopia," *Deutsche Wellem*, October 12, 2015, http://www.dw.com/en.

CHAPTER 30—"NO LAND NO LIFE"

1. "Violent Land Disputes Still Hound Agriworkers 30 Years After Mendiola," UMA Pilipinas, January 19, 2017, https://umapilipinas.wordpress.com/2017/01/19/violent-land-disputes-still-hound-agriworkers-30-years-after-mendiola/.

2. Pan Asia Pacific, "An Appeal to Stop Killing Farmers, Lumad Fighting Land Grabs, and Pursue Peace to Address Land Issue as Cause of Conflict in the Philippines," February 7, 2017, http://panap.net/2017/02/nolandnolife-an-appeal-to-stop-killing-farmers-lumad-fighting-land-grabs-and-pursue-peace-to-address-land-issue-as-cause-of-conflict-in-the-philippines/; Pan Asia Pacific "PANAP Joins Solidarity Mission vs. Land Grabbing, Repression of Farmers in Philippine Banana Plantation," December 16, 2016, http://panap.net/2016/12/nolandnolife-panap-joins-solidarity-mission-vs-land-grabbing-repression-farmers-philippine-banana-plantation/.

3. BAYAN, "Summary of Relevant Information," November 16, 2004. http://www.bayan.ph/2004/11/16.

4. Lumad Portal, *To Hacienda Luisita and Back: The Forlorn Journey of the Lumad Sacadas* (Manila: Mindanao Interfaith Institute on Lumad Studies, January 5, 2017), http://www.miils.org/type/reports.

5. Author's visit to Lumad occupation, Manila, November 23, 2015; Katrina Santiago, "Meet the Lumad," *Manila Times*, October 24, 2015; Reynaldo Navales, "Stop Killing Farmers," *SunStar*, April 1, 2017.

6. Ruth Pina and Julia Dolce, "Spectacular Protest of Landless Women," *Dawn News*, March 7, 2017.

7. "Landless Women Denounce Vale," March 8, 2017, Friends of the MST, http://www.mstbrazil.org/news.

8. Michael Fox, *Landless Women Stage Protests Across Brazil*, NACLA report (March 2009).

9. "Bharatiya Kisan Union Backs Protesting Tamil Nadu Farmers in Delhi; Call That Demands Be Met Immediately," Focus on the Global South, March 28, 2017, https://focusweb.org/content/bharatiya-kisan-union-backs-protesting-tamil-nadu-farmers-delhi-call-demands-be-met.

10. "FTAs and Agriculture," *Nyéléni Newsletter*, March 29, 2017; "Five Indian Farmers Killed During Protest," *Al Jazeera*, June 6, 2017.

11. Tom Philpott, "No, GMOs Didn't Create India's Farmer Suicide Problem, But . . . ," *Mother Jones*, September 30, 2015.

12. Tinyade Kachika, *Land Grabbing in Africa: A Review of the Impacts and Possible Policy Responses* (Oxford, UK: Oxfam International, 2010), 42.

13. Khuon Nairm, "Government Threatens Land Rights Protesters," *Cambodia Daily*, March 27, 2017.

14. "ChavezResist Marches," United Farm Workers, http://ufw.org/chavezresist-marches, accessed October 6, 2017.

15. PAN AP, *The Right to Resist Land Grabs*, film, posted on YouTube March 29, 2017.

16. Elizabeth Mpofu/La Via Campesina, "Building an International Movement for Food and Seed Sovereignty," *Other Worlds*, 2016, http://africaspeaks4africa.org/7592-2/, accessed October 10, 2017.

17. "Manifesto: Rights of Peasants," La Via Campesina, March 17, 2017, www.viacampesina.org.

18. "The Time Is Ripe," La Via Campesina, May 22, 2017.

CHAPTER 31—"AGRARIAN REFORM IN REVERSE"

1. David Adam, "Food Price Rises Threaten Global Security," *Guardian*, April 9, 2008.

2. Till Bruckner, "The Myth of the African Land Grab," *Foreign Policy*, October 20, 2015; Lutz Goedde, Maya Horii, and Sunil Sanghvi, "Pursuing the Global Opportunity in Food and Agribusiness," *McKinsey Quarterly* (July 2015), http://www.mckinsey.com.

3. "The Global Farmland Grab in 2016: How Big, How Bad?," *Against the Grain*, June 2016.

4. Carolyn Kamm, "Why European Dairy Farmers Are Protesting," *Christian Science Monitor*, February 12, 2017.

5. "Asia's Agrarian Reform in Reverse," *Against the Grain*, April 2015; "Will Cambodia's Kleptocrats Finally Face Justice?," *Cultural Survival*, November 28, 2016.

6. David Blair, "Liberia Sells Almost Quarter of Country to Logging," *Telegraph*, September 4, 2012.

7. Kachika, *Land Grabbing in Africa*; T. S. Jayne et al., "Africa's Changing Farmland Ownership," July 24, 2015, unpublished paper, UN Economic Commission for Africa conference; K. Deininger et al., *Rising Global Interest in Farmland: Can It Yield Sustainable and Equitable Benefits?* (Washington, DC: World Bank Publications, 2011); K. Deininger,

X. Fan, and S. Savastano, "Smallholders' Land Ownership and Access in Sub-Saharan Africa," Policy Research Working Paper 7285, World Bank, 2015.

8. Antonio Onorati and Chiara Pierfederici, "Land Concentration, Land Grabbing and People's Struggles in Europe," 2012, https://www.tni.org/files/download/05._italy .pdf; "Biggest Farms in the World," http://www.worldatlas.com/articles.

9. "Europe: Land Concentration and Land Grabbing Reaching Blatant Levels," La Via Campesina, August 19, 2013.

10. Nafeez Ahmed, "UN: Only Small Farmers and Agroecology Can Feed the World," *Permaculture News*, September 26, 2014.

11. ILO, "Labor Migration Statistics," http://www.ilo.org/global/topics/labour -migration/policy-areas/statistics/lang--en/index.htm, accessed October 10, 2017.

12. Madison Iszler, "Could a 7-Year-Old Have Picked the Food You're Eating?," *News & Observer*, July 8, 2017.

13. Svetlana Boincean, *Workers and Unions on the Move: Organising and Defending Migrant Workers in Agricultural and Allied Sectors* (Geneva: IUF-UITA-IUL, May 2008), http://www.iufdocuments.org/www/documents/IUFmigrantworkersmanual-e.pdf; Helena Smith, "Bangladeshi Fruit Pickers Shot At by Greek Farmers Win Human Rights Case," *Guardian*, March 30, 2017.

CHAPTER 32—MILK WITH DIGNITY

1. "Selected Statistics on Farmworkers," Farmworker Justice, 2014, https://www.farm workerjustice.org/sites/default/files/NAWS%20data%20factsht%201-13-15FINAL.pdf.

2. Kyle Midura, "How Trump's Immigration Policies Could Reshape Vermont Dairy Industry," WCAX-TV, January 26, 2017.

3. Jonathan Purdy to Brady Goff, October 30, 2014, posted online October 12, 2016, Migrant Justice, https://migrantjustice.net/news/ice-to-vermont-dmv-were-going-to-have -to-make-you-an-honorary-ice-officer; Paul Heintz, "Vermont DMV, State Police Play Nice with ICE," *Seven Days*, April 5, 2017.

4. Greg Asbed and Sean Sellers, "The Fair Food Program: Worker-Driven Social Responsibility for the 21st Century," *TalkPoverty*, May 27, 2014; Coalition of Imakolee Workers, http://www.ciw-online.org/about.

5. Richard Mertens, "Tomato Pickers Win Higher Pay. Can Other Workers Use Their Strategy?," *Christian Science Monitor*, March 9, 2017; Robbie Silverman, "A Big Win for Poultry Workers," *The Politics of Poverty*, Oxfam, April 26, 2017.

6. Migrant Justice, "Milk with Dignity," video on Vimeo, https://vimeo.com /128623142.

7. Sarah Olsen, "Ben & Jerry's Agrees to Negotiate 'Milk with Dignity' Agreement," *VTDigger*, June 21, 2015.

8. "VT Dairy Workers Announce Northeast Milk with Dignity Speaking Tour!," March 16, 2017, https://migrantjustice.net/news/vt-dairy-workers-announce-northeast -milk-with-dignity-speaking-tour.

9. *Silenced Voices*, a film by Sam Mayfield, Brendan O'Neill, and Gustavo Ter'an, March 10, 2014, available at https://www.youtube.com/watch?v=Q3DRQVbV6LM; "RFC and Stanford Students Team Up with Milk with Dignity," Real Food Challenge, February 23, 2017, http://realfoodchallenge.org.

10. "Presbyterian Church to Ben & Jerry's," June 27, 2017, https://migrantjustice net; Michael Colby and Will Allen, "Sweatshop Dairy," http://regenerationvermont.org /regeneration-now.

11. Noam Scheiber, "Ben & Jerry's Strikes Deal to Improve Migrant Workers' Conditions," *New York Times*, October 3, 2017; "'It's a New Day in Dairy': Migrant Justice, Ben & Jerry's Sign Agreement to Launch Milk with Dignity Program in Vermont Dairy Industry!," Coalition of Immokalee Workers, October 3, 2017, http://www.ciw-online .org/blog/2017/10/its-a-new-day-in-dairy.

CHAPTER 33—"LIKE THE TIME OF CESAR CHAVEZ"
1. Larry Copeland, "Life Expectancy in the USA Hits a Record High," *USA Today*, October 8, 2014, https://www.usatoday.com/story/news/nation/2014/10/08/us-life -expectancy-hits-record-high/16874039; Dylan Ruiz and Joseph Smooke, "Surviving the Drought in California," June 15, 2015, *People, Power, Media*, http://www.peoplepowermedia .net/immigration/california-drought-farm-workers.
2. All quotes from interview with Bernardino Martinez, Oxnard, CA, September 6, 2015.
3. "California: Wages, EFI, FLCs," *Rural Migration News*, July 2013, https://migration .ucdavis.edu/rmn/more.php?id=1764.
4. José Luis Rocha, "Strawberry Fields and Undocumented Workers Forever?," *Envío*, June 2008; Vernon Takeshita, "America's Strawberry: Fruit of Our Labor," *Japanese American National Museum Magazine*, October 3, 2007.
5. Tomás Madrigal, "The Role of the Private Security Industrial Complex in 21st-Century Agricultural Strike Breaking," *Káráni: Escribir o Volar*, June 18, 2016.
6. State of California, Agricultural Labor Relations Board, Moving Party and United Farm Workers of America and Constantino Rodriguez, Charging Parties v. Montalvo Farms, LLC, Respondent, May 7, 2012, pp. 4–5.
7. Rebekah Kearn, "Labor Board Alleges Vicious Anti-Unionism," Courthouse News Service, May 22, 2012, https://www.courthousenews.com/labor-board-alleges-vicious -anti-unionism.

CHAPTER 34—BITTER GRAPES
1. Henriette Abrahams, "Farm Workers Are Still Fighting for Dignity and Their Rights in the Western Cape," *Ground Up*, February 20, 2015.
2. Mercia Andrews, "Sleeping Giant Is Stirring: Farm Workers in South Africa," 2014, South African History Online, http://www.sahistory.org.za/article/western-cape-farm -workers-strike-2012-2013.
3. Mandy de Waal, "Striking Workers Burn Vineyards," *Guardian*, November 8, 2012.
4. Sean Christie, "Leaderless Farm Strike Is 'Organic,'" *Mail & Guardian*, November 16, 2012, available at www.mg.co.za.
5. Annie Majavu, "The Farm Workers' Strike, It's Far from Over," South African Civil Society Information Service, November 15, 2012.
6. Kaitlin Cordes and Clive Baldwin, *Ripe with Abuse: Human Rights Conditions in South Africa's Fruit and Wine Industries* (New York: Human Rights Watch, August 23, 2011).
7. Aruna Rao, Joanne Sandler, and David Kelleher, *Gender at Work: Theory and Practice for 21st Century Organizations* (London: Routledge, 2015).

CHAPTER 35—"WHAT ARE WE RISING FOR?"
1. "Sakuma Farmworkers: We Want a Contract!," October 8, 2013, The Stand: News About Working People Standing Together in Washington State, http://www.thestand.org /2013/10.

2. Tomás Madrigal, "Driscoll's Notorious Record on Labor," *Káráni: Escribir o Volar*, November 17, 2014.

3. Interview with Juvenal Solano and Alfreda (pseudonym), Oxnard, CA, September 7, 2015.

4. Dan LaBotz, "Important Strike in Mexico," *Global Research*, April 3, 2015.

5. David Bacon, "Farmworker Rebellion Spreads," *People's World*, August 31, 2015.

6. Information Supplement, *La Jornada*, July 18, 2015.

7. Ibid.

8. Richard Marosi, "Baja Labor Leaders Learned Their Tactics from Their Efforts in US," *Los Angeles Times*, March 28, 2015.

9. Marcos F. Lopez, "Places in Production: Nature, Farm Work and Farm Worker Resistance in US and Mexican Strawberry Growing Regions," PhD diss., University of California, Santa Cruz, 2011; Richard Marosi, "Mexican Farmworkers Target Driscoll's," *Los Angeles Times*, April 10, 2015; Tomás Madrigal, "The Costco Connection," *Káráni: Escribir o Volar*, June 28, 2015.

10. "Farmworkers Win Big Maybe," editorial, *Los Angeles Times*, June 11, 2015.

11. "Washington Farmworkers Union Ends Boycott," *North West Labor Press*, November 14, 2016.

12. Interview with Irene Gomez, Oxnard, CA, September 6, 2015.

CHAPTER 36—"THESE BORDERS ARE NOT OUR BORDERS"

1. Interview with Arcenio Lopez, Oxnard, CA, September 5, 2015.

2. Interview with Anastacia Lopez, Oxnard, CA, September 7, 2015.

3. Michelle Venetucci Harvey, "The Farmworkers' Journey: NAFTA, Agricultural Exceptionalism and California Farmworkers," *Spinning Spoons*, February 16, 2012; Laura Carlsen, "Under NAFTA, Mexico Suffered and the United States Felt Its Pain," *New York Times*, November 24, 2013.

4. Rocha, "Strawberry Fields and Undocumented Workers Forever?"; Miriam J. Wells, *Strawberry Fields: Politics, Class, and Work in California Agriculture* (Ithaca, NY: Cornell University Press, 1996); Julie Guthman, "Life Itself Under Contract: Rent-Seeking and Biopolitical Devolution Through Partnerships in California's Strawberry Industry," *Journal of Peasant Studies* 40, no. 1 (2017): 100–17, posted online October 28, 2016.

5. MICOP, *2016 Annual Report* (December 2016), www.mixteco.org/2016/12/micops-2016-annual-report/.

6. Interview with Maricela Vargas, Santa Barbara, CA, September 7, 2015.

CHAPTER 37—AFTER THE COLONIZERS, RICE

1. All quotes from interview with Vicky Carlos Garcia, Manila, November 21, 2015, and electronic correspondence, November 2016–April 2017.

2. All Mary Hensley quotes from telephone interview, March 17, 2017.

3. Simone Adler, "An Interview with Elizabeth Mpofu," *Other Worlds*, February 2, 2016.

4. Ibid.; "Land and Seed Laws Under Attack," GRAIN, January 21, 2015, https://www.grain.org/article/entries/5121-land-and-seed-laws-under-attack-who-is-pushing-changes-in-africa.

5. "The Global Staple," *Ricepedia*, Project of Global Rice Science Partnership, http://ricepedia.org/rice-as-food/the-global-staple-rice-consumers, accessed October 10, 2017.

6. "Bill Clinton's Trade Policies Destroyed Haitian Rice Farming," *Democracy Now!*, October 11, 2016, https://www.democracynow.org/2016/10/11/bill_clinton_s_trade_policies_destroyed.

7. "Rice Varieties Critical to Culture and Biodiversity at Risk of Extinction," *Food Tank*, December 2014, https://foodtank.com/news/2014/12/heirloom-rice-in-the -philippines-at-risk-of-extinction.

8. Alaric Francis Santiaguel, "The Seed Keepers' Treasure," *Rice Today* (October–December 2010).

9. Robert Domoguen, "Remembering the Old Suyoc Village and Its Generation of Rice Growers," *SunStar Baguio*, March 9, 2011; "Rice Terraces of the Philippine Cordilleras," UNESCO World Heritage List, 1992–2017, http://whc.unesco.org/en/list/722 /multiple=1&unique_number=853.

10. Robert Domoguen, "Cordillera Losing Its Heirloom Rice Varieties," *SunStar Baguio*, February 28, 2011.

11. Alisa Tang, "Malaria, Murder and Occupational Hazards of Indigenous Activists in the Philippines," Reuters World News, November 1, 2016.

12. "The PAKISAMA: Our Mother Organization," PAKISAMA Mutual Benefit Association, http://pakisamamutual.tripod.com/pksm/id12.html, accessed October 10, 2017; La Via Campesina, "Stop Land Grabbing in the Philippines!," March 18, 2014, https://focusweb.org/content/stop-land-grabbing-philippines-statement-la-campesina.

CHAPTER 38—"WE CAN TURN AROUND THE LABOR MOVEMENT.
WE CAN REBUILD POWER AND WE CAN WIN!"

1. Interview with Madeline Janis, Los Angeles, September 9, 2015; Harold Myerson, "LA Story," *American Prospect*, August 6, 2013.

CHAPTER 39—FLASHES OF HOPE

1. Alaa Milbes, "Labor and Community Groups Sign Landmark Agreement," Jobs to Move America, July 17, 2017, http://jobstomoveamerica.org/labor-community-groups -sign-landmark-agreement-electric-bus-manufacturer-byd-los-angeles.

2. Tony Barboza, "Plan Calls for L.A., Long Beach Ports to Go to Zero-Emissions Technology," *Los Angeles Times*, July 19, 2017.

3. Corilyn Shropshire, "First Step to New CTA Rail Cars," *Chicago Tribune*, March 16, 2017.

4. Alaa Milbes, "MTA Commits to U.S. Jobs," Jobs to Move America, July 17, 2016, http:// jobstomoveamerica.org/mta-commits-u-s-jobs-new-3-2-billion-subway-car-purchase.

5. Ibid.

6. Alaa Milbes, "JMA to LA Metro on $1 Billion Purchase of Heavy Railcars," Jobs to Move America, January 11, 2016, http://jobstomoveamerica.org/press-release-jma-to-la -metro-on-1-billion-purchase-of-heavy-railcars.

7. "Our Story," Township Winery, http://townshipwinery.com/our-story.

8. Martin Seemungal, "Cape Town's Urban Vineyard Could Revitalize the City's Poor," *NewsHour*, PBS, November 24, 2016.

9. Pumza Filani, "The Wine Grown in a South African Township," BBC News, December 10, 2015.

10. "Love Is in Our Nature," Thandi Wines, http://thandiwines.com.

11. "About," United States Federation of Worker Cooperatives, https://usworker .coop/about.

12. United States Environmental Protection Agency, "Methyl Bromide," unsigned article, https://www.epa.gov/ods-phaseout/methyl-bromide.

13. "Jim Cochran: Swanton Berry Farm, Cultivating a Movement: An Oral History Series on Sustainable Agriculture and Organic Farming on California's Central Coast,"

University of California, Santa Cruz, Special Collections online, https://library.ucsc.edu/reg-hist/cultiv/home.

14. "History," Swanton Berry Farm, unsigned article, http://www.swantonberryfarm.com/history.

15. "USDA Seeks Applications for Next Round of Food Insecurity Nutrition Program," press release no. 022816, https://www.fns.usda.gov/pressrelease/2016/022816.

16. "Fresh Food Box Locations," Greenmarkets, GrowNYC, https://www.grownyc.org/greenmarketco/foodbox.

17. Eric Holt-Giménez and Miguel Altieri, "Agroecology 'Lite': Cooptation and Resistance in the Global North," Food First, October 18, 2016, https://foodfirst.org/agroecology-lite-cooptation-and-resistance-in-the-global-north.

18. "Global Brands, NGOs, and the Prince of Wales Unite," Better Cotton Initiative, May 26, 2017, http://bettercotton.org.

19. Joe Bozich, "Knights Apparel's Ethical Business Model: The Alta Gracia Project: Changing Lives One Shirt at a Time," https://www.changemakers.com/intrapreneurs/entries/knights-apparels-ethical-business-model-alta-gracia-pro.

20. Ibid.

21. Joanne Lamphere Beckham, "Good Business," *Vanderbilt Magazine*, December 2, 2013.

22. "About Us," Tonlé, https://tonle.com.

23. Chris Teare, "College Students Are Starting to Demand 'Living Wage' Sportswear," *Forbes*, March 31, 2016.

24. Clean Clothes Campaign, "Bangladesh Accord: Brief Progress Report and Proposals for Enhancement," April 21, 2017, https://cleanclothes.org.

CHAPTER 40—BIG IDEAS, NEW MODELS, SMALL COURTESIES
BUILD A NEW WORLD

1. Interview with Madeline Janis, Los Angeles, September 9, 2015.

2. Telephone interview with Roxana Tynan, September 15, 2015.

3. Julian Gross, Greg LeRoy, and Madeline Janis-Aparicio, *Community Benefits Agreements: Making Development Projects Accountable* (Washington, DC: Good Jobs First and California Partnership for Working Families, 2005).

4. "Yale-New Haven CBA," Community Benefits Agreements, January 30, 2008, http://communitybenefits.blogspot.com/2008/01/yale-new-haven-cba.html.

INDEX

Abrahams, Henriette, 207, 209–10
Adidas, response to organizer demands, 152
adjunct professors. *See* contract labor; graduate students, efforts to unionize; teachers, professors, as low-wage workers
agribusiness: in Baja, Mexico, 213–14; bioengineered seeds, 228, 230; dependence on migrant workers, 13, 190; industrial/plantation techniques, 182–84, 188–89; and loss of arable land, 231; and the new "Green Revolution," 187, 190, 228–29; and wage slavery, 185, 191, 194, 207, 209. *See also* farmworkers; land theft; migrant workers/undocumented migrants
Agricultural Labor Relations Board (ALRB), California, 203
agroecology practices, 230–31, 233, 248–49
Aguinaldo, Emilio, 234
airport workers, 79–80
Akhter, Nazma, 139–40
Akter, Kalpona: campaign against workplace violence, 55; changing view of activists, 49; organizing strategies and activities, 32, 37, 39–41, 116, 118–19; 146–47; on the Rana Plaza factory collapse, 135; retaliation against, 139; sponsors, 39; and the Tazreen factory fire, 137–38; on working conditions for Bangladeshi garment workers, 119–20, 131–34, 136–37. *See also* Bangladesh Fire and Safety Accord; garment industry
Alfreda, Zapoteca migrant field-worker, 213–14, 222
alcohol, as wages, 19, 209
ALEC (American Legislative Exchange Council), 81–82, 96, 255

Allen, Will, 197
Alliance of Progressive Labor, 49, 63, 167, 173–74
Alta Gracia Project, Dominican Republic, 249–50
Altieri, Miguel, 248–49
Amazon, working conditions at, 103
American Legislative Exchange Council (ALEC), 81–82, 96, 255
amnesty programs, for migrant workers, 219, 224
Anacapa, frozen berry distributor, 202
Apartheid Group Areas Act of 1950, 244
Aquino, Benigno, III, 180–81
Aquino, Corazon, 172, 180, 235
Aran, Virgilio, 57–59
Arcos Dorados (McDonald's in Brazil), court case against, 73–74
Arroyo, Gloria Macabal, 180
Arthur Svensson International Prize, 154–56
Asbed, Greg, 253
ASEAN-India trade pact, 183
Asia Floor Wage, 152
Asian Indigenous Peoples Pact, 231–32
Asian Peasants' Coalition, "Day of the Landless" actions, 183–84
Ath Thorn, 135, 152, 155–57
Atienza, Em, 45, 49, 99, 240

Bagong Silangan *barangay* dancers, 62–63
Baja California, Mexico, berry picking, 16, 213–15, 216–17
Baker, Ella, 59
Balcazar, Enrique "Kike," 192–93, 195, 197–99
Bangladesh: garment industry in, 119–20, 123–24, 134; minimum wage increases, 141; monitoring of social media in, 44;

organizers/activists in, 45, 139–40, 145, 147; preferential trade status, 19–20; response to protests, 128, 148, 158; Tuba Group demonstrators, 143. *See also* Bangladesh Fire and Safety Accord; garment workers

Bangladesh Center for Worker Solidarity, 138, 146

Bangladesh Fire and Safety Accord: enforcement challenges, 124; focus on pressure at the top of the supply chain, 195; impacts, 124, 128, 140, 251–53; signatories to, 118–19

Bangladesh Garment Manufacturers and Exporters Association (BGMEA), 142, 143, 144

Barber, William, II, 33, 94

Barbero, Rosanna, 163

Barlage, Denise: achievements, 32, 111; on continuing to fight, 259; friendships and shared activism, 113–15; hunger strikes, 86–88, 94; on importance of a living wage, 12, 89; and OUR Walmart, 29–30; Walmart policies and working conditions, 105–7

Bataan Export Processing Zone (BEPZ), 170–72

Battle of Seattle, 1999, 5

Beach, Carolyn "Polly," 76

beer promoters, Cambodia, 17–20

Bellamy, Cole, 66

Bello, Walden, 45

Ben & Jerry's, 195–99

berry farming, organic, 246

BerryMex, 214–25

berry pickers: challenges of organizing, 202–5; interconnections among, 213; ongoing goals and needs, 217; Swanton Berry Farm labor practices, 246. *See also* farmworkers; indigenous workers/activists; Sakuma berry strike and boycott; San Quintín Valley berry pickers strike

Binos, Asuncion "Sion," 55, 126, 167–68, 171, 173–78

biodiversity vs. bioengineering, 228–30

bioengineered seeds, 228, 230

Bitter Grapes (documentary), 210

Black Lives Matter activism, 59, 73, 94

Black Panthers, 73, 76

Boal, Iain, 45–46

Boston, Massachusetts, UNITE HERE actions in, 26–27

Bozich, Joe, 249–50

bracero program, 218, 220. *See also* farmworkers

Brazil: court case against Arcos Dorados, 73–74; port and oil workers' work stoppages in, 73; Senate hearings on McDonald's, 9, 36; struggles over land ownership, 182

Brito, Santa, 25–26, 83–85

Brooks, Kwanza, 100–101

Brown, Michael, 72

Buckner, Ann, 65

Burrow, Sharan, 54

Bustos, Edwin, 24

Butler, Laphonza, 27, 81

BYD (electric-vehicle manufacturer), 242

Cabot Creamery (Agri-Mark), 197

Cáceres, Berta, 43, 46

California Agricultural Labor Relations Board, 16

California United Long-Term Care Workers Union, 27

call center workers, 100

Cambodia: beer promoters, 17–20; destruction of small farms in, 184; "fast fashion"/garment industry, 123–26, 149–50; Food and Service Workers' Federation (CFSWF), 18–19; hotel housekeepers, 22; Pol Pot regime, 155; responses to garment worker protests, 128, 151–53, 158; Tonlé apparel manufacturing, 250–51; urban population growth, 161. *See also* export-processing zones (EPZs); garment workers

Cambodian Alliance of Trade Unions, 157–58

Cambodia National Rescue Party, 150

Cambodian Coalition of Apparel Workers Democratic Union (CCAWDU), 155–56

Cambodian Food and Service Workers' Federation (CFSWF), 18–19
Cambodian Labor Department, 151–52
Cambodian National Rescue Party, 154
Cambrew (beer company), Cambodia, 17–20
campus unions, 91
Cape Flat, South Africa, renewal of wine production in, 244
Carling, Joan, 231–32
Carlsberg Beer, labor practices, 19–20
Carl's Jr. labor practices, 72
Carnegie, Andrew, "Gospel of Wealth," 5
Carrillo-Sanchez, Alex, 192, 198
Carson, Rachel, 246
Catamin, Lei, 63
Cavite Export Processing Zone, Manila, 166–67, 174–75
CBAs (community benefits agreements), 254, 256–57, 258
Central Coast Alliance United for a Sustainable Economy (CAUSE), 225
Chavez, Cesar, 89, 200, 215, 246
Chea Mony, 153–56
Chea Vichea, 154
Chhim Sitthar, 22–24, 28, 45
chicken processing companies, actions against, 195
children: care for as part of organizing strategies, 163; as farmworkers, 190–91; as garment workers, 128; low-cost clothing for, 136; of migrants, and parents' deportation, 198; as reason for migration, 174–75
Children's Place (clothing manufacturer), 136
China: expansion of agribusiness and farmer displacement in, 13–14, 188; marketizing of China, 43; as rice importer, 230; rice plantations in Africa, 184; "Wal-Maoism" in, 103
Christian faith, fusion with activism, 14–15, 49, 70, 77
civil disobedience, 11, 33, 90
CIW. See Coalition of Immokalee Workers (CIW)
Clark, Lauralyn, 33, 75

Clark, Septima, 59
Clean Clothes Campaign, 39, 251–52
Clergy & Laity United for Economic Justice (CLUE), 94, 114–15
Clinton, Bill, 131, 229–30
coalition building/globalized activism: agroecological movements, 183–84, 194–95, 214, 221, 248–49; as key to modern activism, 24, 28, 47, 94–97, 155–56, 167, 240–41, 257–59; and link between civil rights and labor rights, 75–76; as response to a globalized economy, 19, 43, 47, 49–50, 97–98, 167. See also social movement activism
Coalition of Immokalee Workers (CIW): assistance for the organizers of the San Quintín berry pickers, 214; on employer conducted safety checks, 119; gains for tomato field-workers, 194–95; organizing model, global applications, 195; strategic approach, 194
Cochran, Jim, 246–48
collective ownership, 244–46
Collins, Barbara, 111–12
Communist Manifesto (Marx), 86
community benefits agreements (CBAs), 254, 256–57, 258
community benefits movement, 256–57
conflict minerals, 50
Congress of Industrial Organizations (CIO), 97
Conklin, Wim, 155
consciousness-raising/peer discussions: education using, 58, 160, 210; empowerment from, 56, 224; and global organizing efforts, 147. See also education
construction workers, hazards faced by, 22
consumers: consumer boycotts, 41, 216; educating, 158–59, 164; and fast-fashion industry, 129; focusing actions on, 194, 210–11; and ubiquity of low prices, 6; and ready availability of fresh produce, 220
contract labor: call center workers, 100; fast-food workers, 99–100; fostering solidarity among, 66–67; garment

workers, 177; and the "gig" economy, 68; grape pickers, 209; and low wages, 67–68; as product of globalization, 68, 167; as strategy for avoiding corporate responsibility, 177; teachers, 66, 79, 91

Contreras, Miguel, 254

Conway, Jill Ker, 130

Cooper Union, New York, 37

Cordillera region, Philippines: heirloom rice project, 231, 233; indigenous farming communities, 227, 232; migration from, 232; traditional agroecology practices, rice rituals, 230–31; as a UNESCO "Globally Important Agricultural Heritage Site," 231

corn production, Mexico, impact of NAFTA, 15–16

Corona, Bert ("El Viejo"), 94

Coronacion, Joanna Bernice ("Sister Nice"): concept of freedom, 12; on contractualizing fast-food workers, 99; and DUBS, 63; education, 48–49; on globalized social movement activism, 97; on need to dismantle patriarchy, 48; on wage theft, 101

corporations/transnational corporate imperialism: and corporate wealth, 4–5; and industrialized agribusiness, 13–14; and neoliberalism, 5. *See also* agribusiness; McDonald's; Walmart; *and other multinational corporations and industries*

COSATU (South African trade union federation), 93

Cosecha (Harvest) activists, 198

cotton production, transformation of, 249

coyotes (human smugglers), 219

Creech, Chrissy, 104

Crenshaw Walmart, Los Angeles, Girshriela Green's experience working at, 102

Cruise, Tom, 32

Cruz, Evelin: death, 111; and the Pico Rivera Walmart strike, 29, 115; response to managers' bullying, 107–8; on the struggle for justice, 259; work with OUR Walmart, 30

Cruz, Mariano, 83–84

dairy farming: mega-dairies, 189–90; migrant workers, 195–96. *See also* agribusiness

Dancers' Union of Bagong Silangan (DUBS), 63

danger zone areas, Manila, 62

Day of Disruption, 2016, 69

"Day of the Landless" actions, 183–84

debts, national, and corporate control over poorer nations, 6

Deida, Lyle, 192

Deida, Lymarie, 198

Dembélé, Antoinette, 184

Democratic Republic of Congo, sexual violence in, 50

Deng Xiaoping, 43

Department of Motor Vehicles (DMV), Vermont, cooperation with ICE, 193

de Quiro, Conrado, 173

Dhaka, Bangladesh, garment factory, 40, 134, 148

Diamond Island, Cambodia, NagaWorld Casino, 22

Diaz, Victor, 196

Dina (Cambodian Worker Information Center facilitator), 162–64

Disneyland workers, hunger strikes by, 90

divorce rights, 50

domestic workers: invisibility, 21; in Manila, organizing approaches, 52–53; working conditions, 52. *See also* home-healthcare workers; hotel housekeepers

Drayton, Canute, 12, 79–80

Driscoll berries: BerryMex affiliate, 214; costs of San Quintín strike to, 215; international organizing efforts, 16; small farmer partners, 202; and strawberry production, 219–20. *See also* berry pickers; migrant workers/undocumented migrants; San Quintín Valley berry pickers strike

DUBS. *See* Dancers' Union of Bagong Silangan (DUBS)

Dukes, Betty, 106

Duncan, Ruby, 56, 77

Durazo, María Elena: civil disobedience, 90; coalition building, 95–96, 240; and the founding of LAANE, 254; and hotel ownership issues, 25; organizing strategies, 89–90, 95; and paths to citizenship, 28; on power of activist youth, 45; on reasonable workloads for hotel housekeepers, 26; union building, 93–95

Duterte, Rodrigo, 169, 176, 181

Ebenezer Baptist Church, Atlanta, 75–76
Economic Policy Institute, 100
Edmundson, Hilde, 70
education: of consumers, 158–59, 164; of workers, 57–59, 63, 76, 160, 163–64. *See also* consciousness-raising/peer discussions; labor organizers/activists
Eiker, Richard, 70
ejido common lands, Mexico, 45–46
Employee Free Choice Act, 96
"End Our Pain, *No Más Dolor*" rallies, Providence, 85
Ethiopia, labor laws in, 178
European Union, agricultural subsidies and farm consolidation, 189–90
Everson, David, 210–11
export-processing zones (EPZs): establishment 170; low-wage workers in, 173; in the Philippines, 132, 166–67; working and living conditions in, 127–29, 171. *See also* garment workers

Facebook, as organizing tool, 65
Fair Food Program (CIW), 194
Fair Food Standards Council, Florida, 194–95
Familias Unidas por la Justicia (Families United for Justice), 213
Family Medical Leave Act, 106–8
Farfan, Mary Carmen, 87
farmworker-activists: courage shown by, 191–92; Farm Labor Organizing Committee, 184–85; "Farmworker Bill of Rights," 224–25; *horas y cajas* (hours and boxes) pay system, 201; Mexican

berry pickers strike, 13, 15; organizing challenges, 202; protests against free trade pacts, 183; resistance and violence faced by, 16, 191; United Farm Workers, 28, 89–90, 84–95, 200–5
farmworkers: dependence on by agribusiness, 190–91; international organizing efforts, 16; laws affecting, 224; life expectancy, 200; and a path to citizenship, 16; working and living conditions, 180, 185, 189, 191, 200, 246. *See also* agribusiness; migrant workers/ undocumented migrants; United Farm Workers (UFW); *specific types of agricultural production*
fashion show protest, Cambodian garment workers, 121–23
"fast fashion." *See* garment industry
fast-food workers: contractualization of, 99; Day of Disruption actions, 70–71; on-demand scheduling, 44; global actions and solidarity, 35, 7–74; organizing strategies and activities, 11, 34–35, 49; and student guest workers, 35. *See also* Fight for $15 movement; McDonald's
"Fast for $15" hunger strikes, 88
"Fate of Garment Workers" (Messenger Band), 131
Faulkner, Tyfani, 87, 94–95, 112, 114–16
feminist activists, 48–55, 105, 121, 208, 210. *See also* women
Fernandez, Eloy, 215
Ferraris, Ylleny, 83–84
Fight for $15 movement: coalition building, 94; and contract/part-time labor, 100; determination, 70; educational workshops, 75; origins, 33, 44, 96–97; participants' backgrounds, 65–66;
Fight for a Fair Economy, 96
flash strikes/flash mobs, 11, 35, 64
Flores, Norma, 90
Florida, worker-run farm labor inspections, 194
food, as wages, 191, 209
Food Chain Workers' Bill of Rights, 248

food costs: and access to fresh, affordable food, 248; and agribusiness/bioengineering, 229; following creation of the Bataan EPZ, 171; and hunger among low-wage workers, 88–89, 174–75, 187; and the living wage movement, 165; and meeting nutritional needs, 88; rising, in face of corporate farm consolidation, 190; and use of Food Stamps among low-wage workers, 7; and workers' participation in the Food Stamp program, 88. *See also* living wage movement

Food Justice certification, 246

Food Policy Councils, 248

food-service workers, 79

Foxx, Anthony, 243

Frattini, Massimo, 21, 24, 27–28, 35, 56

freedom fighters, 75

freedom schools, 59

Free Trade Union of Workers of the Kingdom of Cambodia (FTU), 149, 153–54

Friedman, Thomas, 71

Gallin, Dan, 97

Gandhi, Mahatma, 89–91

Gap (clothing manufacturer), 152, 253

Garcia, Vicky Carlos, 13, 227–28, 230, 232–35, 237

garment industry: environmental costs, 127; ethical apparel manufacturing, 249–50; globalization of, 123–27, 139; profits and earnings, 164–65; "run-away shops," 129; response to worker demands, 37, 145, 153–56, 171–73, 175; use of migrant workers, 161. *See also* export-processing zones (EPZs); *specific garment factories*

garment workers: achievements, 172–73, 251–52; bravery in face of state violence, 154–56, 171–73; as contract workers, 177; costs of living, 132–33, 150; educating about global supply chains, 164; exposure to toxic chemicals, 2, 146, 160, 165, 251 factory fires, 136–39; and fast-fashion production techniques, 128; forced labor, 128;

Girl Effect campaign/foundation, 130–31; global vision, 174; hunger and mental illness among, 146; identifying manufacturers, challenges of, 149–50; labor laws and protections, 169–70; living wage rallies, 173; minimum wage increases, 172; New York strike, 1909, 38; organizing strategies and actions, 39–41, 53–54, 121–22, 139–40, 148, 154; production quotas, 131; protests organized against the Tuba Group, 142–45; risks faced by, 37; and union tradition, 169; working conditions, 39–40, 119, 126–28, 132, 134, 149, 166–68, 170. *See also* Bangladesh Fire and Safety Accord

Garment Workers Unity Forum, 141–42, 146, 160, 165, 251

Garner, Eric, 59, 72–73

Ghana, farmworker protests in, 184

"gig economy," 68

Girl Effect campaign/foundation (Nike), 130–33

Global Day of Action to Stop Gender-Based Violence in the Workplace, 54

globalization: and changing patterns of corporate ownership and management, 25; as "good" for female workers, 130; and low-priced goods, 6, 128–29. *See also* agribusiness; coalition building/globalized activism; garment industry; neoliberalism; and *specific countries and corporations*

Global Peasants' Rights Congress, 185

GMO (genetically modified) crops, 229–30

Gomez, Irene, 217, 222–24

Gomez, Thelma, 197

Gonzalves, Rudy, 243

Gorbea, Nellie, 85

graduate students, efforts to unionize, 67, 79, 90–91

Great Peasants' War, 185

Great Recession, 2008, 7

Green, Girshriela, 102–4, 106, 110–11

Greenberg, Aaron, 91

Greenpeace, 229
GrowNYC initiative, 248
Guangzhou, China, garment workers in, 129
Guáqueta, Alexandra, 194
Guttal, Shalmali, 54

H&M (clothing manufacturer), 122, 151–52, 249, 253
Häagen-Dazs ice cream boycott, 216
Hacienda Luisita sugarcane plantation, Philippines, 180
Hamer, Fannie Lou, 34
Hampton, Fred, 73
Hanauer, Ana, 182
Happy Happy program, 164
Harvest of Shame (documentary), 194
Hasina, Sheikh, xiii, 148
Henry, Mary Kay, 96
Hensley, Mary, 228–34, 236
Herrera, Justino, 215
Hicks, Rusty, 27, 93
Hil Chandy, 123
Holmes, Bene't, 105
Holt-Giménez, Eric, 248–49
home-healthcare workers: challenges faced by, 70; as part of the living wage movement, 33, 65; wage increases, 78; working conditions, 65
horas y cajas (hours and boxes) pay system, 201
hospital workers, unionizing of, 78–79
Hossain, Delwar, 141, 143–44
hotel housekeepers: $15 wage initiative, 83; global organizing/activism among, 24; health risks/working conditions, 21, 24–26, 83–85; and identifying hotel ownership, 25; invisibility of, 21; outsourcing, as anti-union strategy, 24; Providence, RI, $15 wage initiative, 85–86
huelga de hambre (hunger strikes), 84, 86–91, 94, 144
Huerta, Dolores, 28, 91, 94
human-centered work environments, 12
Human Rights Watch (HRW): charges of labor abuses against

garment manufacturers, 152–53; on slave-conditions of South African wine workers, 209
human trafficking, and the trade in migrants, 74, 180–81, 191. *See also* migrant workers/undocumented migrants; wage slavery
Hungerford, Amy, 91
hunger strikes, 84, 86–91, 94, 144
Hun Sen regime (Cambodia), repression of activists, 22–23, 150, 154
"Hyatt Hurts" boycott, 26–27

"I Can't Breathe," 59, 72–73
Immigration Act of 1924, 193
Immigration and Customs Enforcement (ICE): arrests of migrant dairy workers, 192; and deportation dangers, 14, 28, 72, 85, 191, 197–98, 204; Rhode Island laws related to, 85; treatment of detained activists, 197. *See also* migrant workers/undocumented migrants
Immigration Reform and Control Act (IRCA), 219
India, agribusiness in, 182
indigenous workers/activists: Asian Indigenous Peoples Pact, 231–32; dangers faced by, 42–43; global perspective, 46; growing militancy among, 225; and indigenous identity, 215; land protests, Philippines, 172, 180–81; and land thefts, 6; La Voz Indígena, 223; long-term perspective, 217; Luzon area rice farmers, 227–28, 230, 232; Mixteco/Indígena Community Organizing Project (MICOP), Oxnard, California, 15, 221–24; Oaxacan farmers, 218; rice farmers on Luzon, 227–28; tradition of *tequio* (communal service), 224; use of racial prejudice to control, 201–2; varying views on unionizing, 224
IndustriALL, global linkages, 54
Industrial Workers of the World (IWW), 174
injuries, scars: among activists/organizers, 150, 153, 155; among berry pickers, field-workers, 2, 206; among dairy

workers, 196; among fast-food workers, 2–3, 10; among garment workers, 2, 118, 131, 136, 143, 163; among hotel housekeepers, 2, 26, 84; among Walmart employees, 6, 103–4, 108, 113
International Brotherhood of Electrical Workers, 242
International Domestic Workers Federation, 52
International Labor Rights Forum, 39
International Labour Organization (ILO), 21–22, 127, 147
International Ladies' Garment Workers' Union (ILGWU), 94–95
International Monetary Fund (IMF), 6, 125, 170
International Rice Research Institute (IRRI), 228
International Trade Union Confederation (ITUC), 54–55, 167, 229
Islam, Aminul, 120, 139
IUF (international federation of food, farm, and hotel workers), 21, 24, 28, 35, 97

Jackson, Prince, 79–80
Jambela, Kate, 244
Janis, Madeline, 240–43, 254–58
Jeftha, Rydal, 245
Jobs to Move America (JMA), 242–43
J. P. Stevens strike, North Carolina, 23–24

karaoke singers, organizing/unionizing by, 18–19
Kasich, John, 96
Katsiaficas, George, 56
Kem Lay, 151
Kentex flip-flop and sneaker factory explosion, 177
Khloek Outrok, 149–51
Khmer Rouge genocide, 161–62
King, Martin Luther, Jr., 75
Klein, Jonathan, 115
Kline, John, 251
KMU (May First Movement), 170, 172, 173
Knight, Phil, 122

Knox, Graham, 244
Koch brothers, 5–6
Koopmanskloof estate winery, South Africa, 245
Korean Arbeit Workers Union, 73
Kuala Lumpur, Malaysia, Nepali migrants in, 74

label searches, and garment worker organizing, 32, 40, 135–38, 146, 149–50, 176
labor laws and protections: and the Alta Gracia Project, 249; in California, 203; dismantling/undermining of, 5–6, 42, 100, 158, 172–73, 175, 177; following Bataan EPZ general strike, 172; following the Triangle fire, 38; for garment workers in Cambodia, 152, 155, 250–51; for migrant farmworkers, 224; NYC rules benefiting fast-food workers, 34–35; in the Philippines under Marcos, 169–70; and practices at Swanton Berry Farm, 246–48; preemption bills, 82, 84, 255; and the right to organize, 32, 67, 90, 111, 178, 213; "right-to-work" legislation, 81–82; and worker-led social responsibility codes, 193. See also Bangladesh Fire and Safety Code; National Labor Relations Board (NLRB)
labor organizers/activists: community building by, 56, 163–64; concept of freedom, 12; connection with civil rights struggles, 75; dangers faced by, 42–43, 47, 49, 53, 110, 120, 145, 150–51, 153–58, 167, 169–70, 176, 180, 203–4, 215–16, 234; dominance of women among, 17; feminist activists, 48; focus on young people, 63, 97, 108, 223; friendships and support systems, 113–14; fusion of activism with faith, 14–15, 49, 70, 77; handling despair/losses, 112–13, 59, 173, 240; new strategies and approaches, 11, 44–45, 51–52, 63–65, 86, 96–97, 119, 121–23, 126, 165, 167, 195, 256; and running for office, 85; as service providers,

222–24. *See also* education; social movement activism; *specific activists and job categories*

"Land and Life" (Messenger Band), 132

land theft: in Cambodia, 18; expanding levels of, 188; and the exploitation of indigenous lands, 6; and food insecurity, 185; in Mexico, 45–46; organized responses to, 14; in the Philippines, 52, 181–82; in South Africa, 209. *See also* agribusiness; migrant workers/undocumented migrants

Lapanday Foods, Mindanao, Philippines, 180

Las Vegas, Nevada, 26, 76–77

La Teresita Cafe, Tampa, FL, 65

Laundry Workers Center (LWC), 57–59

Lauren, Ralph, 122

La Via Campesina, Philippines: agroecological coalitions, 249; Global Peasants' Rights Congress, 185; and the international peasants' movement, 14–15; organizing to limit pesticide use, 233; promotion of seed exchanges, 228

La Voz Indígena (the Indigenous Woman's Voice), 223

LeGrand, Naquasia, 34–36

Lemlich, Clara, 37–38, 40–41

Lenca, Honduras, dam project, 43

Lewis, John L., 97

LICADHO (the Cambodian League for the Promotion and Defense of Human Rights), 151

living wage movement: and the living wage concept, 56–60, 88, 173, 256–57; and multicultural/multi-issue organizing, 72–73, 95; need to work at multiple jobs, 35, 70; rallies for, 59, 72–73, 76, 78–81. *See also* food costs; social movement activism; *specific low-wage jobs*

Lockheed Martin, surveillance work by, 32

Lopes, Maribel, 192

Lopez, Abelardo, 218–19

Lopez, Alfonza, 220

Lopez, Anastacia, 218, 225

Lopez, Arcenio, 15, 218–21, 225

Lopez, Delfino, 220

Lopez, Mahoma, 58–59

Lopez, Nicanor, 220

Los Angeles, California: living-wage ordinances, 256; Los Angeles Alliance for a New Economy (LAANE), 240, 254–55, 259; Los Angeles Federation of Labor, 26–27, 93, 255; Metro contract award criteria emphasizing local employment, 243–44; "Women Fast for $15," 86

low-wage workers: concepts of freedom, 12; demand for respect and visibility, 11, 16, 57, 71; demands for paid time off, 79; and the Moral Mondays campaign, 33; as the precariat (postindustrial working class), 67–68; predominance of people of color among, 75; predominance of women among, 48. *See also* contract labor; food costs; living wage movement; *specific low-wage jobs*

Lumad communities, Philippines, 181

Luna, Venanzi: arrest during Walmart strike, 114–15; on empowerment from organizing, 102, 113–14; friendship with Barlage and shared actions, 113–15; losses experienced by, 116; and strike against the Pico Rivera Walmart, 29; Unfair Labor Practices complaints by, 30; union background, 29; at Walmart shareholders' meetings, 115–16; on Walmart's response to Pico Rivera strike, 32; working experience at Walmart, 106–7, 112–13

Luzon, Philippines: forced displacement of small farmers, 13; indigenous farming communities, 227. *See also* Cordillera region, Luzon, Philippines

Mack, Reika, 75–76

"Made with Love" label, Children's Place, 135–36

Madotyeni, Nkosi, 245

Malcolm X, 76

Maldonado, Shelby, 83–85

Manila, Philippines: danger zone areas, 13, 48; demonstration for decent jobs, 62; low-wage workers in, 48, 176, 236;

resistance to unionizing efforts in, 24; signs of colonialism in, 166; Tondo shanty town, 13; Visayan-speaking domestic workers, 52. *See also* garment workers; hotel housekeepers; Philippines

Marcos, Ferdinand, 45, 169, 172, 234

Margules, Rita, 40

Mariveles Export Processing Zone, Philippines, 166–67

Market Match program, 248

Martinez, Bernardino, 16, 200–206

Martinez, Bonifacio, 214

Martinez, Gloria Gracida, 217

Marx, Karl, 86

massage workers, organizing by, 18–19

Mata, Josua, 45, 93–94, 97–98, 166–67, 172–74

May First Movement (KMU), 170, 172, 173

McDonald's: actions against by European governments, 74; bike deliverymen, 10–11; case against in Brazil, 10, 73–74; profits from real estate and franchises, 71; responsibility for working conditions of franchisees, 44, 71; as target of labor activists, 11, 59, 70–71, 77; trafficking charges against by Nepali migrants, 74; use of labor from exchange students, 35; wages and employment practices, 9–11, 34, 71, 79; wage theft by, 99–101. *See also* fast-food workers; Fight for $15 movement

"McJobs" term, 35, 71

McMillon, Doug, 115, 122

Mendiola massacre, 171–72, 181

Messenger Band (Cambodian garment workers), 53, 126, 131, 156

methyl bromide pesticide, 246

Mexico: Oaxacan teachers' strike, 46–47; rebellion against globalization and neoliberalism, 45; San Quintín Valley berry pickers strike, 13, 15, 213–16; treatment of indigenous peoples in, 220–21. *See also* indigenous workers/activists; migrant workers/undocumented migrants

middle class, destruction of, 7

Migrant Justice, Vermont, 193–94, 198

migrant workers/undocumented migrants: amnesty programs, 219, 224; Bracero Program, 218, 220; dairy workers, 193–95, 198; discrimination against, 57; exploitation/mistreatment of, 14, 27–28, 72, 191, 201; and export-processing zones, 127–29; fear of deportation, 14, 28, 72, 85, 191, 197–98, 204; fear of speaking up for rights, 57–59, 69; illegal border crossings by, 221–22; importance of path to citizenship, 16, 28; increasing numbers of, 13–14, 132, 161, 184–85, 187, 219, 232; and land theft, 132; organizing and motivating, 57, 69, 257; use of racial prejudice to control, 201. *See also* farmworkers; indigenous workers/activists

Milk with Dignity campaign (Migrant Justice), 194, 195–97

Miller, George, 121

Mills, Jenny, 108–9

Mindanao, Philippines, forced displacement of small farmers, 13, 180–81, 189

minimum wage increases: among berry pickers, 212, 216; Cambodian garment workers, 150–52; for federal employees, 34; as focus of feminist activists, 50; following Bataan EPZ general strike, 172; and the Moral Mondays campaign, 33; in the Philippines, 173; in the US, 78. *See also* Fight for $15; living wage movement

Mishu, Moshrefa, 45, 141–45

Mixteco farmers: in California, identity issues, 221; migration by as result of NAFTA, 15; and small farming in Oaxaca, 220; and social movement activism, 221, 224; strike against Driscoll, 202; traditional farming practices, 220

Mixteco/Indígena Community Organizing Project (MICOP), Oxnard, California, 15, 221–24

models, as spokespeople for garment workers, 119

Modi, Narenda, 182–83

Monsanto, bioengineered seeds, 228

Montcrief, Maia, 76

Montenegro, Jamaia, 52–53
Moore, Thelma, 105
Mora, Sar, 18–20
Moral Mondays campaign, 33
Movement of Landless Workers (MST),
    182
Mpofu, Elizabeth, 14–15, 185, 229
Mudanjiang, China, 189
Multi-Fiber Agreement, 125
Murillo, Benedict, 10–11, 99

NAFTA. *See* North American Free Trade
    Agreement (NAFTA)
NagaWorld casino, Cambodia, 22–23
National Guestworker Alliance, 35
National Labor Relations Board (NRLB):
    and the firing of workers for orga-
    nizing, 110; ruling allowing graduate
    students to unionize, 91; ruling on
    McDonald's, 71; and suits against
    Walmart, 111
Navarro, Luis Hernandez, 47
neoliberalism, 5–7, 12–13, 42
"new economy movement," 241
New York/New Jersey Airport Workers
    Bargaining Committee (SEIU Local
    32BJ), 80
Nguyen, Linda, 242–43
Nichols, Heather, 84–85
Nike: Girl Effect campaign/foundation,
    130–31; price of shoes vs. wages paid
    workers, 159; resistance to unionizing
    efforts, 133; supply chain improve-
    ments, 253; Vietnam factories, 132
Nobre, Miriam, 50
Noi Supalai, 133
No Land No Life farmers' group, 188
Noquit, Joshua, 99–100
North American Free Trade Agreement
    (NAFTA), impacts on Mexican small
    farmers, 15–16, 213, 218–19
NUWHRAIN (Philippine hotel workers'
    union), 24

Oaxaca, Mexico, 46–47, 212, 218. *See also*
    indigenous workers/activists
Obama, Barack, 34, 80, 243

Occupy Wall Street, 4, 47
Olalia, Rolando, 170
OUR Walmart (Organization United for
    Respect at Walmart). "Black Fri-
    day" protests, 31–32; empowerment
    through, 102–3; Manhattan hunger
    strike, 87–88; Jennie Mills's activism in
    association with, 108, 110; NY rally for
    a living wage, 59; Park Avenue sit-in,
    112; Pico Rivera strike, 29, 31, 114;
    Walmart's response to, 32, 107, 111
Oxfam, 6, 195

PAKISAMA (Philippine smallholders'
    confederation), 233
Palacios, Victoria "Zully," 192–93, 197–98
palm oil plantations, 13, 52, 180, 188–89
PAN AP (Pesticide Action Network-Asian
    Pacific), 183–85
Pao Chhumony, 23–24
Parada, Mirjoam, 83 84, 86
Parker, Mark, 122
Park Geun-hye, 73
Parks, Rosa, 76
Partnership for Working Families, 256
patriarchy, language of violence and sup-
    pression at the heart of, 51
"Peasant Marches," 184–85
peasant movement, international, 14. *See*
    also farmworkers; migrant workers/
    undocumented migrants
Pekeur, Wendy, 209
Penner, Greg, 88
People Power movements, 43, 56, 172,
    235
Perez, Luc, 72
Pesticide Action Network-Asian Pacific
    (PAN AP), 183–85
philanthropy, and the "Gospel of
    Wealth," 5
Philippi, South Africa, farmers' coopera-
    tive, 244–45
Philippine Alliance of Progressive Labor,
    93–94
Philippines: armed struggle in, 173; aver-
    age age of workers in, 63; displacement
    of farmers in, 13, 188–89; export of

workers from, 174–75; financial crises, 170; garment industry in, 126; as global trade crossing, 167; GMO crops in, 229; musical theatrical protests, 64; People Power revolution, 235; rapid loss of arable land in, 231; role of Americans in, 234–35; tradition of unions and organizing in, 45, 169; violence against organizers and activists, 169. *See also* export-processing zones (EPZs); garment workers; rice production

Phnom Penh, Cambodia. *See* beer promoters, Cambodia; garment workers

Pineda, Filemon, 212, 214

Ports of Los Angeles and Long Beach, electric vehicles for, 242

Powers, Julia, 91–92

precariat (postindustrial working class), 67–68

preemption bills, 81–82, 84–85, 255

pregnancy discrimination: CCAWDU's efforts to counter, 156; Pregnant Workers' Fairness Act, 105; Respect the Bump advocacy group, 102, 104–7

Pregnancy Discrimination Act, 1978, 105

Pritzker, Penny, 27

Procaccianti Group (hotel management), 25–26, 83, 85

professors, adjunct, unionizing, 79

"Profits, Pain, and Pillows" campaign (UNITED HERE), 27

Providence, Rhode Island. *See* hotel housekeepers; Procaccianti Group

Providence's Pain Problem, 85

public services, privatization, 126

Puzder, Andrew, 72, 77

racism, racial prejudice: faced by Visayan-speaking domestic workers, 52; teaching about history of, 58; as tool for controlling farm workers, 201–2

Rainer, Bleu: on the broken American Dream, 66; demand that McDonald's accept responsibility for labor practices, 11; and the "Fast for $15" hunger strike, 88; on impatience for change, 34; on links between poverty and police violence, 72–73; living conditions as a low-wage worker, 35; on McJobs, 71; on the "new civil rights movement," 75; protests and actions, 9, 36, 59, 74, 77; on ubiquity of low-wage labor, 67; on working and living conditions, 34–35

rain forest destruction, 188–89

Rally for a Living Wage, NY, 2015, 57–60

Rana Plaza factory collapse, Bangladesh, 32, 118, 120, 135. *See also* garment workers

Reagan, Ronald, "A Time for Choosing," 5

REAP (Resist Expansion of Agricultural Plantations), 181

Reiter, J. Miles, 215, 225

Remontal, Irene, 63

Republican Party, 70, 81–82, 96

RESPECT Fast Food Workers Alliance, 51–52, 62–64, 99. *See also* Dancers' Union of Bagong Silangan (DUBS)

Respect the Bump advocacy group (Walmart employees), 102, 104–7

Restaurant Opportunities Centers (ROC), 57–58

Revitalize Indigenous Cordilleran Entrepreneurs (RICE) Project, Cordillera, Philippines, 232–34, 236

rice production: acceleration of, 188; arguments in favor of plantation approach, 229; and bioengineered seeds, 228; and destruction of smallholder farms, 184; and extinction of rice species, 229–30; indigenous approaches to, 227–28; and poor nutritional quality of "modern" rice, 231; and "seed keepers," 230; as a staple, 229

Ride for Respect (Our Walmart), 110–11

"right-to-work" legislation, 81–82

Robertson winery strike, South Africa, 210–11

Rodriguez, Rosanna, 57–59

Rolf, David, 97, 100

Roots of Change foundation, 248

Roth Minea, 122, 165
Rousseff, Dilma, 73
"run-away shops," 129
Ryan, Paul, 70

Safe Cities for Women movement, 163
Sakuma, Steven, 213
Sakuma berry strike and boycott, 16, 212,
    216–17
Salovey, Peter, 91
Sanchez, Fidel, 214–15
Sanders, Bernie, 45
Sanders, Vance "Stretch," 33–34, 70, 72,
    76–77
San Diego Hilton, response to union
    demands, 27–28
San Quintín Valley berry pickers strike,
    13, 15, 213–16
Santiz-Cruz, José Obeth, 196
São Paolo, Brazil, farmworker action
    against Vale Fertilizer plant, 182
Savar Building collapse, Dhaka, Bangla-
    desh. See Rana Plaza factory collapse,
    Bangladesh
Searcy, Rhett, 203–4, 212–13
security guards, unionizing by, 79–80
"seed keepers," seed exchanges, 228, 230
SENTRO (Philippine union federation),
    97, 174
Seoul, South Korea, protests against
    McDonald's in, 73
Service Employees International Union
    (SEIU), 24, 96
service workers, unionizing of, 79–80
sexual harassment/exploitation/violence:
    Cambodian beer promoters, 18;
    campaigns against, 49–50, 54–55; and
    domestic violence, 49–50; educating
    workers about, 58; of garment workers,
    147, 172; of hotel housekeepers, 24;
    protections against in the Philippines,
    172. See also women
Shepard, Keegan, 67–68
Shiva, Vandana, 183, 228
Sifang (Chinese railcar manufacturer),
    Chicago factory, 242
Sikder, Reba, 120–21

Sikhula Sonke farmworkers' union, South
    Africa, 207–11
Singh, Manmohan, 183
SMART (sheet metal workers' union), 242
Smit, Stewie, 245
SNAP (Supplemental Nutrition Assis-
    tance Program), 88
Social Accountability in Sustainable Agri-
    culture (SASA), 246
social media, as organizing tool, 11, 44, 86
social movement activism: and coalition
    building, 95–96; effectiveness as a
    strategy, 224; and the Filipino Alli-
    ance of Progressive Labor, 173–74;
    global reach, 97; impact on workers'
    lives, 93; and provision of health
    services, 222–23; and the Sikhula
    Sonke farmworkers' union, 208–9;
    in the US, 94
social responsibility codes, worker-led,
    253–54
social safety net, cuts to, 5–6, 70
Sok Kin, 22
Sok Thareth, 122, 131, 160, 162–64
Solano, Juvenal, 205, 213, 224
Solheim, Jostein, 196–97
Solidarity Center, Phnom Penh, 155,
    161–62
South Africa: displacement of small
    farmers, 14; grape pickers strike, 15;
    organizing in, 208–9; social movement
    activism, 93; wine industry in, 207
South Korea, 10–11, 188
Sreypon (Cambodian union president),
    165
Station Casinos, Las Vegas, 90
Stratospheric Ozone Protection Award
    (EPA), 246
strawberry production, California:
    conditions and wages, 201; lucrative
    nature of, 219–20; and methyl bromide
    pesticide, 246
sub-Saharan Africa, land lost by small
    farmers since 2008, 188–89
"Suffer from Privatization" (Messenger
    Band), 126
Sustainable Cotton Communiqué, 249

Sutton, Crystal Lee ("Norma Rae"), 23
Swanton Berry Farm, 246
Syngenta, bioengineered seeds, 228

Tampico Foils Company fire, Bangladesh, 145
Tazreen factory, Dhaka, Bangladesh, 136–38
teachers, professors, as low-wage workers, 7, 66
Temer, Michel, 73, 182
Tep Saroeung, 17–20
Tep Vanny, 184
Tiananmen Square uprising, 43
Timberlake, Justin, 11
"A Time for Choosing" (Reagan), 5
Tolbert, Jeremiah, 85–86
tomato fields, Florida, 194–95
Tonlé apparel manufacturer, Cambodia, 250–51
Torres, Ramon, 212
Touch Seou, 154
Township Winery, Philippi, 244–45
toxic chemical exposures: farmworkers, 180, 185, 189, 246; garment workers, 2, 146, 160, 165, 251; hotel housekeepers, 24, 84; Walmart workers, 105
Trade Facilitation and Trade Enforcement Act, 124
transnational organizing efforts, 54
Transport Workers Union, 242–43
TransWorld Security Forces, 212–13
Triangle Shirtwaist Factory fire, New York City, 37–39, 41
Triqui farmers, 15, 221
Trump, Donald: dismantling of immigrant and women's rights, 70; dismantling of social safety net/worker protections, 5–6; election of, fear engendered by, 226; philanthropic stinginess, 5; rescinding "U.S. Employment Plan," 243
Trump, Ivanka, 124
"Truth Tours" (CIW), 194
Tuba Group, Bangladesh, strike against, 137, 141–45
Tubman, Harriet, 76
Tynan, Roxana, 254–59

UFW. See United Farm Workers (UFW)
unemployment, 7
Unfair Labor Practices (ULP), 30, 107
UN Food and Agriculture Organization, 190
UNI Global Union, 31, 54
Unilever, 195
unions: and anti-union activities, 81; and challenges of changing property ownership patterns, 25; changing definition of, 94; dominance of males in, 17; and importance of strikes, 87, 158, 204–5; neoliberal attacks on, 7. See also coalition building/globalized activism; labor laws and protections; labor organizers/activists
United Farm Workers (UFW): California strawberry pickers' strike, 200–203; coalition with UNITE HERE, 28; hunger strikes, 89–90; as paradigm for social movement organizing, 94–95; tactics used against, 202–5
United Food and Commercial Workers (UFCW), 29, 30–31, 104
United Mine Workers, 97
United Parcel Service (UPS), 105–6
United Sisterhood Alliance: on conditions faced by Cambodian garment workers, 131; focus on violence against women, 163; Happy Happy program, 164; Messenger Band, 53; support from the CCAWDU, 156; worker drop-in centers in Phnom Penh, 162–64; Worker Information Center discussions, 160
United Students Against Sweatshops, 39, 159
United Voice and Strength of the Working Class, 167
UNITE HERE (hotel and restaurant workers' union): achievements, 79; organizing strategies and activities, 26–27, 86, 89–90; "Profits, Pain, and Pillows" campaign, 27; ties to the UFW, 28; on working conditions in Providence, RI, 25–26
urban development, and community benefits contracts, 256

"U.S. Employment Plan," 243
US National Labor Relations Board (NLRB), 44
US Supreme Court, and rights for pregnant workers, 105

Vale Fertilizer, 182
van Wyk, Arlene, 245
Vargas, Maricela, 225
Vathanak Serry Sim, 22, 161–62
Vermont dairy industry, migrant workers in, 192–97
VF (clothing manufacturer), 118–19
violence against women: Akter's ongoing efforts to stop, 146–47; domestic violence, 49–50; as focus of Sikhula Sonke, 209; and the language of patriarchy, 51
Virgin Wines, UK, investment in Township Winery, 244
Vivid Picture Project, 248
Vun Em: and the creation of the Messenger Band, 163; English studies, 53; "Fate of Garment Workers," 131; on the Khmer Rouge genocide, 162; "Land and Life," 132; organizing activities, 53–54; "Suffer from Privatization" song, 126; Womyn's Agenda for Change, 53. See also Messenger Band (Cambodian garment workers)

wage slavery: by agribusiness companies, 180, 185, 194; CIW efforts to expose and end, 195; and human trafficking, 74, 191; ITUC focus on, 54; in Kuala Lumpur, 74; in South Africa, 207. See also migrant workers/undocumented migrants; wage theft
wage theft: and contractualization in the fast-food industry, 99–100; from graduate students, 67; from indigenous berry pickers, 201–2; from migrant farmworkers, 191
Walker, Scott, 96
Walmart: anti-union efforts, 32; "Black Friday" protests against, 31–32;

bullying by managers, 106–8; and the CIW Fair Food agreement, 194; expansion into India, 31; Pico Rivera strike, 29–32; Respect the Bump advocacy group, 102–5; response to employee injuries, 108–9; response to organizers and strikes, 102–3, 107, 110–13; response to Tazreen factory fire, 138; San Quintín Valley berry pickers strike, 13, 215–16, 220, 225; scope of global operations, 31, 103; sex discrimination lawsuit against, 106; ULPs filed against, 107; working conditions at, 29, 102–4, 108–9
Walmart Global Union Alliance, 31
Walton, Alice, Walton family, 5, 7, 87–88, 115
Washington State, Sakuma berries boycott, 212
Webb-Fiske, Eric, 66–67
Western Cape Winelands strike, South Africa, 15, 207–8
Williams, Lukia, 100–101
Williams, Samuel Homer, 36, 69
Wilmar, and palm oil industry, 189
wine production, South Africa, 207, 244–45
Wisconsin, response to anti-union actions, 96
women: as food producers in Asia and Africa, 184; and the 1909 NYC garment workers' strike, 38; organizing by, leadership roles, 14–15, 17, 23, 68, 157, 208; resistance to commodification of, 51; and women's rights organizing, 95; World March of Women, 49–51. See also feminist activists; pregnancy discrimination; sexual harassment/exploitation/violence; social movement activism; specific organizers and organizations
"Women Fast for $15," 86
"Women's Manifesto for Peace," 51
Women Without Land, 182
Womyn's Agenda for Change (WAC), 53, 163

Woolworth saleswomen's strike, Detroit, 115

Worker Information Centers, 156, 162–63

Worker Rights Consortium, 39

workers, changing definitions of, 94

World Bank: on benefits of globalized garment production, 130; export-processing zones (EPZs), 127, 170; power of, in the twenty-first century, 6; role in globalizing the garment industry, 125

World Trade Organization (WTO), 5–6, 125

Xabanisa, Judith, 245

Yale University, graduate student hunger strike, 90–91

Yang Sophorn, 157–58

Yim Sothy, 53

You Can't Jail Hope! video (Migrant Justice), 198

Young, Peggy, 105–6

Young, Sandy, 222–23

Zapatistas, 46

Zapoteco farmers, 15, 224

zero-waste manufacturing techniques, 250–51

Ziff, Sarah, 119

Zondani, Nomhle, 244–45

ABOUT THE AUTHOR

Photo by Joel Benjamin

ANNELISE ORLECK is the author of five books and coeditor of two. Her previous books include *Common Sense and a Little Fire: Women and Working-Class Politics in the United States* (1995/2017), *Soviet Jewish Americans* (1999), *Storming Caesars Palace: How Black Mothers Fought Their Own War on Poverty* (2005), and *Rethinking American Women's Activism* (2014). She is the coeditor of *The Politics of Motherhood: Activist Voices from Left to Right* (1997) and *The War on Poverty, 1964–1980: A New Grassroots History* (2011). She teaches at Dartmouth College in the departments of History; Women's, Gender, and Sexuality Studies; and Jewish Studies. Born and raised in Brooklyn, New York, she lives in Thetford Center, Vermont, with her partner, journalist Alexis Jetter. They have two children—Evann and Raphael—and several cats, including a series of majestic Maine coons.